4

Studies in US politics

This volume is dedicated to the family of John D. Lees

Studies in
US politics

edited by
D. K. ADAMS
Department of American Studies,
University of Keele

Manchester University Press
Manchester and New York
Distributed exclusively in the USA and Canada by St. Martin's Press

Published by
Manchester University Press
Oxford Road, Manchester M13 9PL, UK
and Room 400, 175 Fifth Avenue, New York, NY 10010, USA
Distributed exclusively in the USA and Canada
by St. Martin's Press, Inc.,
175 Fifth Avenue, New York, NY 10010, USA

British Library cataloguing in publication data

Studies in US politics.
 1. United States. Politics
 I. Adams, D.K.
 320.973

Library of Congress cataloging in publication data

Studies in US politics.
  Includes index.
  1. United States—Politics and government.
I. Adams, David Keith. II. Title: Studies in United
States politics.
JK21.S78   1989   320.973   88-8300

ISBN 0-7190-2584-2 hardback

Printed and bound in Great Britain
by Anchor Press Ltd, Tiptree, Essex

Contents

Contributors

Dr Colin Bonwick is Senior Lecturer in the Department of American Studies, University of Keele, England.

Dr John Hart is Senior Lecturer in the Department of Political Science, The Australian National University, Canberra, Australia.

Dr Richard Maidment is Lecturer in Government in the Faculty of Social Sciences, The Open University, England.

Dr David Morgan is Reader in the Department of Political Theory and Institutions, University of Liverpool, England.

Professor Nelson W. Polsby is in the Department of Political Science and is Director of the Institute of Governmental Studies, University of California, Berkeley, USA.

Professor Göran Rystad is in the Department of History, University of Lund, Lund, Sweden.

Professor Clive S. Thomas is in the Department of Political Science, University of Alaska, Juneau, Alaska, USA.

Dr James A. Thurber is Professor at and Director of the Center for Congressional & Presidential Studies, School of Public Affairs, The American University, Washington, D.C., USA.

Professor James P. Young is in the Department of Political Science, University Center at Binghamton, Binghamton, New York, USA.

Preface

This volume of essays by some of his former students, colleagues and professional associates is presented in memory of John David Lees (1936–1986), whose early death deprived the American Studies movement of one of its leading practitioners. Trained as a political scientist at Oxford, he took his master's degree at the University of Michigan, Ann Arbor, and his doctorate at the University of Manchester. He joined the American Studies programme at the University of Keele in 1964, was one of the founding members of the Department of American Studies in 1965, and of the David Bruce Centre for American Studies in 1969.

He is remembered by successive generations of students in both American Studies and Politics as a caring and resourceful tutor, whose commitment to the standards of his discipline invoked the best of their talents. His enthusiasm for political science was conveyed to both undergraduates and graduate students alike, and carried by many of them to later careers in public service and teaching at all levels.

Beyond Keele he gave much of his time to the British Association for American Studies and to the Politics Association, and was a founder member of the American Politics Group. In great demand as reviewer, consultant, external examiner and lecturer, he could always be counted upon to make time for others without sacrificing his own research output. He was also assiduous in maintaining his professional academic links, not only throughout the United Kingdom but also in the United States and Canada, well aware of what Nelson Polsby has called the danger of reasoning by analogy, and of what he himself termed 'the loneliness of the long-distance observer of American politics'.

John Lees established his early reputation with his work on congressional committees (*The Committee System of the United States Congress*, London, 1967), which was extended in his book, *Committees in Legislatures: A Comparative Analysis* (Durham, NC, 1979, with Malcolm Shaw). The breadth of his interests was revealed in a stream of articles on most aspects of American political culture, and in his pamphlet, *The President and the Supreme Court: New Deal to Watergate* (London, 1980). Working as he did side by side with historians, geographers and literary specialists in the area studies programme, he became absorbed in the general environments from which political structures and ideas emerge. His considerable understanding of American historical development was amply displayed in *The Political System of the United States* (London, 1969, rev. edns 1975, 1983). The success of this text was paralleled by *American Politics Today* (Manchester, 1982, rev. edns, 1983, 1985, with R. A. Maidment and M. Tappin) which sought to initiate 'students with no prior background in politics into the "merry-go-round" of politics in the United States', and established itself as a leading and widely-used text.

The essays in this volume reflect the scope of John Lees' professional interests, and the writers are a representative group of his friends who wish to memorialise his contributions to the study of the United States and to the teaching of American politics. In the preparation of this volume we acknowledge with gratitude the skill and patience of Karen Harrison, the American Studies secretary, as John Lees himself so often did.

D. K. Adams
Keele, Staffordshire
January 1988

Part 1

Political history and theory

English principles and American constitutionalism

Celebrations of the bicentennial of the Philadelphia Convention encourage scholars once more to explore the ever fruitful subject of American constitutionalism and its relationship to English practice. E. C. S. Wade and G. Godfrey Phillips have argued that writers on the British Constitution could be divided into three types: historians, political scientists, and lawyers.[1] Much the same taxonomy can be applied to writers on the United States Constitution, and in each instance the insights of one discipline inform and illuminate the analyses of the others. It is particularly appropriate in this volume that an historian should examine the relationship between English and American constitutionalism since John Lees was especially conscious of the historical dimension to political science. Certainly scholars on both sides of the Atlantic have long acknowledged the significance of English principles to the development of American ideas and practices even though they recognise the distinctiveness of key elements such as federalism. It is therefore possible to argue that the United States Constitution was the product of particular circumstances and provided unique solutions to particular political problems, yet also insist that its familial relationship to English constitutionalism remains a rewarding subject for historical analysis. Perhaps A. V. Dicey's opinion that the historian 'is primarily occupied with ascertaining the steps by which a constitution has grown to be what it is' is too narrow, but such an investigation is undoubtedly important.[2]

I

There has, of course, been considerable argument over the attitudes and perspective of the founding fathers themselves. Two of the most influential historians of the Philadelphia Convention, Max Farrand and R. L. Schuyler, insisted that its members were not historically oriented; rather, they were practical men whose political conclusions derived almost entirely from wrestling with the problems of the Confederation years. Yet when John Dickinson of Pennsylvania declared that 'experience must be our only guide' he was comparing it with philosophical axioms and the logic of abstract reason, and had something broader in mind than the lessons of the immediate Revolutionary past. It was not reason, in his opinion, that discovered the 'singular and admirable mechanism of the English Constitution', but extended experience, and he went on to ask rhetorically, 'shall we oppose to this long experience, the short experience of 11 [sic] years which we had on this subject?'[3] For Dickinson and his contemporaries the past was a valuable guide to the solution of contemporary problems though they treated it in a manner different from that of twentieth-century academic historians. They possessed ample libraries of classical, medieval, and modern history in which they read extensively, less to understand the past for its own sake and more to find evidence and examples pertinent to contemporary issues. History was 'philosophy teaching by example' in the English writer Lord Bolingbroke's words, and a tutor in wisdom; human nature and behaviour were constant in all society and ages, and according to the Scottish philosopher David Hume, the study of history was useful preeminently as a means of enabling the reader *'to discover the constant and universal principles of human nature'*.[4]

Whether or not history contained evidence of universal propositions, there is no doubt that the Revolutionaries' minds were influenced by their understanding of the past. It was a broad historical experience since the United States was intellectually a child of Europe as well as Britain. Much American public thought was rooted in the record of the ancient classical world, and the colonial sense of admirable characteristics was fuelled by the traditional Roman virtues of 'restraint, temperance, fortitude, dignity and independence'.[5] Revolutionary leaders deeply admired the Greek city states and especially the Roman republic as models of political organisation, though they were alarmed by the internal decay which they diagnosed as the prime cause of failure in the classical world. They were also aware of other more contemporary models of confederation. John Adams's *Defence of the Constitutions of Government of the United States of America*, which he prepared while minister to London, was full of quotations and commentary on political systems ancient and modern, and when James Madison was preparing himself for the Philadelphia Convention he systematically analysed Dutch, German and Swiss confederations as well as those of Greece. J. G. A. Pocock has also demonstrated the existence of an attenuated thread which took American Revolutionary debates back to those of Renaissance Florence.[6] But within this broad historical framework, the Revolutionaries were especially familiar with English historical writing, the major commentaries on English law, and a substantial number of studies on political theory. Together these works formed an important element in the historical context of American constitutionalism and supplemented their experience of colonial politics.

This emphasis on the intellectual ancestry of the American mind is not to deny the importance of social context and immediate circumstances that shaped the Revolutionary process and prompted Congress to accede to the nationalists' demands for a Convention in 1787. Every element was interactive and each informed and shaped the others. The Constitution grew out of the political problems generated by the decision to declare independence eleven years earlier, and was the climax of a process that had begun with the consequent need to establish new systems of government in each of the states. It was this experience that provided the medium and catalyst through which English principles were translated, adapted, and incorporated into American constitutionalism − and sometimes rejected. The fact that it took some time was helpful, for the war years provided a period of experimentation during which the individual states could test their colonial experience and English intellectual inheritance against the needs and imperatives of contemporary circumstances. Crucially, it permitted the states to be selective from among the alternatives available to them, and to be innovative if they wished. It also posed a particular problem that would require great adaptive ingenuity for which there was no obviously pertinent counterpart in the English experience: the need to construct a national union out of thirteen states.

II

In evaluating the contribution of English principles to American constitutionalism it is necessary to attempt some definition of the English
constitution. The task is not easy. Alexis de Tocqueville suggested
that 'the English constitution has no real existence', which is especially
unhelpful since the greatest eighteenth-century legal commentator,
Sir William Blackstone, believed there was indeed such a thing and
that it was perfect, and many Americans as well as Englishmen shared
his opinion.[7] At this point a further complication emerges, since
there were two distinct yet cognate definitions. Firstly, there was
the received version, so admired by Blackstone, which formed the
reigning structure of English political and legal conduct. The second
was a radical understanding of the constitution which derived from
the upheavals of the previous century and was adhered to by the small
group of true believers known as Commonwealthmen or Real Whigs.

The 'official' constitution was anything but codified. It consisted
of the common law and customs, statute law (including major claims
of rights such as the Bill of Rights and Habeas Corpus Act), associated
decisions of the courts of laws, and above all the institutions of
government such as the Crown and Parliament together with the
conventions which made it operational and the practices by which it
adjusted to changing circumstances. As its principal interpreter
Blackstone attached little importance to the theoretical source of
legitimacy, though he did postulate a pre-social state of nature and
then sketch a rudimentary contract theory of authority. He conceded
that the purpose of the constitution flowed from the purpose of
society, which was to protect individuals in the enjoyment of absolute
rights vested in them by the 'immutable laws of nature', and
acknowledged that the people possessed the ultimate power to withdraw their trust in parliament, but argued the consequences would
be so cataclysmic as to make the exercise of it wholly impracticable.[8]
What concerned him and his orthodox readers were pragmatic considerations; for them the sovereign power meant the making of laws.
Thus the central element of the constitution was the sovereignty of
parliament, whose power and jurisdiction Blackstone followed Sir
Edward Coke in insisting 'is so transcendent and absolute, that it
cannot be confined either for causes or persons, within any bounds'.
It had 'sovereign and uncontrollable authority' in matters relating
to the law, could alter the succession of the crown and change the

established religion, and could go so far as to 'change and create afresh even the constitution of the kingdom and of parliaments themselves'.[9] Such absolute power was potentially dangerous, but Blackstone argued that the parliamentary components of King, Lords, and Commons functioned as a system of reciprocal checks and they prevented each other from exceeding the proper limits of their respective powers. A second key to the system's success lay in its structure as a mixed government of balanced estates of monarchy, aristocracy and democracy. Within this balance the House of Lords functioned as a crucial intermediary between King and Commons, thus preventing the crown and people from encroaching on each other's rights. He conceded an abstract equality for all members of society, but believed that government should be placed in the hands of those whom he deemed most fitted to exercise it.[10]

Like their orthodox counterparts the radical Commonwealthmen greatly admired the English constitution, yet they conceptualised it in a distinctly different manner which in practice was far more congenial to Americans. What they admired was what they considered to be its 'genuine spirit and purity'. Whereas Blackstone and the orthodox explicated and defended the constitution as it currently functioned, the radicals defended fundamental principles, among them being liberty. Two of their most influential publicists, John Trenchard and Thomas Gordon, authors of *Cato's Letters* in 1721–2, argued that liberty was unalienable and 'the Parent of all the Virtues', but could not exist without equality. Government was a trust, and its duty was to promote the general welfare; moreover, the people were fully capable of judging its competence.[11] James Burgh, writing just before the American Revolution, explicitly challenged Blackstone's theory of sovereignty by insisting on the sovereignty of the people who, he argued, were superior to government and possessed the authority to remodel it if they wished. In his view, and that of other radicals, 'all lawful authority, legislative, and executive, originates from the *people*. Power in the *people* is like light in the sun, native, original, inherent and unlimited by anything human. In governors, it may be compared to the reflected light of the moon'.[12] Radicals insisted that the separation of powers between legislature, executive and judiciary should be genuine rather than nominal, but the heart of their constitutional theory lay in its system of representation. Few were prepared to advocate universal suffrage, even though they believed government was a task requiring only common sense and diligence, but all insisted that the legislature was crucial since it was elected by the people. Two things became essential: electors should be capable of exercising genuinely independent political judgment, and parliaments should refresh their authority yearly, for as Obadiah Hulme argued, 'where annual election ends, slavery begins'.[13] What radicals feared particularly was uncontrolled power, especially executive power. Though necessary and useful when regulated, it was naturally expansive and constantly threatened the liberty of the people, hence the imperative need to impose limits on the extent of government authority.[14]

In the mid-eighteenth century the contrast between theoretical principles and actual political behaviour was in radicals' eyes deeply alarming. Most were persuaded that their theoretical axioms had been operational in the so-called ancient or Anglo-Saxon constitution but had been destroyed by the Norman Conquest; what was needed was its revival, not a new system. They deplored the corruption and distortions condoned by Blackstone, and in particular abhorred the perversion of the system of representation, the over-long parliaments, and the Crown's use of bribery, pensions and places to ensure its control of the House of Commons.

III

The circumstances of their growing disagreement with Britain after 1763 made Americans especially sensitive to issues of constitutional interpretation. Although much of their revolutionary rhetoric, as exemplified by the Declaration of Independence, was couched in terms of natural rights and the doctrine that legitimate authority rested on consent, they were much more concerned before 1776 with the structural engineering of government as a means of protecting individual liberty.[15] English radical definitions of constitutional principles and programmes for reform were especially attractive. Tracts by writers such as Joseph Priestley, Richard Price and John Cartwright were reprinted in the colonies during the revolutionary era, as was Catharine Macaulay's 'republican' *History of England*. Above all, *Cato's Letters*, which was widely popular for many years, and James Burgh's *Political Disquisitions*, whose subscribers included George Washington, John Adams, John Dickinson, and Thomas Jefferson when it was reprinted in Philadelphia in 1775, served as influential primers for interpreting events and constructing governments.[16] As

Bernard Bailyn has brilliantly demonstrated, the issues that alarmed Englishmen resurfaced in America; the colonists were convinced that the disposition of power lay behind every political controversy and that liberty was the natural victim of its inherent aggressiveness. Constitutions thus became the necessary instruments for curbing and confining governmental power.[17] Such opinions became ever more persuasive as the Anglo-American crisis deteriorated, for Americans stood in the same relation to the politics of the court and government as did the opposition writers. They saw the abuse of representation as evidence that the English constitution had been corrupted, but still insisted on their desire to return to the purity of the putative ancient constitution, for as a North Carolina delegate to the Continental Congress insisted in 1776, 'I am well assured that the British constitution in its purity (for what is at present styled the British constitution is an apostate), was a system that approached as near to perfection as any could within the compass of human abilities'.[18] Americans were especially impressed by the division of powers, which seemed to match the structure of their own governments, though they were unsure whether it was a mixed constitution of counterpoised social estates or a balanced constitution of legislative, executive and judicial functions.[19]

Yet the radical thesis did not occupy the entire field in America, even for those who were about to advocate independence. Blackstone's *Commentaries* were available in the colonies and were to be widely read for many years; there was also the experience of domestic politics to serve as both a context and a guide to future action. Thus when American revolutionaries formed their own independent governments they were able to draw on a range of cognate but competing sets of precedents, and did do so under the pressure of circumstances and the need to attract the support of the majorities of their communities. Furthermore, they were obliged to construct an additional tier of central government above the states if they were to create a nation as well as independence, and there was rivalry among conservatives and radicals for command of this process, for the constitutions as well as governments had policy as well as structural objectives. Not surprisingly, the consequent constitutionalism was eclectic as well as innovatory.

IV

Independence provided a rare chance to formulate a new political system. As John Adams said,

How few of the human race have ever enjoyed an opportunity of making an election of government − more than of air, soil, or climate − for themselves or their children! When, before the present epoch, had three millions of people full power and a fair opportunity to form and establish the wisest and happiest government that human wisdom can contrive?[20]

The task was far from simple. Construction of new governments was completed separately in each of the states between 1776 and 1780. Connecticut and Rhode Island modified their charters and continued much as before; all the others drafted formal codified constitutions to replace the governors' commissions, which had provided the basis for legal authority in most colonies, or royal charters. Superficially the state-written constitutions had much in common with the unwritten constitution of the rejected mother country. Apart from their affirmation of republicanism in place of monarchy, they appeared to rest on the same principles and deploy much the same machinery. Many long-cherished procedural protections for individual rights which derived from English law reappeared in declarations of rights or elsewhere, as did prohibitions of such practices as general warrants and the suspension of laws. Each state had its own particular concerns, including the right to free elections, toleration of religious belief and freedom of the press, and the right to trial by jury, but representation remained a central issue as it had been on both sides of the Atlantic before independence. The principles that voters should have a commitment to the interest of the community and be capable of exercising a free and independent judgment, dear to Blackstone, English radicals and American colonials alike, resurfaced in the states' requirement of property qualifications for voting − a criterion accepted by Burgh and most English radicals and, to a degree, even in the radical Pennsylvania Constitution.[21] There were also a separation of powers between legislature, executive, and judiciary, and (except in Pennsylvania and Georgia) a two-house assembly.

In some respects the impression of similarity is misleading, for there were important differences. Royal charters and instructions to governors provided some limited precedents for a constitutional system predicated on written principles and practices as opposed to the uncodified propositions of the English constitution, but only in a double-edged way. Over the years Americans had come to interpret them as expressions of fundamental laws, but their faith had little basis in reality. Legally the charters were no more than concessions or grants of privileges which could be modified or withdrawn at will, as Massachusetts discovered to its cost in 1774 when Parliament drastically altered its political structure by means of the Massachusetts Government Act. Implicitly – and sometimes explicitly – Parliament and the royal governors had claimed to be superior to the members of the local communities and their representatives, if only because they possessed reserved powers to invalidate colonial legislation. Legally and often substantively, imperial authority had flowed downwards from the crown and was imposed on the people; the colonial legislatures had acquired considerable powers but were formally no more than consultative bodies whose function was to ease the administration of royal power.

By contrast the new states incorporated the radical principle of popular sovereignty in their new institutions. Before setting out the technical details of procedural protection, the Virginia Declaration of Rights spelled out the philosophical foundations of lawful government in a manner replicated by Pennsylvania and other states. Section 1 baldly stated 'that all men are by nature equally free and independent and have certain inherent rights, of which, when they enter into a state of society, they cannot, by any compact, deprive or divest their posterity'; and when the self-consciously elitist gentlemen of Virginia could agree with their fellow citizens 'that all power is vested in, and consequently derived from, the people; that magistrates are their trustees and servants, and at all times amenable to them', they were dramatically altering the ground rules of constitutionalism and opening a Pandora's box of trouble for themselves, for even in the absence of universal suffrage this represented a significant social advance.[22] Legitimate authority in the new states now flowed upwards from the people and would control and limit the contingent authority of governments. The revolutionaries in Virginia and elsewhere further adjusted the relationship between the people and government by following Hulme's warning that slavery began where annual election ended. Most states extended the principle beyond the legislature to include rotation in executive office, and Pennsylvania continued it to include seven-year elective terms for judges. Within the legislatures the balance between the two houses was altered. In England the House of Commons had become by far the more important of the two houses; in the American states the senates were considered to be equal with the lower houses. Like the English radicals and with recent memories of the behaviour of some royal governors, the framers of the new constitutions were cautious in granting powers to the state presidents, as the chief executives were often called. They were appointed commanders-in-chief and were permitted emergency powers, but though their powers were not explicitly limited to executing laws enacted by the legislature, only New York permitted its governor to initiate legislation. In general the authority granted to the executives was circumscribed and followed the radical prescription that a constitution should define the limits of power so as to frustrate its natural tendency to encroach on public liberty.[23]

In other respects the development of American constitutionalism was more experimental. It took most of the war period to construct a model which would formulate a satisfactory relationship between constitutions on the one hand and governments on the other. When completed, the new system proved to be strikingly different from the reigning English model and in important respects more advanced than the proposals of the radicals. Its originality was symbolised by Virginia's decision to publish its declaration of rights first, and only secondly to draft a constitution. Here was the genesis of a new regime which would progress from a statement of philosophical principles to the construction of a constitution which would articulate them into a structure of government and permit the exercise of administrative authority within defined limits. Although the Virginia reorganisation of government was complete before Congress declared independence in July 1776, it was only four years later that the period of experiments in the states came to a conclusion with the implementation of the 1780 Constitution in Massachusetts. At its heart the Massachusetts Constitution and the process by which it came into existence fulfilled the potential inherent in its Virginian procedessor. Three features were especially important. It was drafted by a convention elected solely for the purpose on a universal manhood franchise, and was then formally (if only technically) ratified by the voters of the states' townships, thus articulating the principle of popular sovereignty. Lastly it confirmed the supremacy of the constitution as a grant of power and a definition of rules superior to government and imposing limits on it. It also spelled out a new balance between the three elements within government.

Retrospectively it can be seen that the Massachusetts system became the standard model for general emulation as the nation expanded and more states were admitted to the union. Even so, it was by no means the only possible pattern. During the Revolution the distinction between constitutions and constitution-making on the one side and the operations of government on the other remained unclear in spite of every state's possession of a written constitution. The pressures and exigencies of circumstance did much to influence the process of constructing the independent regimes and their political practices. From 1774 onwards, as the institutions of royal authority disintegrated, they were first replaced by provincial congresses which exercised *de facto* power but whose legitimacy was questionable even though they were elected by members of their local communities. The pressing need to regularise their status persuaded most states to move quickly to form new governments with insufficient attention to the importance of the procedures by which the constitutions were to be drafted if the principles of popular sovereignty and limited government were to be implemented. In Connecticut and Rhode Island the task was easy, but other states found the task much more difficult. Military operations delayed the process in New York, but also made its completion more urgent as a means of consolidating support in a state whose capital had been occupied by the British within weeks of the Declaration of Independence. New Hampshire was only able to sketch a very brief constitution in 1776 and had to wait until 1784 before a more permanent and detailed constitution was approved. Significantly, however, the delay in Massachusetts was the consequence of an extended public debate on the ideological principles and structure of the new regime.

In most states the procedure by which constitutions were formed was substantially different from that of the Massachusetts model. Often the document was drafted by the current provincial congress and approved as if it were a normal bill; New York explicitly declined to elect a convention.[24] Although several congresses claimed popular authority for their actions and were aware of its significance, articulation of the concept of the people as constituent power was still uncertain and remained open for alternative development. Thomas Jefferson was highly critical of the Virginia Constitution for this reason. He denied that the 1776 provincial congress had possessed any superior authority, and argued that the constitution possessed no more authority than any other laws. It could not bind its successors, but legislation could be and already was being enacted in contradition to it and, he concluded, it could be amended by the legislature.[25]

The significance of this practice is especially evident in South Carolina. Its provincial congress had no special instructions from the people, yet at the same time as conducting other business it drafted a temporary constitution in 1776 which it brought into immediate effect without attempting to consult its constituency. Thereafter the first general assembly proposed amendments, and the second drafted another constitution the following year. Among other things, the new version substantially altered the balance between legislature and executive by removing the president's absolute veto. Not surprisingly John Rutledge, the incumbent president, vetoed the proposal but to no effect. Lacking sufficient support in the assembly he felt obliged to resign and the revised constitution became operational in March 1778.[26] Pennsylvania, the most radical state, went as far as to elect a special convention to draft its constitution, but it too conducted normal business and (like its neighbours Delaware and Maryland who also elected constitutional conventions) it brought its fundamental law into effect without any process of popular ratification.

These examples demonstrate that an alternative set of constitutional law and practices was developing as a rival to the emerging Massachusetts model. In spite of the rhetorical affirmation of popular sovereignty in the state declarations of rights and the United States Declaration of Independence, the written constitutions still lacked clear supremacy over legislative action and municipal law. The extent to which constitution-making and legislation were intertwined, as in England, is evident in the amending process. Although Pennsylvania, Georgia and Massachusetts separated amendments from legislation, other states did not; Maryland allowed amendments to be ratified by two-thirds majority in successive assemblies, and South Carolina's 1778 Constitution permitted a simple majority in each house to alter the constitution.[27] Here was the embryo of a system congruent with the Blackstonian concepts of constitutionalism and perhaps even parliamentary sovereignty.

V

Another great change had similar potential. It lay in the treatment of the relationship between the three elements of government — legislature, executive, and judiciary — and was partly a consequence of the social rivalry symbolised by the radicalism of Thomas Paine's *Common Sense* (1776) and the strikingly democratic Pennsylvania constitution on the one hand, and John Adams's *Thoughts on Government* (also 1776) and the more conservative Maryland and New York constitutions on the other. This contest between popular interests and elites for control of the machinery of government raised a constitutional issue of great importance. In England the constitutional balance of mixed government was one of social estates, as well as governmental functions, in which an aristocratic House of Lords purportedly maintained a crucial balance between the monarchic principle exemplified in the Crown and the democratic principle contained in the House of Commons; in practice it worked because the landed aristocracy dominated the Crown and controlled many members of the Commons even though their own house was politically weaker. Such a balance was impossible to achieve in America for two reasons. First, the constitutions articulated the controlling principle that all legitimate authority derived from the people, thus making it theoretically impossible to devise any adequate countervailing power against it. Second, the wealth, status, privileges and cultural supremacy over their fellow citizens enjoyed by American elites was so inferior to that enjoyed by the English aristocracy that there could be nothing comparable to the peerage. In spite of efforts to equate membership of state senates with social status, the upper houses rapidly diminished into revisory chambers enjoying little if any social significance.[28] Such difficulties demonstrated the crucial principle that members of the executive and judiciary as well as the legislature were effectively representatives of the people.[29] It was therefore necessary to construct a balance that would accommodate the necessary power or authority of executive government to the protection of the rights of the citizen, in a manner that would function differently from any previous practice.

A solution was found by modifying drastically the overlapping processes that enabled the English trinity to operate so confidently during the eighteenth century. Instead of mixed constitutions of social categories, the American systems attempted to divide the legislative, executive and judicial branches of government so that none would be dependent on another, and the constitutions would become balances of separated powers.[30] This balancing structure was incorporated in every state constitution in a manner generally far more explicit than in England. The Massachusetts Constitution spelled out the principle in detail: according to Article 30 of its Declaration of Rights,

The legislative department shall never exercise the executive and judicial powers, or either of them: the executive shall never exercise the legislative and judicial powers, or either of them: the judicial shall never exercise the legislative or executive powers, or either of them: to the end it may be a government of laws and not of men.[31]

Yet close analysis of political behaviour and constitutional law again suggests the existence of an embryonic alternative. The frequent dysfunctions between royal executives and colonial legislatures, so evident before independence, had demonstrated both the need to impose formal limits on executive power and the necessity of co-operation between it and the legislature if public business was to be conducted effectively. It was easy to meet the first requirement by spelling out the governors' responsibilities, but memories of the immediate past made it more difficult to cope with the second. In practice the states addressed the problem reluctantly. Their constitutions deliberately weakened the executives and erected legislatures so powerful as to dominate the new machinery in spite of the rhetoric of entrenched popular rights and the efforts to construct a system of checks and balances. Outside New York and Massachusetts, where separate gubernatorial elections were held, all governors were elected by their legislatures (usually for a one-year term), and were politically dependent on them. The consequences were evident in every state. Even an absolute veto proved to be a broken reed for President Rutledge of South Carolina, and such distinguished and able politicians as Patrick Henry and Thomas Jefferson faced considerable difficulty as governors of Virginia; at their most extreme the president of Pennsylvania was little more than a cypher. Ironically, it was a system that could only function satisfactorily if governors built up bodies of supporters in the legislature, thus opening the possibility of a shift towards the English system of interlocked executive and legislature.

VI

Parallel with the states' efforts to order their domestic affairs, Congress was wrestling with the problem of national union. Success required the creation of a stable and permanent level of government additional to, and possibly superior to, the states. The magnitude of the challenge was evident in the need to make two attempts at solving it. As the first national constitution, the Articles of Confederation provided for a central government so limited that its critics began agitating for its replacement even as it became operational in 1781. Arguably, the English process of constitutional growth and adjustment an appropriate model by which it could be strengthened, but this was rejected in favour of what, following the Massachusetts precedent, was becoming the standard American procedure of a constitutional convention.

The new system would have to address once more the conflict of interest between the protection of liberty and the need for effective power, and simultaneously devise a viable balance between central and local governments. For this there was no English precedent, for the apparent similarity between the United States and the British empire is misleading. In the British imperial system a chain of authority flowed downwards from the Crown and parliament. As inferior bodies, the colonies were the creatures of a superior government and were directable by it; the Declaratory Act of 1766 went to the heart of imperial organisation when it stated that parliament could legislate for the colonies in all cases whatsoever. In Revolutionary America the situation was totally different. The thirteen states were the primary units of political community, and Congress was obliged to acknowledge their sovereignty as the price for securing ratification of the Articles. As George Dargo has pointed out, in this respect the American system was the reverse of British centralism.[32]

Replacement of the Articles of Confederation by the United States Constitution marked the climax of Revolutionary constitutional development. When drafting the document, members of the Philadelphia Convention had a number of policy objectives, including containment of what they mistakenly believed were democratic excesses in the states, but though these considerations influenced its final format they were less important in the long run than its structural features. These were partly innovative, partly drawn from the options developed by the states since 1776, and partly derived from English principles and practices.

Of the two English traditions – orthodox and radical – the federal Constitution rested more comfortably within the commonwealth tradition, as had the state constitutions. Though its austerely pragmatic language was notably less elevated than the grand rhetorical phraseology of the state declarations of rights, it included many of their procedural protections for individual rights in the main body of its text or in the first ten amendments. More importantly, it rested on the same ideological principles. It confirmed that the people, rather than the legislature, were the active constituent and sovereign power; it consolidated the procedures of constitutional drafting and ratification along the lines of the Massachusetts model, and it affirmed in Article 6 the primary principle of the supremacy of constitutions over government. It also confirmed that separation of powers would be the key to frustrating potential executive excesses, and instructed the federal government to guarantee a republican form of government to every state. By so doing, the federal Constitution substantially extended the logic of commonwealth principles. In England, radicals were essentially critics who wished to purge contemporary politics of its imperfections and to restore constitutional integrity by purifying the structure of representation and by reviving legislative supremacy; they had been less concerned with other aspects of government. This was an inadequate basis for an entire political system, and the new machinery filled out the gaps and in one respect significantly altered the radicals' structure. Whereas the states conformed to the commonwealth doctrine of legislative superiority, the federal constitution was able to implement the principle that all power and authority derived from the people by constructing a much more even balance among the three elements.

In two respects, moreover, the United States Constitution implicitly went further than the states in repudiating the orthodox version of English constitutionalism. The first instance was its treatment of religion, in which it also went to the limits of commonwealth principles. Eighteenth-century English orthodox constitutionalism was not restricted to secular matters. It was a diarchy of church as well as state, for the established Church was an essential and legally protected prop to the secular regime, and enjoyed both privileges and authority over all members of the community. Several colonies had possessed establishments, some of which (notably the Congregational church in Massachusetts, Connecticut and New Hampshire and the Anglican church in Maryland, Virginia and South Carolina) occupied positions proximately similar to that of the English church, including, in the case of the Anglican church, some authority over non-members. During the Revolution the individual states moved only hesitantly. All those that had possessed Anglican churches disestablished them, but in Connecticut and Massachusetts the Congregational establishments staggered on until 1818 and 1833 respectively. Moreover every state constitution retained some form of religious test – usually requiring profession of some form of Christianity – as a demonstration of adherence to the values of the community and a qualification for voting or public office. Only in Virginia – and only later – were all forms of ecclesiastical privilege, authority and confessional discrimination abolished in the statute for religious freedom of 1786.[33] The process itself was significant for it demonstrated uncertainty as to the boundaries of constitutional principles and practice, by asserting the citizens' rights to the free exercise of religion in the Declaration of Rights, yet using only statutory procedures to dismantle the previously constitutional apparatus of establishment and religious tests. By contrast, the United States Constitution only mentioned religion in order to outlaw any form of religious test for federal office, and the First Amendment abruptly prohibited Congress from establishing any religion at all.

The second respect in which federal constitutionalism went further than the states was in forsaking English common law. Since this had been an integral component of colonial law before the Revolution, and according to James Otis, based on 'the law of nature and its author', the Continental Congress had considered that it formed part of Americans' entitlement of rights; by 1784 eleven states had incorporated the principles of common law and certain categories of British statute law into their own legal systems.[34] Thereafter the states adjusted and developed the common law to their own particular purposes, hence the continuing popularity of Blackstone's *Commentaries* in American as well as English editions. No such explicit provision for the reception of English common law was included in the national Constitution, but the few references to it in the Convention debates and the wording of the Eighth Amendment imply that delegates assumed that it would form part of federal law.[35] Thereafter the evidence is inconclusive. Congress probably intended to grant common-law jurisdiction to federal courts but did not make its intention clear. Also, many members of the Supreme Court during its first twenty years, including James Wilson, William Paterson and Chief Justice Oliver Ellsworth (all of whom had been influential members of the Convention) accepted jurisdiction of common law crimes; Justice James Iredell in particular argued in 1799 that the First Amendment protection of free speech declared the existence of the common law of seditious libel as described by Blackstone. Yet in 1812

the Supreme Court decided that a defendant could not be convicted in the absence of a statute, and the concept of a federal common law evaporated.[36]

But if the United States Constitution was more in line with the radical version of English constitutionalism, it is wrong to assume that all elements of orthodoxy disappeared. Although both it and the state constitutions were formally written constitutions they could only become operable if they developed a corpus of supplementary law and practice. Diverse treatment of such central constitutional issues as religion and the common law by the state and the federal constitutions illustrates the extent to which constitutionalism quickly outreached the documents themselves. Legislative dominance in the early state constitutions contrasted with the balanced structure of checks and balances in the national constitution, and the debate over federal common law similarly suggests an alternative line of development much more akin to English constitutional practice. Also, conventions (in the English sense of customs and conventional rules) quickly assumed almost as great an importance in American constitutionalism as in its British counterpart.[37] The separation of powers in the U.S. Constitution was never total if only because the processes involved in such matters as legislation and the appointment of high officials and judges required formal collaboration. Successful government also required the development of informal codes of co-operative conduct in relations between the three branches of government. As first president, George Washington devoted much attention to establishing suitable non-statutory precedents for the conduct of the executive office on such matters as relations with Congress, his authority over members of the cabinet and the prosecution of foreign policy. Some later presidents have wished to emulate the supremacy over the House of Commons enjoyed by British prime ministers, and although they have been unsuccessful there can be no doubt that the early supremacy of the legislature in the states has given way to increased executive authority in the federal government and most states. Also, although unmentioned in the Constitution and considered dangerous by members of the Philadelphia Convention, political parties quickly developed during the 1790s and have acquired quasi-constitutional status in America as in England. Other constitutional understandings quickly altered the founding fathers' original intentions. Thus the presidential electoral college has never functioned as intended, and when Franklin D. Roosevelt flouted the custom that presidents should serve only two terms, the convention was converted into a constitutional principle.

Above all there was the question of interpreting the document itself. Almost inescapably the framers were obliged to use a conjunction of precise and general phraseology in order to construct viable machinery capable of achieving their philosophical goals. By listing a series of specific powers and restrictions such as those in sections eight and nine of Article 1 yet using phrases such as the 'general welfare' and 'necessary and proper' clauses, the issue was raised of whether the Constitution should be construed broadly or strictly. There was also the crucial need to establish an ultimate authority with power to determine its meaning, a matter on which the Constitution itself is silent. Neither question was capable of a quick and ready solution, but in each case the answer brought American constitutionalism closer to the English formula of a bundle of customs, practices and conventions supplementing positive law. The greatest difference between English and American practice is, of course, the doctrine of judicial review, by which Chief Justice John Marshall on behalf of the Supreme Court laid successful claim to possession of the final right to interpret the meaning of the Constitution. Precedents existed in English law, notably in the pronouncements of Sir Edward Coke, but were developed into a principle profoundly different from the prevailing doctrine which places parliament above the courts as the final arbiter of constitutional meaning. Ironically, though, judicial review is a prime example of a constitutional convention so common in English practice.

The formation of the Revolutionary constitutions can and should be analysed from many standpoints. In each case the framers were faced with particular problems — some unique to the new nation — and were obliged to compose fresh solutions. Nevertheless, three related conclusions stand out in any analysis of the relationship between English principles and American constitutionalism. First it is appropriate to discuss the Philadelphia Convention as the climax to a longer but vital phase in the development of American ideas on the principles and structure of government. Second, if the example of that eighteenth-century botanical classifier Linnaeus were to be followed, American and English constitutionalism in both forms would be located in the same family of governments. Last, though English models were useful and sometimes persuasive, they had to adjust to particular circumstances and needs, and accommodate necessary innovations. American usage of English constitutionalism has clearly been eclectic and adaptive rather than simply adoptive.

Notes

1   E. C. S. Wade and G. G. Phillips, *Constitutional Law*, 6th edn, London, 1960, p. 12.

2   A. V. Dicey, *Introduction to the Study of the Law of the Constitution*, 10th edn, London, 1960, p. 16.

3   Douglass Adair, *Fame and the Founding Fathers*, ed. Trevor Colbourn, New York, 1974, pp. 109–10.

4   Trevor Colbourn, *The Lamp of Experience*, Chapel Hill, NC, 1965, pp. 4–20; Adair, *Fame and the Founding Fathers*, pp. 110–11.

5   Gordon S. Wood, *The Creation of the American Republic: 1776–1787*, Chapel Hill, NC, 1969, pp. 49–50.

6   John Adams, *A Defence of the Constitutions of Government of the United States of America*, 3 vols, London, 1787–8; Robert A. Rutland *et al.*, eds, *The Papers of James Madison*, vol. 9, Chicago, 1975, pp. 4–22; J. G. A. Pocock, *The Machiavellian Moment*, Princeton, NJ, 1975, esp. pp. 506–52.

7   Alexis de Tocqueville, quoted in Dicey, *Law of the Constitution*, p. 22; Gareth Jones, ed., *The Sovereignty of the Law*, London, 1973, pp. xxxi–xxxiii.

8   Dicey, *Law of the Constitution*, pp. 23–8; Sir William Blackstone, *Commentaries on the Laws of England*, 17th edn, ed. Edward Christian, 4 vols, London, 1830, I, pp. 63, 124, 161–2.

9   *Ibid.*, pp. 48, 160, 161.

10   *Ibid.*, pp. 154–5, 157–8, 47.

11   David L. Jacobson, ed., *The English Libertarian Heritage*, Indianapolis, 1965, pp. 106, 131, 91, 93–5.

12   James Burgh, *Political Disquisitions*, 3 vols, London, 1774–5, reprinted New York, 1971, III, pp. 277–8, I, pp. 3–4; for the English radical tradition see Caroline Robbins, *The Eighteenth-Century Commonwealthman*, Cambridge, Mass., 1961.

13   Quoted in Burgh, *Political Disquisitions*, I, p. 83.

14   Jacobson, ed., *English Libertarian Heritage*, pp. 80–7, 256–60.

15   Stanley N. Katz, 'The origins of American constitutional thought', *Perspectives in American History*, III, 1969, p. 474.

16   Thomas R. Adams, *American Independence*, Providence, RI, 1965, pp. 81, 100–1, 172–7; Colbourn, *Lamp of Experience*, pp. 11, 19.

17   Bernard Bailyn, *The Ideological Origins of the American Revolution*, Cambridge, Mass., 1967, pp. 55073, 175–84.

18   William Hooper, quoted in Elisha P. Douglass, *Rebels and Democrats*, Chicago, 1965 [originally 1955], p. 123.

19   Wood, *Creation of the American Republic*, pp. 10–20, 25–8, 30–1, 33–4.

20   John Adams, 'Thoughts on Government' in *The Political Writings of John Adams*, ed. George A. Peek, Jr., Indianapolis, 1954, p. 92.

21   Burgh, *Political Disquisitions*, I, pp. 38–9; Colin Bonwick, *English Radicals and the American Revolution*, Chapel Hill, NC, 1977, pp. 19–20.

22   Francis Newton Thorpe, comp. and ed., *The Federal and State Constitutions, Colonial Charters, and Other Organic Laws of the States, Territories, and Colonies Now or Heretofore Forming the United States of America*, 7 vols, Washington, DC, 1909, VII, p. 3813.

23   For a general discussion of the state constitutions see Willi Paul Adams, *The First American Constitutions*, Chapel Hill, NC, 1980, on which much of the following description is based. Cf. William Clarence Webster, 'Comparative study of the state constitutions of the American Revolution', *Annals of the American Academy of Political and Social Science*, IX, 1897, pp. 380–420.

24   *Ibid.*, pp. 63–93.

25   Thomas Jefferson, *Notes on the State of Virginia*, ed. Thomas Perkins Abernathy, New York, 1964, p. 116.

26   Fletcher M. Green, *Constitutional Development in the South Atlantic States*, New York, 1966 [orig. 1930], pp. 106–12; Adams, *First American Constitutions*, pp. 70–2.

27   Adams, *First American Constitutions*, p. 140.

28   Jackson Turner Main, *The Upper House in Revolutionary America*, Madison, 1967, p. 241.

29   Wood, *Creation of the American Republic*, pp. 447–9.

30   *Ibid.*, pp. 450–3.

31   Adams, *First American Constitutions*, pp. 266–71; Thorpe, ed., *Constitutions*, III, p. 1893.

32   George Dargo, *Roots of the Republic*, New York, 1974, p. 30; *U.S. Articles of Confederation*, Article II; Thorpe, *Constitutions*, I, p. 10.

33   For constitutional provisions regarding religion see Thorpe, ed., *Constitutions, passim*; for the process in Virginia, see Thomas E. Buckley, *Church and State in Revolutionary Virginia, 1776–1787*, Charlottesville, 1977.

34   Morton J. Horwitz, *The Transformation of American Law, 1780–1860*, Cambridge, Mass., 1977, p. 4; William E. Nelson, *Americanization of the Common Law*, Cambridge, Mass., 1975, p. 8.

35   Max Farrand, ed., *The Records of the Federal Convention of 1787, rev. edn*, 4 vols, New Haven, Conn., 1966 [orig. 1937], II, pp. 316, 431; III, p. 130; IV, p. 95.

36   Leonard W. Levy, *Emergence of A Free Press*, New York, 1985, pp. 274–9.

37   Cf. Dicey, *Law of the Constitution*, p. 28n.

The Hartz thesis revisited

For a generation the paradigmatic analysis of American political thought has been *The Liberal Tradition in America* by Louis Hartz. This study represents the high point of the consensus school of historiography initiated by the publication of Richard Hofstadter's *The American Political Tradition* in 1948. Clearly, though unsystematically, Hofstadter shifted the focus of attention away from conflict to a consensus rooted in an ideology of 'self-help, free enterprise, competition, and beneficent cupidity'.[1] This stress on the basic principles of liberal capitalism was echoed by Hartz while being broadened with a perception of the importance of Lockean political theory in American life.

Hartz contends that American thought is deeply, irrationally Lockean in character. In an analysis that, as Samuel Huntington has observed, fruitfully uses Marxist categories to reach Tocquevillian conclusions, Hartz argues that America has experienced an inverted law of combined development, with the United States skipping the feudal stage of history as Trotsky contended that Russia leaped over the bourgeois interlude. Following Tocqueville, Hartz notes that Americans are 'born equal' rather than having to become so. The result is that American thought is profoundly middle-class liberal in its basic orientation with Locke standing rather vaguely as the symbol for this viewpoint. Precisely what 'Lockean' means is never quite defined, though Hartz does refer to 'the reality of atomistic social freedom' as the 'master assumption' of American political theory.[3] Beyond this, Lockeanism clearly refers to such key elements in liberalism as constitutionalism, capitalism and at least a formal commitment to equality. The depth of this attachment has been such as to freeze American politics and thought in the centre of the ideological spectrum, thus foreclosing the development of either a traditionalist, European-style conservatism or any politically serious socialism. The danger, therefore, is not so much the majority tyranny that has preoccupied so much American theory, as it is a paralysing unanimity. We are dominated, says Hartz, by a powerful liberal 'absolutism'.[4]

This is a theory of significant explanatory power. Much falls into place when we realise the extent to which consensus has been the norm for American politics. And, in comparison with Europe, America has been relatively free of overtly class-based politics. However, the Hartz thesis has not by any means gone unchallenged. It is not possible here to examine the whole range of criticisms. Instead, a number of particularly important problems will be singled out. First, one must note that Hartz's discussion suffers by starting with the Revolution, thus leaving out the long heritage of colonial history. Here the most notable analytic loss is any serious treatment of Puritanism, which may well have unwittingly contributed to the development of liberalism, but which is surely not itself liberal. Second, since Hartz wrote, there has been the historical rediscovery of civic republicanism, its connection with Puritanism, and its role in shaping the Revolution. Third, on the face of it, a history whose central event has been a bloody civil war is difficult to interpret in terms of a monolithic consensus. Also, as Robert Dahl has pointed out, serious conflict has erupted on the average of once a generation.[5] Finally, in the years since the publication of *The Liberal Tradition in America*, there has been a recurrent sense that the tradition may have run its course, a development not predicted by Hartz, though it must be said that portions of his work display a sense of forboding. A survey of contemporary alternatives to liberalism, as well as the many attempts to resuscitate it, can provide much insight into the present state of American politics, and into the continued validity of the Hartz thesis.

Puritanism, republicanism, and the liberal tradition

Some of these complexities reveal themselves in a consideration of Puritanism and the ideas of civic republicanism. One implication of the Hartz thesis is that, since liberalism is an essentially modern theory, the United States has been from the beginning a quintessentially modern nation. However, both Puritanism and republicanism are theories with distinctively pre-modern characteristics.

Puritanism is a particularly complex case since, in spite of having roots in an earlier time, it also looks forward in significant ways to some of the most striking features of modernity. Some of this ambiguity is suggested in the late Perry Miller's observations about the requirements of interpreting Puritanism to a changing audience. In the thirties, he points out, it was common, as a reaction to pietistic writers who insisted on making Puritans into prophets of the Constitution and the Bill of Rights, to stress that the Puritans were not at all liberal and to point to the 'authoritarian, the totalitarian element in a complex and sophisticated philosophy'. Later, a contrary disposition took hold and it became usual to 'dwell upon the inherent individualism, the respect for private concience, the implications of revolution, nurtured by Puritan doctrine'. Neither interpretation, Miller adds, constituted more than a 'partial apprehension of the reality'.[6]

That reality must be ascertained through the screen of mythology which, at least for Americans, tends to obscure Puritanism. First, the Puritans were not defenders of religious Liberty; they were not advocates of toleration, but rather 'professed enemies of it'.[7] Nor were they concerned with the principle of separation of church and state. Their government was a theocracy. There could be some debate over the use of this term since the civil magistrates were not ministers. However, the Puritans themselves used this word to suggest the coming together of the sacred and the secular. Moreover, as Miller notes, at this time, 'very few men would even have grasped the idea that church and state could be distinct. For the Puritan mind it was not possible to segregate a man's spiritual from his communal life'.[8] Society was conceived as an organic unit in which government was to play an active part. There was no Jeffersonian ideal of the minimal state. The prevalent conception of liberty was not the negative idea of the absence of external restraints. As John Winthrop put it, there is 'liberty to that only which is good, just and honest', a conception which is closer to the positive liberty of a Rousseau than to anyone in the liberal tradition.[9]

The community was bound together by a strong sense of religious fellowship. Individuals were expected to subordinate their personal interests to the common good. Again Winthrop: 'the care of the public must oversway all private respects ... for it is a true rule that particular estates cannot subsist in the ruin of the public'.[10] Puritanism, Michael Walzer tells us, was a revolution of the saints[11] and the governmental result was a dictatorship of the saints. Note, however, that it was 'a dictatorship, not of a single tyrant, or of an economic class, or of a political faction, but of the holy and regenerate'.[12] Active participation in the governance of the community was restricted to members of the church and non-members were expected to hold their silence, but even for the 'saved' this was not an egalitarian society. 'In all times,' Winthrop told his flock, 'some must be rich, some poor; some high and eminent in power and dignity, others mean and in subjection.'[13] And the magistrates were expected to be obeyed. 'Liberty is maintained and exercised in a way of subjection to that authority.' As a result, men should 'quietly and cheerfully' submit to authority.[14] That they should do so is simply to give proper recognition to the fallen state of man.

These are clearly not the principles of a liberal democratic society and yet they are at the foundation of American politics. But Puritanism is more complex than these ideas alone suggest, and it is necessary to examine some other dimensions of the thought of colonial New England before completing a sketch of the early origins of American political culture. Whatever the predelictions of their creators, in an illustration of the law of unintended consequences, Puritan ideas often led toward some of the basic ideas and practices of liberal democracy.

First, the 'dictatorship of the saints' was not absolute. The Puritans took over the position stemming from the Parliamentary side in the English Civil War which held that government must be governed by a fundamental law.[15] In New England, of course, the source of such law was the Bible, but the entrenchment of the idea survived into a more secular age. Moreover, closely related to the emphasis on fundamental law was the idea of social compact.

Second, in spite of the strong communitarian impulse of the Puritans, there was also, nonetheless, a real individualistic, voluntarist side to both theory and practice. Because of its emphasis on predestination, this side of Calvinist theology is often overlooked. At the end of time individuals had to face God alone,[16] the 'saints' entered the church voluntarily, and this voluntarism carried over into politics. Citizens were expected to submit to authority, but this submission was likewise voluntary.[17] The similarity to liberal contract theory hardly needs remarking.

Third, for the citizens, in spite of the disbelief in egalitarianism, there was a commitment to a high degree of political participation.

As George Armstrong Kelly writes, 'one can recognize in early Massachusetts and Connecticut the sprouting germs of republican civic co-operation. Citizenship and mutual help were strict duties in these communities'.[18] Moreover, in spite of the pervasiveness and power of the religious creed, it is still possible to argue that 'the clergy had less control over politics than anywhere in Europe'.[19]

Fourth, and most controversially, one must consider Max Weber's powerful thesis of the relation between Protestantism and the development of the liberal capitalism which has played so vital a role in American society. It is not possible here to enter into the controversy surrounding Weber's argument. However, even if it is conceded that he sometimes overstates his case,[20] it is still a wonderfully suggestive theory when applied, as it was by Weber, to the American scene. In particular, it is difficult to avoid the conclusion that the fact that Puritanism took root in New England in a way that it never did in the South played a significant role in the profoundly different economic and above all cultural development of the two regions.[21] Little in American history is more important.

Capitalism and secularisation played a notable part in the development of puritan culture. This was a society dependent on a high degree of religious enthusiasm, and as secularism inexorably advanced, aided and abetted by a developing capitalist economy, a degree of stress was virtually inevitable. The dictatorship of the saints began to find that saints were in short supply.[22]

This was a genuine problem for a society based on an set of religious and political ideals and possessed by a high sense of moral mission. In fact, the conflict between these standards and the actual behaviour of Puritans as it was perceived in the real world posed difficulties almost from the very start. John Winthrop had announced, before setting foot on land, that 'we must consider that we shall be as a city upon a hill, the eyes of all people are upon us'.[23] But as early as 1662, Michael Wigglesworth was crying out that 'God has a controversy with New England'. And the Puritan divines seemed to be saying, as Perry Miller notes, 'that New England was sent on an errand, and that it has failed'.[24] This is clear when one reads the passionate sermons which lamented the falling away from the true path whose pursuit was the essence of the Puritan sense of mission. These Jeremiads, whether one stresses the dark side, as does Miller, or finds in them a message of hope, as does Sacvan Bercovitch, became one of the most characteristic forms of American political rhetoric, and a clue to some of the moralistic, even messianic, aspects of American politics.[25]

Puritanism, then, looks both ways. It is not liberal and thus does not easily fit the Hartz thesis. On the other hand, it lays the foundations for what, in secular form, becomes liberal constitutionalism, and also perhaps for the capitalist economy and a peculiarly American form of political morality.

One other form of pre-modern thought must be considered, namely civic republicanism. Until the mid-sixties it would have been taken for granted that at least the American Revolution could be explained in terms of Lockeanism. However, it is now clear that this interpretation in its simplest form will not do. It would be more accurate to contend that Lockean ideas provided the 'deep background and gave a general coloration' to the beliefs of the period.[26] Whether these ideas alone were enough to spark a rebellion is more doubtful. There was a less sober side, a frenzied, visionary, nearly hysterical mood which reflected deep psychological tensions.[27] Indirectly, this stream of thought came from ancient political thought and more immediately from Machiavelli, by way of James Harrington and other seventeenth-century Republicans.[28] The ideas of this civic humanist tradition became part of the revolutionary ideology derived from the 'country' opposition against the 'court' position of the Walpole ministry. In the version set forth by J. G. A. Pocock, Locke and liberalism virtually disappear and the Revolution becomes one of the last acts of the Renaissance.[29]

Republican theory goes well beyond essentially conservative arguments for revolution based on the rights of Englishmen, and also beyond the most radical Lockean positions. The starting point was the instability of the much-admired ancient republics coupled with the belief that this stemmed from corruption due to the pursuit of factional interest. The antidote to corruption was to sacrifice private interest to the common good. This was the essence of republicanism and the defining characteristic of civic virtue. But this, as Gordon Wood has pointed out, was a vision quite divorced from reality as perceived by the colonial leaders.[30] Faction, defined as the pursuit of self-interest, was a sign of social pathology which must be rooted out. Despite liberal contractarian principles, in this aspect of revolutionary thought there is clearly an image of pre-modern organic unity that John Winthrop would have understood. And since individuals and groups did, of course, pursue factional interests, this created a problem of some urgency. The question became whether the colonists had the moral strength to become good republicans.[31] From this viewpoint, Wood argues, the Revolution was more than an anti-colonial rebellion; it was also an effort at moral regeneration. And, it might be added that it is entirely reasonable for these civic humanist themes to find deep resonance in an increasingly secularised Puritan culture. A society raised on the Jeremiad clearly responded to themes of corruption and the falling away from virtue.[32]

What begins to emerge is that the rebels held to two sets of not fully compatible ideas. Harvey Mansfield has posed the alternatives sharply, if over-schematically. 'Civic humanism', he writes, 'is the republican virtue of citizens participating in rule'. This is a body of ideas distinct from liberalism which 'favors rights over community, liberty over duty, representation over participation, and interest over virtue'.[33]

From this perspective the theory of monolithic liberal dominance will not do. But neither will a theory which insists on the dominance of civic humanism. This is particularly clear on even the most cursory examination of the Constitution and *The Federalist*. There is little hint of republican virtue there and, in fact, Madison's Tenth Federalist explicitly concedes that there is no hope of eradicating faction; indeed the pursuit of interest is made the centerpiece of the constitutional system, although there is a nod in the direction of a theory of the public interest that distinguishes Madisonianism from more modern versions of pluralism.

Yet only fourteen years separate the end of the Revolution from the framing of the Constitution. I suggest that the ideological difference developing in this time can be accounted for in two ways. First, the framers were simply not engaged in doing political theory for its own sake; they were political actors and intellectual consistency was doubtless not their main goal. More important, I would suggest, is that the late eighteenth century was a period of very rapid socio-economic transformation. It is perhaps to be expected that such a period would generate a number of conflicting definitions even of the meaning of basic concepts such as liberty.[34] And I would suggest, though I cannot establish it here, that the most basic of these changes was the rapid emergence of capitalism. This is consistent with the growing influence of Locke, after a period of lowered importance, in the latter part of the century.[35] We do not have to accept C.B. Macpherson's view that Locke could only have been produced in a capitalist narket society to see that Locke's theory of property and labour is particularly compatible with such a society; and it may be worth noting that Locke's ancestry was Puritan so that a Weberian interpretation linking him to the development of capitalism is quite plausible. If these hypotheses are correct, then they help to account for the decline of civic humanism and the emergence of a liberal society in America. It should also be noted that this view modifies, but does not replace, the Hartz thesis, while taking into account the persistence of a republican rhetoric that continues to have some real force in American politics.

The problem of conflict

Consider next the problem of the high level of conflict which has characterised so much American politics. This is a much more telling line of argument against Hartz. As Richard Hofstadter so cogently observed, even if one grants the existence of an unusually high level of consensus, that alone is not enough. 'Consensus,' he writes, 'to be effective, must be a matter of behavior as well as thought, of institutions as well as theories.'[36] Indeed, consensus may in itself be a source of substantial conflict. As Huntington shows, a deep attachment to a widely-held set of values can breed discontent as the inevitable gap opens between the ideals and the institutions of the society. The result, in his view, is a periodic outburst of political moralism that tends to challenge the legitimacy of governmental institutions.[37] In his reading of history, these periods of 'creedal passion' have occurred four times in America: during the founding period, the Jacksonian era, the age of Populism and Progressivism, and the tumultuous sixties and seventies of the twentieth century. Much of this theory is persuasive, though many dissent from its normative implications, but it signally fails to account for either the Civil War or the New Deal, perhaps due to Huntington's indifference to social and economic reform.[38] Dahl's list of conflict periods is more comprehensive and shows a major crisis on the average of once a generation including the Civil War and the Great Depression, as well as the crises over the Alien and Sedition Acts, the Hartford Convention, the tariff and nullification, the turmoil over the post-Civil War conversion to corporate capitalism and the civil rights revolution of the fifties and sixties.[39]

All of these periods place a certain stress on the explanatory powers of the Hartz thesis. Still, however violent they sometimes were, Hartz could respond that these events took place within a framework dedicated to the principles of capitalism and liberal constitutionalism. There can be no doubt, as J. David Greenstone has argued, that if these principles do not cause the peculiarities of American politics, they at least are an important limiting factor on its development.[40] The obvious exception to the dominance of the liberal tradition is the Civil War, which is very difficult indeed to interpret in light of a theory of monolithic consensus. The war destroyed forever the Jeffersonian/ Jacksonian idyll of pastoral democracy which de Tocqueville had so brilliantly observed. In the election of 1860, anti-slavery forces won out even in the total absence of support from the sectional minority which defended the ante-bellum *status quo*.[41] The conflict that followed led to the completion of an American nation; the house divided was united by force. As Eric Foner has put it,

We can paraphrase John Adams's famous comment on the American Revolution and apply it to the coming of the Civil War – the separation was complete in the minds of the people before the war began. In a sense the Constitution – and the Lockean framework that supported it – 'failed in the difficult task of creating a nation' – only war could accomplish that.[42]

But more than national unification flowed from the war. The state that emerged was decisively a large-scale liberal capitalist state. Here too is irony, for the Union Lincoln fought to preserve was the world of Jacksonian America – in some respects pre-modern – 'the world of the small shop, the independent farm, and the village artisan'. In the South the end of slavery gave to the principal subordinate, pre-modern classes – the poor whites and the former slaves – a chance, not fully used to be sure, to express their grievances against the upper class. In the north the war stimulated a tremendous growth of large-scale capitalist enterprise and began a process of institutional centralisation. To quote Foner once more, 'each side fought to defend a distinct vision of the good society, but each vision was destroyed by the very struggle to preserve it'.[43]

The liberalism which Louis Hartz proclaimed as triumphant from the start was at last firmly established. The last major non-liberal institutional structures were removed and with them their supporting ideologies. The hegemony of a Lockean world-view, incipient from the start, was now complete, and the history of the United States has been largely dominated since then by the logic and constraints of such a view.

These upheavals cannot be fully explained by the theory of a liberal consensus. Hartz's attempt to do so is one of the most stimulating sections of his great book, but in the end it does not succeed. Of course Hartz knew that the system of slave labour was neither liberal nor capitalist. But at the same time, he seems to see the southern system as simply an aberration, a fact attested to by its rapid disappearance after the war. However, his inistence on the importance of what he calls the 'reactionary enlightenment' and the thought of George Fitzhugh go a long way toward undercutting his argument. Fitzhugh's position was based on the most fundamental rejection of all aspects of liberal theory and practice.[44] Fitzhugh's argument is relentless and, unlike the more celebrated John C. Calhoun, it is clear that he fully grasped the necessary logic of a slave society. He repudiates any form of natural rights theory, any doctrine of consent and in fact asserts the natural right of most men to be slaves.[45] This is combined with a rejection of capitalism so sweeping as to impress even a Marxist historian such as Eugene Genovese.[46] The special villain in free society is *laissez-faire* capitalism, which Fitzhugh sees as at war with slavery.[47] Northern labourers, he claimed, were already slaves without knowing it and their employers were their oppressors. This situation requires, in Fitzhugh's view, the abolition of free labour and the institution of nation-wide slavery. Free labour and slave labour cannot co-exist indefinitely. 'One set of ideas', he writes, 'will govern and control the civilized world. Slavery will everywhere be abolished or everywhere be instituted'.[48]

This is the critical point, for this is the also logic of the situation as seen by key segments of the northern anti-slavery forces. This is most clearly seen in Lincoln's 'house divided' speech. The most profound observers on each side of the sectional divide realised that much more was at stake than a quarrel among capitalist factions. Economic factors certainly played a part, but even more it must be stressed that two fundamentally different ways of life were in conflict. These ways of life included deeply opposed intellectual commitments. A system based on free labour was quite naturally compatible with ideas which were essentially liberal in character, though of course this is not to suggest that racism was not widespread in the north, even in abolitionist circles. The theories of Locke had a genuine resonance and were rooted in the institutional structures of the north. The South, for all its Jeffersonian heritage, was pulled strongly toward a viewpoint with pronounced anti-liberal, pre-bourgeois, anti-capitalist attitudes. It came to exhibit, as Eugene Genovese suggests, a 'special social, economic, political, ideological and psychologial content'.[49] From a Lockean perspective such a civilisation could certainly be seen as aberrational but, more important, it posed a threat to the immediate well-being of the free northern labouring classes. The logic of the two societies was perhaps nearly as clear to them as it was to Lincoln and Fitzhugh.

Perhaps, as Genovese and others have suggested, southern society can best be understood in the light of Hegel's theory of the master—slave relationship. The slaveholders

had the habit of command, but there was more than depotic authority in this master-slave relationship. The slave stood interposed between his master and the object his master desired ...; thus the master related to the object only mediately, through the slave. The slaveholder commanded the products of another's labor, but by the same process was forced into dependance on the other.[50]

This may be somewhat speculative, but it suggests complex problems that cannot be explained by a theory of America built on the assumption of monolithic liberalism. Only the excision of slavery fully opens up the possibility of such a theory.

That possibility depends further on the formation of a new national culture. Part of the significance of the war was that it led to the creation of such a culture, but even that process was incomplete and, as Anne Norton has argued, it was a culture forcibly imposed by the north on an unwilling south.[51] And that new consensus, if it can be called that, was itself complex and divided. The victorious northern forces were themselves characterised by regional differences and, indeed, it was part of Lincoln's achievement to weld the north-east and west together in his creation of a new basis for a Weberian rational—legal legitimacy.[52] And, by a careful examination of the ideas of Lincoln, Daniel Webster, and Stephen Douglas, J. David Greenstone has shown that political leaders who fall recognisably into the liberal camp nevertheless exhibited major differences,[53] with Lincoln emerging as the champion of Lockean ideas of natural right and consent. This, after all, is the essential meaning of his ringing appeal to re-enact the Declaration of Independence.

What these considerations make clear is that the Hartz thesis, for all its brilliance, is too simplified to account for the rich variety of conflicts in the pre-Civil War period. Hartz is aware that what he offers is a single factor analysis[54] but, like many such theories, it sheds an intense but narrowly-focused light. It is not so much that

Hartz is wrong, but that he claims too much. To adapt the famous phrase from de Tocqueville, the United States was not born liberal, but had to become so. Lockean liberalism was important from the start, but Lockean ideas were only part of a richer cultural fabric. But the war transformed the nature of liberalism and especially its economic foundations.

The contemporary crisis of the liberal tradition

Louis Hartz captures some of this transformation; however he is not precisely on the mark. As he puts it, 'after Lincoln, the slate is wiped clean for the triumph of a theory of democratic capitalism implicit from the outset in the American liberal world'.[55] But, John Diggins argues, the most important change precipitated by the Civil War was rather the emergence of large-scale *corporate* capitalism.[56] Of course, this development had pre-war roots[57] and de Tocqueville had predicted the emergence of a harsh new industrial aristocracy.[58] But even his formidable powers could not anticipate the magnitude of the change. Earlier social theories had been based on the predominance of agriculture and the legitimating ideal of the Jeffersonian dream of a republic of yeoman farmers. But the post-Civil War system did not remotely approach the old forms of economic organisation. As John Blum has written, 'man became economic man, democracy was identified with capitalism, liberty with property and the use of it, equality with opportunity for gain, and progress with economic change and the accumulation of capital'.[59]

The new socio-economic order required a new legitimating theory. This need was met by the importation of the Social Darwinism of Herbert Spencer, with William Graham Sumner as the most important American exponent.[60] The result was a bizarre mixture of Darwinian natural selection, the Protestant ethic, and the economics of Adam Smith[61] which, while deeply liberal in its underlying assumptions, has come to be seen as the essence of American conservatism. This is a theory with deep roots in America, all of which represent powerful intellectual currents in the modern world. Possessive individualism became the dominant national creed, rapidly eclipsing the Tocquevillian vision of a country of co-operative voluntary association with strong traces of civic humanist republicanism. What was especially remarkable, as Dahl has pointed out, was the extent to which the system clothed itself 'in the recut garments of an outmoded ideology

in which private ownership was justified on the ground that a wide
diffusion of property would support political equality'. The result,
Dahl concludes, was that Americans have never asked themselves if
there is an alternative to corporate capitalism.[62] But whatever the
virtues of corporate capitalism, promoting equality is not one of them.
Nor, as many contemporary critics would argue, is it clear that corporate capitalism and democracy are not at least in tension and at
most incompatible.[63] In any case, the perpetuation of an outmoded
pre-corporate justification of private property must be seen as one
of the lasting triumphs of conservative Darwinism. This heady body
of thought has come to be at the core of much of American conservatism, up to and including the Reagan administration, which is
understandable, if paradoxical. The preservation of the economic
order is a natural function for conservatives but, since to preserve
capitalism is to preserve a system dedicated to change, there is a certain
often remarked irony here. But this, as Hartz well knew, is the natural
fate of 'conservatism' is a society in which much of what is to be
conserved is liberal. This has been the basic dilemma of American
conservatism: the preservation of the *status quo* in a society dedicated
in principle to a dynamism that is bound to upset the *staus quo* and,
more subtly perhaps, to support hedonistic consumption in a system
putatively based on the Protestant ethic.

However powerful, this was a system of ideas that could not go
unchallenged for long. The reform movement which responded came
in three waves: Populism, Progressivism and the New Deal. On one
level, Populism was a reactionary attempt to cling to an already
doomed agrarian past, but it also injected into American politics a
fundamental critique of the new industrial order and a new conception
of a positive role for government on behalf of the victims of the
corporate system which, in the long run, contributed to the emergence
of the modern activist state. But the form of the new state has hardly
what the agrarian rebels might have hoped for.

That state was largely the creation of the ambiguous movement
known as Progressivism. Exactly whose interests were served by the
progressives is a matter of considerable dispute. There is no doubt,
however, that these reformers were responding to the new and
dominant forms of social and economic organisation which developed
following the Civil War.[64] Although Progressivism was a very loose
movement which is hard to describe in brief, David Price is surely
right to argue that its principal ideas were community and control.[65]

A wide range of theorists, of whom John Dewey is the most important, attempted to soften the intense individualism of the conservative Darwinists in favor of a more social, less competitive view of human nature.[66] There was similarly wide agreement in Progressive circles that the pursuit of Darwinian competition was a prescription for chaos and that some form of social control using the agencies of government was necessary. Here the most interesting, if not the most influential, thinker was Herbert Croly. In *The Promise of American Life*, Croly proposed the pursuit of Jeffersonian ends by Hamiltonian means. Clearly this meant the development of a larger state whether in the guise of Wilsonian New Freedom or Rooseveltian New Nationalism. Perhaps the major question was who to benefit from this new effort at control. Theodore Roosevelt proclaimed his aim to bring the 'malefactors of great wealth' to heal, but some of those same malefactors saw an opportunity to assert control over the ostensible controllers. The extent to which they succeeded is still a matter for debate, but there can be little doubt that some of the more sophisticated business leaders reacted in those terms.[67] A partnership between business and government began to emerge which 'gave the appearance and some of the substance of reform', though whether Jeffersonian ends were ever actually pursued under this system has been challenged, in spite of the social democratic aspects of the New Deal.[68] This Yankee capitalism, as some have called it, became the core of establishment ideology and its apparent collapse in the late seventies was a major political and intellectual development.

Several factors contributed to the decay of the reform liberal consensus. From 1948 on the New Deal electoral coalition began to crumble. Further strains were added as conservative elements of the coalition began to react against the civil rights movement and the campaign against the war in Vietnam. On the left, that war was seen as a liberal war and the system which produced it came to be known as 'corporate liberalism'. Even moderate critics of the reform consensus began to write of the 'end of liberalism' and to attack the pathologies of 'interest group liberalism'.[69] Toward the end of the seventies, the situation was exacerbated by apparent inability to deal with foreign policy problems such as the Iranian hostage crisis and the seemingly intractable domestic problem of 'stagflation'. This helped bring to power a presidential administration dedicated, at least rhetorically, to ending many of the achievements of the reform movement of the preceding decades.

Some theory would predict a crisis of legitimacy in a system in which the basic supporting theories of the past generation and more had come under sustained attack.[70] Politically the problem is quite clear. Public opinion polls have revealed a decline of confidence in all elites, although political leaders have recovered somewhat during the Reagan years. However, that recovery appears fragile and may well prove temporary.[71] Perhaps more important is the long secular decline in voter turnout, a particularly disquieting fact in a political system where voting is the central act of the citizen and in which other forms of participation are often discouraged.[72]

Nonetheless, it would be a serious exaggeration to say that the United States is in a legitimacy crisis. Still, a 'legitimacy deficit' leading to considerable social and political strain is a real possibility.[73] No doubt as a partial consequence, recent years have seen a major revival of political theory in general and a renewed interest in authority and the state in particular.

The list of works is long and by no means every major contribution to the debate can be mentioned. The responses cover a wide ideological range. Some of the most powerful work, such as that of Hannah Arendt, virtually deny the continued existence of meaningful authority.[74] Others view American discontents as a product of an excess of authority, and hope, like Robert Nozick and members of the Chicago school of economics, to return to the never-never land of the minimalist state, a view which strikes responsive chords in parts of the Reagan administration.[75]

More theoretically interesting are the attempts to revive or reconstruct specifically liberal versions of democratic theory. Nozick's *Anarchy, State and Utopia* falls into this category at the liberarian end of the scale, but by far the most discussed example is John Rawls's *A Theory of Justice*.[76] This is a work whose practical thrust is to defend the theoretical underpinnings of the modern welfare state, although it must be said that it does so on the most abstract level and that it exhibits a most disconcerting lack of concern for institutional considerations.[77] However, in spite of this, the egalitarian implications of the well-known difference principle point in this direction. The political impact of Rawls's work is difficult to ascertain, though it is possible that, over time, the sheer magnitude of the discussion surrounding it will make at least an indirect mark, as will the widespread attention paid to Rawls in the law schools.

Ideologically very different is the work of the students of the late Leo Strauss who make up an intellectually and perhaps politically important school. The precise import of this version of neo-classical political philosophy is not clear. For some it is nothing much more than a form of Platonic elitism based on dubious classical scholarship.[78] For sympathetic critics the picture is more complex. Here the argument is often made that the principal defect of liberal democracy is its hesitancy to defend itself against other, more virulent, forms of modernity and that we can learn most from classical philosophy if we read it as an injunction against any and all forms of utopianism.[79] In this perspective modern liberal democracy is the best alternative open to the Western world. How weak a reed this is can be seen if one considers Leo Strauss's own severe strictures against Locke.[80] In any case, the impact of the Straussians in a number of elite universities opens up the possibility that we are seeing here the start of a genuine American conservative theory, although the dominance of capitalist principles continues to haunt this version of conservatism as much as its predecessors.

Other theories also break interesting new ground. Two are virtually polar opposites. The first is the Hegel-inspired approach to authority and the state developed by George Armstrong Kelly. The situation Kelly sees is one in which there have been 'injuries against state-mindedness by the highest state authorities themselves'.[81] Neither liberals nor Marxists have developed adequate conceptions of authority, he suggests. The liberal image of the patrolman merely directing the flow of free transactions in a society has been called into question and Marxist or elitist theories of domination lead, he argues, either to cynicism or to apocalypse. As a substitute, the Hegelian view that, 'political authority is there to amplify and sustain the solidarity of a people by acting as a focal point of reverence and by suspending particular wills and interests' has its attractions.[82] Some of the conditions specified by Hegel for the appearance of such a state have developed in America: the stabilisation of the frontier, the increasing competition over scarce goods, the potential for class antagonism to increase, and a general sense of physical and psychological cramping.[83] Kelly clearly does not believe that a Hegelian state is about to emerge in the United States or that it would provide miraculous solutions were it to do so. However it is fair to say that he is among those powerfully drawn to a strong state as a necessary component of any real alleviation of present discontents. And it might be noted that, while Kelly is no civic republican, the emphasis on solidarity and the suppression of particular interests is nonetheless in keeping with a strong current in contempory thought.

That current runs strongly in the next group of theorists. At the other end of the continuum from Kelly is the view advanced most powerfully by John Schaar and Sheldon Wolin. Here the themes are even more strongly reminiscent of the civic republican tradition. The emphasis is on small-scale political units, citizen participation, close popular control of government, and the priority of politics over economics. They, like Arendt, seem to believe that humanly mean-ingful authority is near to extinction and that one of the reasons is the modern state itself, a state which is deeply implicated in the modern Faustian project − the attempt to subordinate nature, and the correspondingly inevitable rise of large, bureaucratic, technocratic organisations associated with what they feel to be an ultimately Sisiphean project. The humane gains even the welfare state brings are paltry in comparison with the dangers of the modern state itself. Schaar argues that only radical decentralisation can save us. Our watchword must be 'all power to the fragments'.[84]

Sheldon Wolin's views are, if anything, even more deeply critical of the condition of contemporary American democracy.[85] He sees profound dangers emerging in liberal society. The United States today threatens to become one of those societies which chooses to take its identity from economic performance 'while allowing political life to languish from corporate and bureaucratic centralization and from the steady corruption by commercial television of public perceptions of a public world'.[86] The United States is faced with a form of rule anticipated, though imperfectly, by de Tocqueville in his notion of democratic despotism. It is a society of dependants rather than active citizens. Life has been depoliticised by trivialising the commonality of politics, 'and then claiming that it is represented by the public opinion poll and mass elections dominated by the powers big money can buy'.[87] The strong state must be case aside because such a state and democracy are contradictions in terms.[88] Democracy requires participation and it demands diffusion rather than centralisation of power. However, not all problems can be defined in smaller terms and it is therefore 'not necessary to abolish the state'. What is impor-tant is to move toward a politics of smaller groupings.[89]

The views of Schaar and Wolin are in some ways very attractive. They are deeply committed to a politics of democratic participation which is difficult, if not impossible, to achieve in the modern state. But the state is hardly likely to wither away. It is difficult to imagine what forces, short of thermonuclear holocaust, would bring about its final destruction. Kelly on one side, and Schaar and Wolin on the other, have presented us with a gigantic historical dilemma. We need the large state; the suffering that would be brought about by its demise is frightening to contemplate. And, after all, modernity has not been a total loss. But the costs just as clearly have been enormous. The security the state provides is frequently minimal at best and it offers little to anyone imbued with the ideals of participatory democratic citizenship. It is hard to imagine life without the state and it may well yet prove impossible to live with it. The dilemma was captured aphoristically by Henry Kariel a number of years ago: 'Just as small-scale, humanly comprehensible groupings are essential, so are large-scale humanly incomprehensible ones'.[90]

That it seems impossible for modern states to resolve this dilemma either in theory or in practice is a measure of the problems inherent in achieving a meaningful form of democratic authority under the conditions of contemporary American politics. It may be that the recent work of Michael Walzer begins to offer a glimpse of a way out consistent with the American tradition of political theory. Walzer too stresses that the state will not wither away; instead, he argues, it must be 'hollowed out'.[91] Precisely what this entails is not fully specified, but it clearly involves at least a democratisation of the 'local units of work, education, and culture' and the great functional organisations of contemporary society, a rethinking of the relation of economic to political institutions, an increase in levels of participatory, mass-based, movement politics, and some elements of decentralised market socialism.[92]

Walzer's very moderate reform socialism appears consistent with the tradition of American politics. His important theory of justice rests on the view that there is no simple distributive principle which covers all cases or, still less, that justice can be imposed by some central authority. We can draw a map of a society, in Walzer's view, by specifying the various goods which must be distributed and then determining the relevant principles which, consistent with the shared social understandings of the society, should govern the distribution in a particular social sphere.[93] No single distribution will work in and a complex, differentiated social system it is a mark of tyranny when a good, even if properly acquired, is used to achieve dominance in another distributional sphere, with the most obvious example the frequent hegemony of money in the realm of politics.

Two things should be noted; the first is that, in Walzer's view, it has been the historical role of liberalism to create this complex of distributional arenas out of the organic structure of feudal society[94] and second, that the concern for shared social understandings ensures that, in America, the just society must be rooted in liberal principles, though it almost certainly will need to range beyond them. This at least opens up the possibility that Walzer's theory might be translated into practice. This is not to suggest the emergence of a politically viable American socialism at any time in the forseeable future. However, there is the possibility of redrawing the line between the economic and political spheres, a line which, in Walzer's view, has been wrongly drawn for a long time.[95] There is widespread evidence of distrust of business elites which could lend impetus to a new wave of reform.[96] Second, there is the recurrent cyclical pattern of American politics which suggests that it is time for a new period of emphasis on public rather than private concerns.[97] The strength of the business community and the much discussed weakness of the party system are, however, formidable obstacles in the way of such a change. The continued vitality of the Hartz thesis may depend on the capacity of the liberal tradition to reorient itself once again, perhaps by drawing on the long submerged themes of republican virtue and on new currents in democratic socialist thought.

Notes

Some parts of this essay have been drawn from the English original of *Amerikanisches politisches Denken: Von der Revolution bis zum Bürgerkrieg*, in Iring Fetscher and Herfried Münkler, eds, 3 *Pipers Handbuch der Politischen Ideen*, Munich, 1985, pp. 617–53. The article here is a summary of arguments to be developed in book form and published by Westview Press. It is a matter of the deepest personal and professional regret that I was unable to discuss these themes with John Lees.

1   Richard Hofstadter, *The American Political Tradition*, Twenty-fifth anniversary edition, New York, 1973, p. xxix.
2   Samuel Huntington, *American Politics: The Promise of Disharmony*, Cambridge, 1982, p. 7.
3   Louis Hartz, *The Liberal Tradition in America*, New York, 1955, p. 62.
4   Hartz, *Liberal Tradition*, p. 58.

5   Robert A. Dahl, 'The American oppositions: affirmation and denial' in Dahl, ed., *Political Oppositions in Western Democracies*, New Haven, 1966, pp. 34–69.

6   Perry Miller, *Errand Into the Wilderness*, Cambridge, 1956, p. 141. My interpretation of Puritanism has been deeply influenced throughout by Miller's work.

7   Samuel Willard quoted in Miller, *Errand*, p. 145.

8   Miller, *Errand*, p. 142. On the question of terminology I follow Sacvan Bercovitch, *The American Jeremiad*, Madison, 1978, p. 3.

9   John Winthrop, 'Speech to the general court' in Perry Miller and Thomas H. Johnson, eds, *The Puritans*, I, New York, 1963, p. 207.

10   Winthrop, 'A model of Christian charity' in Miller and Johnson, *The Puritans*, p. 197. Spelling modernised.

11   Michael Walzer, *The Revolution of the Saints*, Cambridge, 1965.

12   Miller, *Errand*, p. 143.

13   Winthrop, 'A model' in Miller and Johnson, *The Puritans*, p. 195.

14   Winthrop, 'Speech to the general court' in Miller and Johnson, *The Puritans*, p. 207.

15   Miller, *Errand*, p. 146.

16   Miller, *Errand*, p. 143.

17   Miller, *Errand*, pp. 147–50.

18   George Armstrong Kelly, 'Faith, freedom, and disenchantment', *Daedalus*, 111, 1982, p. 132.

19   Kelly, 'Faith', p. 132.

20   Walzer, *Revolution of the Saints*, p. 304 and John Shi, *The Simple Life*, New York, 1986, p. 10. For Weber, see *The Protestant Ethic and the Spirit of Capitalism*, trans. Talcott Parsons, New York, 1958.

21   C Vann Woodward, *American Counterpoint*, Boston, 1971, pp. 13–46.

22   Alan Simpson, *Puritanism in Old and New England*, Chicago, 1955, p. 35.

23   Winthrop, 'A model', p. 199.

24   Miller, *Errand*, p. 2.

25   Sacvan Bercovitch, *The American Jeremiad*, Madison, 1978 and Miller, *Errand*, esp. pp. 1–15. See also Huntington, *American Politics*, pp. 14–15, 154–66.

26   Bernard Bailyn, 'The central themes of the American Revolution' in Stephen Kurtz and James Hutson, *Essays on the American Revolution*, Chapel Hill, 1973, p. 7.

27   Bernard Bailyn, *The Ideological Origins of the American Revolution*, Cambridge, 1967; Bailyn, 'Central themes'; Gordon Wood, *The Creation of the American Republic*, Chapel Hill, 1969, pp. 46–125, esp. p. 121.

28   J. G. A. Pocock, 'Virtue and commerce in the eighteenth century', *Journal of Interdisciplinary History*, 1972, p. 120 and *The Machiavellian Moment*, Princeton, 1975.

29   Pocock, 'Virtue and commerce', p. 120.

30   Wood, *Creation*, p. 53.

31   Wood, *Creation*, p. 95.

32   Shi, *The Simple Life*, p. 52 and the literature cited therein.

33   Harvey Mansfield, Jr., 'Review of Pocock, *The Machiavellian Moment*', *American Political Science Review*, 71, 1977, p. 111.

34   Joyce Appleby, *Capitalism and a New Social Order*, New York, 1984, pp. 14–23.

35   Isaac Kramnick, 'Republican revisionism revisited', *American Historical Review*, 87, 1982, pp. 629–64.

36   Richard Hofstadter, *The Progressive Historians*, New York, 1968, p. 457.

37   Huntington, *American Politics*, pp. 64–8.

38   Samuel H. Beer, 'The Democratic Temper', *The New Republic*, 11 November 1981, p. 32.

39   Dahl, *Political Oppositions*, pp. 48–53.

40   J. David Greenstone, 'Political culture and American political development: liberty, union, and the liberal bipolarity', *Studies in American Political Development*, I, 1986, pp. 1–49.

41   Eric Foner, *Politics and Ideology in the Age of the Civil War*, New York, 1980, p. 52.

42   Foner, *Politics and Ideology*, p. 53.

43   Foner, *Politics and Ideology*, p. 32–3.

44   George Fitzhugh, *Cannibals All, or Slaves Without Masters*, ed. C. Vann Woodward, Cambridge, 1960 and 'Sociology for the South' in Harvey Wish, ed., *Antebellum*, New York, 1960.

45   Fitzhugh, *Cannibals All*, p. 69.

46   See Eugene Genovese, *The World the Slaveholders Made: Two Essays in Interpretation*, New York, 1969, pp. 118–244.

47   Fitzhugh, 'Sociology for the south', p. 47.

48   Fitzhugh, 'Sociology for the south', p. 95.

49   Eugene Genovese, *The Political Economy of Slavery*, New York, 1967, p. 13.

50   Genovese, *Political Economy*, p. 32. Cf. David Brion Davis, *The Problem of Slavery in Western Culture: 1770–1823*, Ithaca, 1975, pp. 557–64.

51   Anne Norton, *Alternative Americans: A Reading of Antebellum Political Culture*, Chicago, 1986, p. 6.

52   Norton, *Alternative Americas*, p. 295, pp. 293–314 *passim*.

53   Greenstone, 'Political culture and political development', pp. 28–47.

54   Hartz, *Liberal Tradition*, 20–23.

55   Hartz, *Liberal Tradition*, pp. 198–9.

56   John P. Diggins, *The Lost Soul of American Politics*, New York, 1984, p. 322.

57   Norton, *Alternative Americas*, p. 33–63.

58   Alexis de Tocqueville, *Democracy in America*, trans. George Lawrence, Garden City, 1969, p. 558.

59   John M. Blum, quoted in Robert A. Dahl, *A Preface to Economic Democracy*, Berkeley, 1985, p. 72.

60   Richard Hofstadter, *Social Darwinism in American Thought*, Boston, 1955.

61   Hofstadter, *Social Darwinism*, p. 51.

62   Dahl, *Preface to Economic Democracy*, p. 73.

63   Charles Lindblom, *Politics and Markets*, New York, 1977, p. 356.

64   Robert Wiebe, *The Search for Order: 1877–1920*, New York, pp. 164–95.

65   David Price, 'Community and control: critical democratic theory in the Progressive period', *American Political Science Review*, 68, 1974, pp. 1663–78.

66   John Dewey, *The Public and its Problems*, New York, 1927 and *Liberalism and Social Action*, New York, 1963.

67   Huntington, *American Politics*, p. 119.

68   Kenneth Dolbeare, *Democracy at Risk*, Chatham, NJ, 1984, p. 30, p. 158.

69   Theodore Lowi, *The End of Liberalism*, New York, 1969.

70   Jürgen Habermas, *Legitimation Crisis*, trans. Thomas McCarthy, Boston, 1975.

71   Seymour Martin Lipset and William Schneider, *The Confidence Gap*, 2nd edn, Baltimore, 1987, pp. 415–40.

72   Walter Dean Burnham, 'The changing shape of the American political universe', *American Political Science Review*, 59, 1965, pp. 7–28.

73   William Connolly, *Appearance and Reality in Politics*, Cambridge, 1981, p. 133.

74   Hannah Arendt, 'What is authority?', in *Between Past and Future*, New York, 1968, pp. 91–141.

75   Robert Nozick, *Anarchy, State, And Utopia*, New York, 1975 and Milton Friedman, *Capitalism and Freedom*, Chicago, 1963.

76   John Rawls, *A Theory of Justice*, Cambridge, 1970.

77   Benjamin Barber, 'Justifying justice: problems of psychology, measurement, and politics in Rawls', *American Political Science Review*, 69, 1975, pp. 663–74.

78   M. F. Burnyeat, 'Sphinx without a secret', *New York Review of Books*, 30 May 1985, pp. 30–6.

79   For a range of views on Strauss and the implications of his work, see Kenneth Deutsch and Walter Soffer, *The Crisis of Liberal Democracy*, Albany, 1987, esp. the essays of John Gunnell, Hilail Gilden, and Stephen Salkever.

80   Leo Strauss, *Natural Right and History*, Chicago, 1953, pp. 202–51.

81   George Armstrong Kelly, *Hegel's Retreat from Eleusis*, Princeton, 1978, p. 231.

82   Kelly, *Hegel's Retreat*, p. 222.

83   Kelly, *Hegel's Retreat*, p. 189.

84   John Schaar, *Legitimacy in the Modern State*, New Brunswick, 1981.

85   In addition to the essays cited here, Wolin's views can be seen in *democracy*, the quarterly he edited from 1981 to 1983.

86   Sheldon Wolin, 'Counter-enlightenment: Orwell's *1984*', in Robert Mulvihill, ed., *Reflections on America, 1984*, Athens, 1984, p. 110.

87   Wolin, Counter-enlightenment', pp. 111–13.

88   Wolin, 'Contract and birthright, '*Political Theory*, 14, 1986, p. 191.

89   Wolin, 'Contract and birthright', p. 191.

90   Henry Kariel, *The Promise of Politics*, Englewood Cliffs, 1966, p. 66.

91   Michael Walzer, *Radical Principles*, New York, 1980, p. 46.

92   *Radical Principles*, pp. 46–7 and Michael Walzer, *Spheres of Justice*, New York, 1983, p. 318.

93   Walzer, *Spheres of Justice, passim*.

94   Walzer, 'Liberalism and the art of separation', *Political Theory*, 12, 1984, p. 315.

95   Walzer, 'Liberalism and separation', p. 328.

96   Lipset and Schneider, *The Confidence Gap*, pp. 163–98.

97   Arthur M. Schlesinger, Jr., *The Cycles of American History*, Boston, 1987, pp. 23–48.

Part 2

Governmental adaptations: presidency, Congress and judiciary

Who makes war? The President, Congress, and the War Powers Resolution

The separation of powers and the checks and balances which are inherent in the American political system and which also form the very basis of the Constitution amount to a built-in institutional conflict between the executive and the legislative branches in government. This is especially important in the foreign policy area where the division between the two branches is much more problematic and vague than in the domestic field. The wording is often ambiguous, and frequently the Constitution does not deal with the problems at all.

Arthur Schlesinger, Jr. has characterised the Constitution as 'cryptic, ambiguous and incomplete' in its allocation of powers affecting foreign policy.[1] One expert calls the provisions 'general, indefinite, and ambiguous',[2] another finds them 'elusive',[3] and a third concludes that 'as they have evolved, the foreign relations powers appear not so much 'separated' as fissured, along jagged lines indifferent to classical categories of governmental power'.[4] Edward S. Corwin has argued that the American Constitution 'is an invitation to struggle for the privilege of directing American foreign policy'.[5]

The growing power of the Executive at the expense of Congress in the decades preceding the Vietnam War and the Watergate crisis came mainly about via foreign policy. It is frequently seen as a consequence of the emergence of American globalist policy and the 'imperial extension of American influence throughout the world'.[6] The need for 'authority, speed and discretion' enhanced the power of the Presidency. However, the development of the dominance of the Executive in foreign policy has a long history. It is, in fact, as old as the Union. Madison called the result of the constitutional provisions concerning foreign policy 'a partial mixture of powers', and Hamilton referred to the war-making and treaty-making powers as 'joint

possessions'. Other commentators have used words such as 'inter-woven responsibilities and competing opportunities'.[7]

Congress has been anxious to protect its constitutional prerogatives: it alone can authorise hostilities against a foreign state. However, in various ways the Executive has succeeded in wresting these powers from Congress. It was the development of the President's war-making power, which to a great extent stemmed from his position as Commander-in-Chief, that enhanced his dominance in the foreign policy area. The premises for the expansion of the presidential powers were well summed up by Hamilton when he stated that 'it is impossible to foresee or define the extent and variety of national exigencies'. World War II decisively contributed to the emergence of the 'Imperial Presidency'. An important step had, however, been taken in the years immediately preceding the war. In its famous decision *United States v. Curtiss-Wright Export Corporation* in 1936, the Supreme Court made some sweeping statements: the President is vested with 'delicate, plenary, exclusive power' as 'the sole organ of the federal government in the field of international relations'. 'In this vast external realm, with its important, complicated, delicate, and manifold problems, the President alone has the power to speak or listen as a representative of the nation... Into the field of negotiations the Senate cannot intrude; and Congress itself is powerless to invade it.'[8]

The war powers resolution

Considering the pivotal character of the war powers in the balance between the executive and the legislative branches it was only natural that the resurgence of Congress in the early 1970s should manifest itself in this part of the institutional conflict. From 1970 onwards Congress tried to stop the Indo-China war by cutting off funds, i.e. by using its power of the purse.[9] Eventually, in the summer of 1973, it succeeded. More important, however, was the War Powers Resolution, which was passed over Nixon's veto on 7 November of the same year. It immediately became the most important symbol of the congressional reassertion in foreign policy.

The War Powers Resolution (Public Law 93–148) was passed by a Congress that aimed at putting an end to what its members deemed to be a usurpation of power, the assertion of executive power to make presidential war. In Section 2(a) the purpose of the joint resolution is said to be to ensure 'that the collective judgment of both Congress and the President will apply to the introduction of United States Armed Forces into situations where imminent hostilities is clearly indicated by the circumstances, and to the continued use of such forces in hostilities or in such situations'.[10]

Section 3 provides that the President 'in every possible instance' shall consult with Congress before introducing United States Armed Forces into hostilities and after such introduction consult regularly with Congress. The applicability of this provision later turned out to be one of the most heatedly debated issues regarding the resolution.

Section 4 is one of the key sections of the resolution, not least because its provisions serve to trigger the congressional actions outlined in the following section. Section 4 requires the President to report in writing to Congress within forty-eight hours after the introduction of United States Armed Forces: 4(a)1 into hostilities or imminent hostilities; 4(a)2 into a foreign territory while equipped for combat except for deployments relating to supply, replacement or training of such forces; 4(a)3 in numbers which substantially enlarge such forces already in a foreign country.

The consultations and reporting requirements of Sections 3 and 4 lead up to the provisions of Section 5, concerning congressional actions. Section 5(b) requires that the President shall within sixty days after a report is submitted or is required to be submitted pursuant to Section 4(a)1 withdraw the Armed Forces deployed in the action with respect to which the report was submitted, unless Congress has 1) declared war or specifically authorized the use of the Armed Forces for the action,[2] extended by law the sixty-day period,[3] is unable to meet as a consequence of an armed attack upon the United States. The sixty-days period shall be extended by another thirty days if the President determines that it is necessary for military reasons and so certifies to Congress in writing.

Section 5(c) is one of the most controversial parts of the War Powers Resolution as it concerns the use of concurrent resolution, legislative veto. It provides that regardless of Section 5(b) the President shall at any time withdraw United States Armed Forces engaged in hostilities outside the United States if Congress so directs by concurrent resolution.

Considering the conflict between the executive and the legislative branches concerning the interpretation of the various provisions of the War Powers Resolution as well as their constitutionality, Section 8 is of special interest, stating that nothing in the joint resolution

'1) is intended to alter the constitutional authority of the Congress or of the President; or the provisions of existing treaties; or 2) shall be construed as granting any authority to the President... which authority he would not have in the absence of this joint resolution'.

Noteworthy in this context is also Section 9, a separability clause, stating that if any provision of the resolution was held invalid or non-applicable the reminder of the joint resolution should not be affected thereby.

Reporting and advance consultations

The provisions in Section 3, requiring presidential consultations with Congress prior to the introduction of armed forces into actual or imminent hostilities, has been a bone of contention in many instances. It is closely related to Section 4, which requires the President to report to Congress in writing within forty-eight hours after such deployment of troops.

Evacuations and rescue operations

During the Cyprus crisis in July 1974 the American ambassador to Cyprus requested a military evacuation of American citizens caught in the hostilities. The action was undertaken by US Marine helicopters. No prior consultations between the President and Congress took place and no report was filed. Senator Eagleton, one of the leading activists in the struggle for congressional reassertion, argued that Cyprus was the first test case of the War Powers Resolution and that Nixon had failed the test. The Department of Defense argued, however, that the War Powers Resolution did not apply as the areas where the helicopters landed were not part of a combat zone, the mission was purely humanitarian and the troops deployed were not equipped for combat. Most members of Congress accepted this line of argument and Senator Eagleton failed to win support for his position.

The first real challenge to the War Powers Resolution came in 1975 with the evacuations and rescue operations in Indo-China.[11] In April American personnel and refugees were rescued by a sealift from Danang. President Ford reported to Congress, but there were no advance consultations. In his report Ford cited his constitutional authority as Commander-in-Chief and as Chief Executive in the conduct of foreign affairs. There was criticism, not surprisingly, but Ford also pointed out that the circumstances of the Danang sealift clearly demonstrated the unworkable nature of the War Powers Resolution. When the crisis that made the operation necessary broke out, Congress and its leadership were on the annual Easter recess, and the consultation provisions were impossible to implement.

After the Danang sealift came the evacuations from Cambodia and, more important, Saigon. The latter rescue operation, which took place in April 1975, was a major military one compared to the other two, and led to the first confrontation between the Executive and Congress concerning the applicability of the War Powers Resolution. President Ford did not consult with Congress. On the other hand, he had previously repeatedly asked the advice and support of Congress as the situation in Vietnam deteriorated. Congress, however, had remained inactive and no legislation addressing the problem had been forthcoming. As in the case of the Danang sealift, Ford cited his authority as Commander-in-Chief. He filed a report with the Speaker of the House, Carl Albert, within forty-eight hours, as required by the War Powers Resolution. In his report he stated that he was 'taking note' of Section 4, and was making his report as he desired 'to keep the Congress fully informed'.[12] However, there is no indication that Ford recognised the War Powers Resolution as binding on him. On the contrary, he obviously took the position that he had constitutional authority to act to save American lives without any kind of special congressional authorisation.

Only two weeks after the final evacuation from Vietnam, the *Mayaguez* incident provided the greatest test up till then of the War Powers Resolution. On 10 May 1975, Cambodian forces seized an American merchant ship *SS Mayaguez* with a crew of thirty-nine Americans. The crew was rescued through an American military operation ordered by President Ford. American losses amounted to forty-one killed. Twenty-three soldiers lost their lives when an Air Force helicopter crashed. On 15 May President Ford reported to Congress that he had ordered US armed forces to recapture *Mayaguez* and rescue the crew. As on previous occasions, he explained in his report that he had 'taken note' of Section 4(a)1 of the War Powers Resolution and that the intention behind the report was 'his desire that Congress be informed on this matter'. The report also gave the information that the ship already had been recaptured and that the American forces were in the process of disengagement and withdrawal.[13]

The immediate acclaim for the successful operation was strong in

the United States. However, critical voices were heard in Congress.
The issues were two. First, had the President complied with the
provisions requiring advance consultations with Congress? Secondly,
Ford had, as before, cited as his authority 'the President's constitutional Executive power and his authority as Commander-in-Chief of
the United States Armed Forces'. Was he within his constitutional
authority when he directed the rescue effort?

In his report to Congress Ford actually used the word 'consultations'. However, as pointed out by some congressional leaders,
it would be more correct to call it 'notification after the fact'.
The position taken by Ford was that the Chief Executive must be
free to deal with Congress as he chooses in an emergency situation,
where he had to act in order to save American lives. He maintained
that his constitutional executive power and his authority as
Commander-in Chief could not be restricted by the War Powers
Resolution.[14]

If the *Mayaguez* incident offered the first great test of the War
Powers Resolution, observers differed when evaluating the results.
I.F. Stone contended that the most important casualty of the
Mayaguez crisis was the War Powers Resolution itself. What Nixon
had failed to achieve with his veto, Ford had accomplished with one
swift stroke. Even critics less harsh than Stone found the outcome
disconcerting. There was a fear that future Presidents would follow
the course taken by Ford, informing members of Congress instead
of consulting with them. Amendments to the War Powers Resolution
were offered in the House as well as in the Senate, but found little
support. Even some activists in Congress, such as Senators Jacob
Javits and Frank Church and Representative Clement Zablocki,
found that the War Powers Resolution had stood up to the test rather
well, pointing not least to the President's compliance with the reporting requirements of the resolution.[15] The main reason for the muted
criticism was, however, the simple fact that no member of Congress
is eager to criticise the President after a successful action which has
met strong popular acclaim.

When, in June 1975, a full-scale civil war broke out in Lebanon,
President Ford in consultation with Secretary of State Henry Kissinger
decided to evacuate United States citizens. Afterwards a discussion
followed whether or not the War Powers Resolution applied, particularly its consultation and reporting provisions. The adverse comment on Capitol Hill was, however, minimal. The main reason was

probably that, as in the case of the airlift from Cyprus in 1974, the evacuation was done by American unarmed personnel.[16]

The War Powers Resolution had become perhaps the most important test of the balance between the Executive and the Legislative branches in foreign policy making. Thus it is natural that there was a great interest concerning how the Carter administration would perform in this area. Jimmy Carter, Cyrus Vance and other members of the administration had made statements that were generally interpreted as promises of strict adherence to the letter of the law and full compliance with its provisions.

Two incidents raised the War Powers Resolution issue during the Carter presidency. The first test came in May 1978 with the outbreak of conflict in Zaire.[17] Carter ordered American transport aircraft to support French and Belgian rescue operations in Zaire and to begin deliveries outside the combat zone. A number of Americans were also evacuated from a copper mining town. Carter did not report to Congress, which led to criticism. In a letter to Clement Zablocki, Chairman of the House Foreign Affairs Committee, a group of Republican congressmen demanded a hearing to determine whether the President had violated the War Powers Resolution. The administration took the position that the resolution did not apply, and Carter explained that he had ordered the rescue operation 'pursuant to present law and under my constitutional powers and duties as Commander-in-Chief'. Hearings were held in August by the House Foreign Affairs Committee. The arguments presented by the administration were developed in a memorandum by State Department Legal Adviser Herbert Hansell. The main point was that the American armed forces had not been introduced into hostilities because the transport aircraft had landed in secure staging areas more than a hundred miles from the sites of the conflict. Even if not all members of Congress were pacified most found the performance of the Carter administration acceptable.

The second incident was a major one. In November 1979 the American diplomats and personnel at the Embassy in Teheran were taken as hostages.[18] On 24 April 1980, an abortive American rescue operation took place, resulting in eight US military deaths. On 26 April Carter submitted a report to Congress, citing his 'desire that Congress be informed on this matter' and also stating that the report was made 'consistent with the reporting provisions of the War Powers Resolution'.

President Carter had neither consulted with members of Congress
nor informed them before the rescue attempt was well under way.
On 24 April newspaper stories about a pending military action had
made Senator Frank Church, Chairman of the Senate Foreign Relations Committee, and Senator Jacob Javits, ranking minority member
of the Committee, send a latter to Secretary of State Cyrus Vance
recommending that consultation procedures should be initiated as
required by the War Powers Resolution. When the letter arrived at
the State Department, however, the operation was already under way
and Cyrus Vance no longer Secretary of State, having submitted his
resignation in protest against the operation.

In his report to Congress Carter stated that the operation was
within 'the President's powers under the Constitution as Chief
Executive and as Commander-in-Chief of the United States Armed
Forces, expressly recognized in Section 8(d)(1) of the War Powers
Resolution'. The Section cited states that nothing in the War Powers
Resolution 'is intended to alter the constitutional authority of the
Congress or of the President'. The position Carter took was obviously
identical with the one argued by President Ford in connection with
the *Mayaguez* incident, which also was cited in the report. However,
the difference was that whereas Ford's action had been successful,
Carter's had ended in disaster. Consequently, the negative reaction
in Congress was stronger.

Hearings were held by the Senate Foreign Relations Committee.
Acting Secretary of State Warren Christopher maintained that it had
not been possible to consult with Congress without jeopardising the
success of the mission and the safety of those involved. The main
argument of the administration was, however, that the President had
no requirement to consult with Congress on the operation, as he
had the constitutional authority, within the Resolution, for rescue
missions. Attorney General Benjamin Civiletti provided a legal
opinion saying that 'the President has the constitutional authority
within the resolution for rescue missions, authority provided by the
Constitution, case law, and the legislative history of the resolution'.[19]
The same point was made by the President's legal counsel, Lloyd
Cutler, who cited previous cases (*In re Neagle*, 135 US 1 /1889/ and
Durand v Hollings, 8 Fed. Cases 111 /1860/). Cutler also argued that
the resolution's Section 8 negated the advance consultations requirement of Section 3.[20] The consequence of the Carter administration's
interpretation of the War Powers Resolution was that when the

President acted within his constitutional powers as Chief Executive and Commander-in-Chief, that is, on his own authority, the consultations requirement of Section 3 did not apply. The Carter administration did not challenge the validity of the War Powers Resolution, and promised to implement it in good faith.

Differences concerning the interpretation of the War Powers Resolution remained. Even so, the criticism in Congress was somewhat subdued. The reason was probably that as long as the hostages remained in danger it was considered inappropriate to take actions against the President's interpretation and application of the resolution.

The same position as Carter had taken in his report on the hostage rescue operation and Ford on the *Mayaguez* action was adhered to by President Reagan when he, on 25 October 1983, advised the Speaker of the House and the President Pro Tempore of the Senate that he had deployed nearly 2,000 marines and airborne troops on Grenada. Even in this case it was a rescue operation, albeit of an entirely different magnitude. About 1,000 American citizens, mostly students, were reported to be on the island, and there was concern that they might be harmed or taken hostage. There was also a second purpose behind the landing, namely to join the Organisation of Eastern Caribbean States' forces to restore law and order to Grenada.[21]

Reagan had met with a number of congressional leaders the evening before the landing. It could hardly be considered 'advance consultations', as orders at that time already were given and the action under way. In his report on 25 October, Reagan noted that he was acting 'consistent with the War Powers Resolution'. He did not cite Section 4(a)1, however, and thus Section 5(b) was not triggered, providing for the withdrawal of the troops within 60 to 90 days in the absence of congressional authorisation.

Obviously, Reagan submitted his report as Ford and Carter had done, that is, without admitting that the War Powers Resolution applied. The congressional response was a joint resolution from the House, H. J. Res. 402, invoking Section 4(a)1, thus starting the sixty-day clock running. The language of H. J. Res. 402 was adopted by the Senate as an amendment to a bill to raise the Federal debt ceiling. The bill failed to pass the Senate, and thus H. J. Res. 402 did not put the President in the predicament of having to either veto or sign it.

The Grenada intervention was successful and met with great

acclaim in the United States. Under these circumstances, few politicians were eager to criticise the President or force the War Powers
Resolution issue. Typically, the presidential hopefuls at the time
refrained almost totally from criticising the action. At first they did
not comment at all, waiting for the popular reaction. And when it
became obvious that there was strong support from the public, most
of them either came out in favour of the operation or continued to
remain silent. An additional factor was, probably, that the President
had followed the precedents from the Ford and Carter administra-
tions, claiming authority under the Constitution to rescue American
citizens endangered abroad.[22]

Enlarging US Armed Forces in a foreign nation

Even if the main provisions of the War Powers Resolution concerned
the situation where American Armed Forces were 'introduced into
hostilities or into situations where imminent introduction in hostilities
is clearly indicated by the circumstances' (Sections 3; 4(a)1; 5), the
reporting requirements also would apply if US Armed Forces were
introduced 'into territory, airspace or waters of a foreign nation, while
equipped for combat' (Sec. 4(a)2) or 'in numbers which substantially
enlarge United States Armed Forces equipped for combat already
located in a foreign nation' (Sec. 4(a)). There are few instances where
the application of these provisions have been debated. It happened,
however, during the Ford administration in connection with the
so-called Korean Tree-Cutting Incident.

On 18 August 1976, a work party of American and South Korean
soldiers were in the process of cutting down a tree in the demilitarised
zone when they were attacked by North Korean soldiers wielding axe
handles and clubs. Two American officers were killed and several
soldiers wounded. President Ford decided on a military response.
On 21 August an American armed force of three hundred soldiers
entered the demilitarised zone and cut down the tree. The soldiers were
accompanied by tactical air support. To convince the North Koreans
of American resolve, F-4s from Okinawa, F-111s from Idaho and
B-52s from Guam were sent to Korea.

The question was raised in Congress by Representative Elisabeth
Holtzman (D−NY) whether the President had correctly applied the
consultation and reporting provisions of the War Powers Resolution.
The response from the administration, offered by Assistant Secretary
of State Arthur W. Hummel, was that Section 4(a)3 did not apply,

since only a handful of pilots had been added to the American forces already in Korea, and because the changes and additions in equipment were not covered by the Sections in the War Powers Resolution. The House Foreign Affairs Committee conducted hearings on 1 September, and harsh criticism was levelled by Elisabeth Holtzman, Dante Fascell, chairing the hearing, Representative Buchanan, and others. The action by President Ford was popular with the public, however, and the administration also had a rather good defence. The build up, which was the matter that might have triggered the application of the War Powers Resolution, did serve to ensure that sending in the American detachment to cut down the tree did not mean introducing them into hostilities or into situations were hostilities were imminent, as it was unlikely that the North Koreans would attack after the American show of strength and resolve. Thus no report was submitted and no advance consultations were called for.[23]

The issue was not further pursued by members of Congress. Thus it can be argued that the Executive managed to maintain a narrow interpretation of the War Powers Resolution, both concerning the application of Sec 4(a)1 and Sec 4(a)3.

Applicability and interpretation: the issue of presidential compliance

Presidents have often reported to Congress, but also made the point that the submission of the report was *consistent with* the requirements of the War Powers Resolution. Thus they have consistently avoided recognising the resolution as binding. The record concerning advance consultations is different. In cases where it has been a matter of evacuations or rescue operations, the Presidents have maintained that they acted within the power granted them by the Constitution as Chief Executive and as Commander-in-Chief. The other main defence used against accusations and criticism for non-compliance with the War Powers Resolution has been challenging the critics' interpretation of the actual situation, that is, contending that the War Powers Resolution did not apply as the actual circumstances did not fit the provisions. The conflict of interpretation was, for example, evident in the case of the Korean tree-cutting incident. There are several others, one of them El Salvador.

During the first Reagan administration the debate turned on whether or not the War Powers Resolution applied to the US involvement in El Salvador. Sec 8(c) states that the term 'introduction of

United States Forces' also included the assignment of combat advisers, 'to command, co-ordinate, participate in the movement of, or accompany the regular or irregular military forces of any foreign country or government', if those forces were engaged in hostilities or if there was a threat of imminent hostilities.

The position taken by the Reagan administration was that US armed forces in El Salvador had not been introduced into hostilities. They were not equipped for combat, and every precaution had been taken to ensure that US military personnel would not become engaged in or exposed to hostilities. The contention was challenged by members of Congress, mostly liberal Democrats. Especially active was Representative Richard L. Ottinger (D–NY), who on 4 March 1981, introduced a resolution into the House calling on President Reagan to comply with the War Powers Resolution and report to Congress about his decision to send military advisers to El Salvador (House Concurrent Resolution 87). The bill was co-sponsored by thirty-seven members of the House, and hearings were held before the Foreign Affairs Subcommittee on Inter-American Affairs. In the Senate, Democratic activist Thomas Eagleton simultaneously called for consultations and reporting in compliance with the War Powers Resolution.

As there was no immediate action by the Foreign Affairs Committee or in the Senate, Representative Ottinger joined with a group of eleven Congressmen headed by Representative George W. Crocket Jr. (D–Mich) and filed suit in the United States District Court for the District of Columbia, seeking to force President Reagan to end any US military involvement in El Salvador. The suit alleged violations of the War Powers Resolution by the President. The court, in *Crocket v. Reagan* dismissed the suit. The argument was the 'Political Question Doctrine', that is, the court ruled that Congress, not the court, must decide whether US forces in El Salvador were involved in actual or imminent hostilities.[24]

The contention over the applicability of the War Powers Resolution to the US involvement in El Salvador did not develop into a major confrontation at this time as Congress in the main as well as President Reagan then seemed to prefer co-operation on the War Powers issue. However, the matter was to reappear later.

Another incident where the executive–legislative confrontation over the War Powers Resolution took the form of differing interpretations of an actual situation took place in 1987. It concerned the US naval presence in the Persian Gulf, where in August that year Kuwaiti tankers had been reflagged and were escorted by US warships. The President did not invoke the War Powers Resolution. As an explanation Secretary of State George Shultz told a Senate Appropriations subcommittee, that there was no 'intention of getting into that war'. He also argued that because of the high incidence of terrorism around the world it would make little sense to invoke the War Powers Act in this instance. The most telling argument, however, was that the administration did not want the Act to be applied as this would start the clock running, forcing a termination of the operation within sixty or ninety days unless Congress specifically authorised the US armed forces to remain.[25] A Senate vote to invoke the War Powers Resolution lost. However, the demand from members of Congress that the resolution should be invoked increased when at the end of September American helicopters attacked an Iranian mine-laying vessel, *Iran Ajr*, in the Persian Gulf. Thus for example Senator John Glenn, a member of the Armed Services Committee, argued, 'if there ever was a situation that called for reporting under the War Powers Resolution, this is it'. However, the Reagan administration refused to give in. Hostilities would have to grow a great deal more to meet the requirements of the War Powers Resolution, contended Caspar Weinberger, Secretary of Defense.

Even if there were many critical voices, Congress was not eager to press the War Powers issue as the military action and the seizure of *Iran Ajr* was politically popular. As in the case of El Salvador, there was an effort by members of Congress to force the President to invoke the War Powers Resolution. A lawsuit was filed by 114 members of Congress. However, there is little chance of the federal courts making a decision, as it would still be a hypothetical case, on which the courts refuse to rule.

The attack on Tripoli on 14 April 1986 led, not surprisingly, to a renewed discussion of the War Powers Resolution. The discussions turned mainly on the question whether or not the President had complied with the consultations requirement of the resolution. This time there could be no doubt as to the applicability of the War Powers Resolution. Advance consultations had also taken place. The problem was whether or not they were adequate. Of special interest in this case is the fact that, while there were the usual demands for more effective constraints on the President's freedom of action, there were counteracting efforts to remove some of the constraints established by the War Powers Resolution.

Some members of Congress, among them House Foreign Affairs Committee Chairman Dante D. Fascell (D—Fla), complained that Reagan's meeting with congressional leaders three hours before the strike did not meet the requirements of advance consultations. Others, among them Speaker of the House Thomas (Tip) O'Neill, contended that the consultations were adequate. Republican Richard G. Lugar, Chairman of the Senate Foreign Relations Committee, took an intermediate position. There was widespread agreement that a refining and formalising of the procedures for consultations was needed in order to assure a congressional role while there were still choices to be made.[26]

Most members of Congress rallied, however, behind the President's air strike against Libya. Pressure also mounted for exploring ways to free the President from some of the constraints of the War Powers Resolution, to amend the act in order to fit what was called the 'new warfare', state-sponsored terrorism. House Republican Policy Committee Chairman Dick Cheney (R—Wyo) questioned not only how deeply Congress should become involved but also how deeply many members of Congress really wanted to get involved. 'This is an area that legitimately belongs to the Commander-in-Chief,' he stated, adding, 'if it gets nasty, a lot of my colleagues will run for the hills.' Cheney implied that deep down many members of Congress did not mind having been reduced by the President to Monday morning quarterbacking.[27]

Only three days after the air strike against Libya Senate Majority Leader Robert J. Dole joined in introducing legislation which would give the President expanded powers to respond to terrorist attacks.[28] Thus counter-terrorist actions would be exempted from constraints on presidential authority, imposed by the War Powers Resolution. The legislation proposed by Dole and his co-sponsors would drop the consultation requirements of the resolution for incidents involving terrorism and also in those cases extend the time within which the Executive had to report to Congress from forty-eight hours to ten days. In presenting his proposal Dole referred to the criticism that the President had failed to give Congress adequate advance notice of the air strikes against Libya, as the bombers were already in the air by the time the White House informed congressional leaders of the mission. Dole now argued that the purpose of his bill was 'to avoid these pointless debates about whether consultations three hours in advance is enough or whether you need four or five hours or whatever'.

Republican Congressman Joe Barton carried the ball in the House, where the bill had forty-six co-sponsors. Hearings on the proposed legislation, 'the Barton-Dole Anti-Terrorism Act 1986', were held before the House Foreign Affairs Subcommittee on Arms Control, International Security and Science. Joe Barton aragued that the act would establish that international terrorism was a form of warfare against the United States.[29] Another witness supporting the bill, Representative Robert Livingston, maintained that Congress should 'stop second-guessing the Commander-in-Chief' and give him 'the latitude he needs to deal with emergencies as they arise'.[30]

Opposition was not lacking, however. The proposals ran counter to simultaneous pressures from, among others, Senate Foreign Relations Committee Chairman Lugar and House Foreign Affairs Committee Chairman Fascell for improved procedures for advance consultations with congressional leaders. Representative Matthew MacHugh opposed any amendment to the War Powers Resolution.[31] He wanted a congressional consultative group to advise the President, a group that should be wide and flexible, unlike the permanent consultative body envisaged by Senator Robert Byrd in a resolution he had offered in the Senate.[32]

There was widespread opposition to a formal reduction of the influence of Congress in the foreign policy process. On the other hand, the public support for President Reagan's attack on Libya had been overwhelming, and even congressional activists were reluctant to challenge the President's behaviour concerning the War Powers Resolution. And as long as the administration had its way concerning the interpretation of the resolution, there was no interest from the White House in forcing the issue. Neither the White House nor Congress were looking for a confrontation on the War Powers Resolution.

The 'Great Debate' and the problem of legislative veto

The MNF in Lebanon Resolution
Section 8 of the War Powers Resolution states that nothing in the resolution was intended to alter the authority of Congress or of the President. Nixon and all following presidents have, however, maintained that certain provisions of the resolution did just that, restricted

the Executive's constitutional power, and were a flagrant violation of a fundamental principle of the Constitution, the separation of powers. This infringement was unacceptable to the Presidents who have been unanimous in their resistance and also have had support from some members of Congress. One key problem concerned the applicability of the War Powers Resolution. Another one, and one of special interest from a constitutional point of view, had to do with the provision in section 5(c) whereby Congress can by concurrent resolution at any time direct the President to withdraw United States Armed Forces engaged in hostilities abroad.

This was one of the central issues in the heated debate that began with the American involvement in Lebanon in the fall of 1982. However, the controversy in this 'Great Debate' was not focused exclusively on Section 5(c). This was only one part of the complex issue of the applicability and constitutionality of various provisions of the resolution. The debate is perhaps the most enlightening of all those that have taken place on the War Powers Resolution.[33] It turned on the veto provision but also on Section 4(a)1, the requirement for reporting. This is, as we have seen, in itself not a very controversial one and it has also frequently been heeded by Presidents. This, however, has been the case when the operations have been limited in time and the problem of the sixty-days period or the legislative veto did not arise. The special function of the provision 4(a)1 was, namely, that it also triggered the application of the provisions of Section 5, that is, started the clock running. Thus the interpretation of the phrase, 'introduce into hostilities or into situations were imminent involvement in hostilities is clearly indicated by the circumstances', is important.

In August 1982, President Reagan ordered the deployment of 800 marines in Lebanon, where they in co-operation with Italian and French military as a multinational force were to assist in the operation whereby the Palestinians would withdraw from Lebanon. On 21 August Reagan reported to Congress. He took the position that the US forces were not introduced into hostilities but had been invited by the Lebanese government. Thus the reporting would be under the 4(a)2 provision ('equipped for combat'), which meant that it did not trigger the provisions of Section 5 and thus did not open the possibility for Congress to determine the length of the deployment. In the report it was contended that it was consistent with the War Powers Resolution, but no specific section was cited. The position taken by

Reagan was challenged by Clement Zablocki, Chairman of the House Foreign Affairs Committee, but the President cited his authority as Chief Executive and as Commander-in-Chief. In his report Reagan followed the example set by his predecessors, insisting his report was consistent with the War Powers Resolution, not conforming to it, thus not explicitly admitting the constitutionality of the resolution.[34]

The American marines were withdrawn from Lebanon on 10 September. On 29 September the President reported to Congress that 1,200 American marines at the request of the Lebanese government 'were assuming peacekeeping duties' at the Beirut airport, joining a multinational force set up in order to help with restoring the authority of the Lebanese government.

The report followed the same line as the previous one, submitted 'consistent with' the War Powers Resolution but with no special provision of the resolution cited. President Reagan cited 'the President's constitutional authority with respect to the conduct of foreign relations and as Commander-in-Chief of the United States Armed Forces'. The marines would serve for an unspecified time, were not to be engaged in combat but would be equipped to exercise the right of self-defence.

Even if Congress accepted the deployment of the marines in Lebanon, there were members who were openly critical of the President's omission to cite Section 4(a)1 in his report. Once again Clement Zablocki protested that Congress thus was deprived of its right to force a withdrawal after sixty or ninety days. He insisted that the marines, in fact, were entering a hostile area and that Section 4(a)1 should apply, starting the clock running. The administration stuck to its position, and the marines remained even after the lapse of the sixty-days period.[35]

On 29 November 1982, the Lebanese government asked that the American armed force serving in Lebanon should be enlarged. As a consequence, hearings were held before the Senate Foreign Relations Committee. Its chairman, Senator Charles Percy, demanded that the President should seek congressional authorisation before increasing the number of marines in Lebanon, in accordance with the provision in Section 4(a)2 of the War Powers Resolution. The same request was made in a letter to the President, signed by fourteen members of the Senate Foreign Relations Committee. In this letter it was also stated that Congress would direct the withdrawal of the marines if they became engaged in hostilities or if their presence in Lebanon no longer served a useful purpose.

During the spring of 1983, an intensive debate took place in Congress concerning what became the Lebanon Emergency Assistance Act of 1983. This act, signed by Reagan on 27 June, was a compromise, which provided that any further increase in the number of marines in Lebanon, or any change in their tasks and function, had to be authorised by Congress.

When fighting erupted in Beirut in August 1983, the marines were fired upon and two of them were killed. President Reagan reported to Congress on 30 August, consistent with the War Powers Resolution, but also this time he omitted citing Section 4(a)1, which would have triggered the sixty-days period provision of Section 5(b). The argument was, as before, that the American force was not introduced into actual or imminent hostilities, but took part in a multinational, peace-keeping operation. The criticism in Congress became vociferous, however, and increased in September when there were new casualties and Reagan ordered Navy and Air Force units to strike terrorist strongholds in support of the marines. Members of the House Foreign Affairs Committee and the Senate Foreign Relations Committee as well as numerous other Senators and Congressmen cited Section 4(a)1 of the War Powers Resolution and demanded that the resolution should be applied.[36]

Senator Charles Mathias introduced a resolution, S.J. Res. 159, according to which the start of the sixty-days period provided in Section 5(b) would be put retroactively to 31 August. At the same time Congress would authorise that the American force would remain in Lebanon for up to 120 days after the end of that period. The proposed time was later changed to a total of eighteen months. At the same time there was considerable support in Congress for a resolution demanding the immediate application of Section 4(a)1 of the War Powers Resolution, triggering the provisions of Section 5(b) and 5(c). Thus Representative Thomas J. Downey (D–NY) introduced H.J. Res. 348 directing the President to report to Congress under Section 4(a)1 and Senator Robert C. Byrd (D–Va) also introduced S.J. Res. 163, noting that Section 4(a)1 applied to the situation in Lebanon.

During the following debates all the vital issues of the War Powers Resolution were argued, by supporters as well as opponents of the congressional efforts to constrain the President's freedom of action in deploying US Armed Forces abroad: the constitutional problem of legislative veto, the consultation and reporting provisions, and, not least, the applicability of Section 4(a)1, that is the interpretation of the concrete situation. Harsh criticism of the position taken by the administration was levelled by, among others, Ernest F. Hollings (D–SC) and Thomas F. Eagleton (D–Mo) in the Senate and by Clement J. Zablocki (D–Wis), Chairman of the House Foreign Affairs Committee, and Dante B. Fascell (D–Fla), later to succeed Zablocki as Chairman, in the House.

Hollings called Reagan's position on the deployment of US Armed Forces in Lebanon 'a travesty' and refused categorically to extend the action for another eighteen months, as proposed in the compromise bill.[37] Thomas Eagleton had been one of the most ardent activists in the efforts to assert the war making powers of the Congress. In 1973 he had eventually ended by opposing the War Powers Resolution as he found it wanting, not going far enough in constraining the President. Eagleton had published a book on the subject, *War and Presidential Power: A Chronicle of Congressional Surrender* (1973).[38] He now expressed his fears that the compromise bill, S.J. Res. 159, 'could result in the worst of all worlds: a blank check for the President'. Reagan's refusal to invoke Section 4(a)1 and his interpretation of the situation in Lebanon was, in Eagleton's opinion, totally unacceptable, amounting to saying: 'Resolution or no Resolution, restrictions or no restrictions, War Powers Act or no War Powers Act, the administration is going to do what it pleases, in Lebanon'. To Eagleton, the controversy concerned a vital constitutional issue:

When you look at the history of the constitutional Convention, it is clear that the warmaking power was intended to be in the Congress. Congress in the War Powers Act does not take anything away from the President. To the contrary, Congress gave to the President 90 days of unilateral warmaking authority which some of us thought was of very dubious constitutionality.

Even if Eagleton opposed H.J. Res. 159, he admitted that he liked one thing in it, namely, Section 2(b) where Congress determines the force and applicability of Sections 4(a)1 and 5(b) of the War Powers Act. He contended that once Reagan had signed H.J. Res. 159, he had officially and legally acknowledged the vital relevant sections of the War Powers Act, 'despite whatever verbal or written reservations and protestations he may make to the contrary. As a result of this Resolution, the War Powers Act lives and lives to be used yet another day.'[39]

It is instructive to compare Eagleton's position with the one argued by a Senator from the other side of the political spectrum, Barry Goldwater (R-Ariz). 'We will not make an unconstitutional piece of legislation valid simply by referring to it in a second piece of legislation', he maintained, adding that the War Powers Act was 'probably the most unconstitutional measure Congress has ever passed'. It would remain unconstitutional even if the President signed the pending resolution. Not only was the War Powers Act unconstitutional, it was an unwise effort by Congress to usurp the President's direction of day-to-day operations of foreign policy. Goldwater also sided with the administration in his interpretation of the actual situation in Lebanon. Besides, Congress in his opinion lacked the constitutional authority to legislate the marines out of Lebanon.[40]

Clement Zablocki, Chairman of the House Foreign Affairs Committee, was a strong supporter of the War Powers Resolution. He held none of the reservations voiced by Eagleton, but saw the resolution as an instrument to achieve 'the balance of congressional controls and Executive flexibility'. The War Powers Resolution should be applied to the situation in Lebanon, but the purpose was not, Zablocki emphasised, to hamstring the President's ability to carry out an effective foreign policy but to achieve the necessary balance between the executive and the legislative branches. Congress now had to decide whether the War Powers Act was operative or whether it was a dead issue. It was 'a very historic day', he maintained, and characterised the pending resolution as 'the first full application of the War Powers Resolution as well as the first de facto endorsement of the War Powers Resolution by the executive branch'.[41] His views were shared by Representative Dante Fascell, who used even stronger words, calling the pending resolution 'one of the most important constitutional statements on the issue of separation of powers in this Nation's 200-year history'.[42] Barry Goldwater, on the other hand, was not alone in his views. The same ideas were expressed in the House by, among others, Representative William E. Dannemeyer (R-Cal). To him the War Powers Resolution was unconstitutional. Its application would also create an impossible situation: 'We can have one President at a time; we cannot have one President in the White House and a Presidential force in the Congress. The President in the White House is in charge of our foreign policy'.[43] In consequence, Dannemeyer voted against the bill. A more curious position was taken by Representative Gerald B. H. Solomon (R-NY). He found the pending resolution 'lousy' because it could be interpreted as acknowledging the constitutional validity of the War Powers Act and was used by Congress in usurping the constitutional authority of the President. He also voiced a complaint more often heard from members of the executive branch, namely, that the members of Congress were setting themselves up as 535 Secretaries of State, the last thing the country needed. Having made this point Solomon nevertheless supported the pending resolution, which he found vitally necessary. It was a compromise, and even if he vehemently opposed certain parts of it, he saw its enactment as the only means of safeguarding continued American participation in the peacekeeping force in Lebanon. And this was in his opinion absolutely necessary in order to avoid disaster in the Middle East.[44]

After heated debates the bill was passed, and on 12 October President Reagan signed the Multinational Force in Lebanon Resolution (Public Law 98–119). The resolution stated that the requirements of Section 4(a)1 of the War Powers Resolution became operative on 29 August 1983. With a reference to Section 5(b) the Multinational Force in Lebanon Resolution then authorised the continued participation of the United States Armed Forces in Lebanon for a period of up to eighteen months from the date of the enactment of the resolution. The resolution also required the President to report periodically to Congress as provided in Section 4(c) of the War Powers Resolution. In no event should he report less often than once every three months.[45]

When signing S.J. Res. 159 into law, the MNF in Lebanon Resolution, President Reagan made a statement of considerable interest in this context. He expressed his great appreciation of the bipartisan support for the policies pursued in Lebanon, mentioning specifically Senate Majority Leader Baker, House Speaker O'Neill, House Foreign Affairs Committee Chairman Zablocki, and Senate Foreign Relations Committee Chairman Percy. Emphasising his support for the policies of the resolution he signed, he also made it clear that he had reservations about some of the 'specific congressional expressions'.[46]

Reagan's reservations were, in fact, not minor ones. For one thing, he disagreed with the congressional position that the requirements of Section 4(a)1 of the War Powers Resolution became operative on 29 August 1983. Isolated or infrequent acts of violence against US Armed Forces should not be interpreted as amounting to a situation where these were introduced into actual or imminent hostilities. Reagan also noted that there had been 'historic differences between the legislative and executive branches of government with respect to the wisdom and constitutionality of Section 5(b) of the War Powers Resolution'. Such 'arbitrary and inflexible deadlines' created unwise limitations on the President's authority to deploy US forces in order to guard US national security. When Reagan here spoke in terms of 'unwise' limitations, it is obviously in an attempt to placate the critics, to avoid provoking a serious constitutional confrontation. In reality it was not a matter of a 'wise' or 'unwise' piece of legislation but of the basic institutional conflict between the executive and the legislative branches of government, the problem related to the separation of powers and the prerogatives of the contending branches.

Reagan made his point emphatically:

I believe it is, therefore, important for me to state, in signing this resolution, that I do not and cannot cede any of the authority vested in me under the constitution as President and as Commander-in-Chief of US Armed Forces. Nor should my signing be viewed as any acknowledgment that the President's constitutional authority can be impermissibly infringed by statute, that congressional authority would be required if and when the period specified in Section 5(b) of the War Powers Resolution might be deemed to have been triggered and the period had expired, or that Section 6 of the Multinational Force in Lebanon Resolution may be interpreted to revise the President's constitutional authority to deploy US Armed Forces.

The outcome was a compromise. On the one hand, the Multinational Force in Lebanon Resolution invoked key sections of the War Powers Act — for the first time since its enactment. On the other hand, the administration avoided legislative attempts at forcing an immediate removal of US Armed Forces from Lebanon and obtained congressional approval of their remaining there for an additional eighteen months. President Reagan also denied that his signing of the resolution implied that he conceded the constitutionality of the War Powers Act. He asserted that he retained his authority as Commander-in-Chief to deploy US Armed Forces where and when he deemed it necessary.

In some quarters the Multinational Force in Lebanon Resolution was hailed as a victory for Congress. This was, in fact, not the case. The gain for Congress was that it was now established that Congress could set the clock running under the provisions of the War Powers Resolution even if the President had not reported under Section 4(a)1. But the MNF in Lebanon Resolution was a compromise, and as such avoided the ultimate confrontation and left the basic issue undecided.

The Chada decision

No president has accepted legislative veto as binding and they have all denied the constitutionality of that instrument. Proponents of the War Powers Resolution have also been troubled by the possibility of adverse court action. In a decision in 1980, the US 9th District Court of Appeals ruled that a concurrent resolution of Congress, over-turning an action by the Immigration and Naturalization Service, was unconstitutional. This so called *Chada decision* was hailed by President Carter as having 'perhaps the most profound significance constitutionally' of anything that happened during his administration. Carter had been plagued by numerous such 'veto' provisions, and his enthusiasm was due to the fact that he interpreted the Chada ruling as a victory for the Executive in the struggle concerning the separation of powers.[47] One legal expert agreed, stating that the decision 'casts doubt on the constitutionality of hundreds of statutes containing similar provisions'.[48]

All experts did not agree that the Chada ruling would affect provisions such as those included in the War Powers Resolution. However, a similar ruling by a Federal Appeals Court in January 1982, added to the worries of congressional activists, who feared the possible consequences for congressional restraining power.

In June 1983 the Chada case, together with two similar cases reached the Supreme Court. Of the rulings that followed, the Chada decision was the most important. It was described by the *Congressional Quarterly* as 'a victory for the Executive Branch', and other commentators used words such as 'a shattering blow to Congressional power'.[49] The Chada ruling was adopted by seven votes to two on 23 June 1983. The Supreme Court ruled that the House of Representatives had acted unconstitutionally when it declared invalid a decision by the Immigration and Naturalization Service. When writing the majority opinion, Chief Justice Warren Burger employed such sweeping language that it meant that, except for special cases like the ratification of treaties and impeachment, Congress can only make laws and regulations by using the traditional and normal procedure. A law has to be passed by both chambers of Congress and then sent to the President for his signature. If it is vetoed by the President, the law can only be passed if both chambers vote by a two-thirds majority to override it. A concurrent resolution, veto-proof as it is not sent to the President for his signature, cannot be binding on the President as it is unconstitutional.[50]

The consequence seems to be that a long series of regulations, which Congress has added to various laws relating to foreign policy, with the purpose of restricting the President's freedom of action, now may be untenable. Thus it would no longer be possible to maintain that Congress can restrict the President's power as Commander-in-Chief by passing a concurrent resolution ordering the withdrawal of US Forces. The Chada decision should also apply, for example, to the stipulation that by a concurrent resolution Congress can veto large armaments sales or purchases by the Armed Forces exceeding 25 million dollars in value. A host of regulations linked to the Trade Act of 1974, the Nuclear Non-Proliferation Act of 1978 and many other laws may also be of questionable constitutionality.[51]

The implication of the Chada decision must be that it is no longer possible to maintain that Congress can restrict the President's power as Commander-in-Chief by passing a concurrent resolution ordering the withdrawal of US Forces. A joint resolution would be needed, which can be vetoed by the President and in that case passed only by a vote of two-thirds majority, a difficult proposition. Another question, as yet not tested, is whether Congress can force the President to relinquish his power as Commander-in-Chief by silence or inaction over a specified time, that is, the provision of the War Powers Resolution, Sec 5(b).

The problem of reconciling 'joint possessions' with the separation of powers

In his veto message to Congress on 4 October 1973, President Nixon characterised House Joint Resolution 542, the War Powers Resolution, as both unconstitutional and dangerous to the best interest of the Nation. Unconstitutional were, in his opinion, both the use of concurrent resolution, legislative veto, in the manner required by the resolution, and the provision which would automatically cut off certain of the President's authorities after sixty days unless Congress extended them. Nixon also found the resolution fraught with dangers, seriously undermining the nation's ability to act decisively and convincingly in times of crisis. Again he pointed to the sixty-day limit, which, in fact, could prevent the United States from acting effectively for peace and instead could prolong or intensify a crisis. An adversary would be tempted to refuse serious negotiations as long as there was a chance of American withdrawal when the sixty days were up. On the other hand, the existence of the deadline could also lead to an escalation of hostilities in an effort to achieve results before the sixty days expired.[52]

Nixon also pointed to the confusion and the dangerous disagreements that could result from the vagueness of the resolution regarding when the sixty-day rule would apply. He was also highly critical of the provision that would automatically cut off the President's constitutional powers as Commander-in-Chief without any overt congressional action. 'It would give every future Congress the ability to handcuff every future President merely by doing nothing and sitting still.'[53]

As we can see President Nixon in his veto took issue with exactly those provisions that became the focus of the conflict that later evolved between Presidents and Congress regarding the interpretation and implementation of the War Powers Resolution. It is also worth noting that Nixon explicitly approved the consultation provisions, which he maintained were consistent with his administration's desire for 'regularized consultations with the Congress before and during the involvement of United States forces in hostilities abroad'. These provisions were also, at least in principle, accepted by his successors in the White House.

President Nixon saw the War Powers Resolution as 'a serious challenge to the wisdom of the Founding Fathers in choosing not to draw a precise and detailed line of demarcation between the foreign policy powers of the two branches'. Members of Congress did not see the problem in the same way. They argued that the problem was an usurpation of powers by the Executive and that, consequently, there was an urgent need to establish constraints on the President's freedom of action in order to ensure 'collective judgment'. The issue at hand was the institutional conflict between the Executive and the Legislative branches in an area were there were – to use Hamilton's phrase – joint possessions. A moment when a balance existed between the presidency and Congress, satisfactory to both sides, has rarely if ever occurred.

Efforts have been made to have the third branch decide the problem. However, the problem is a political one and the courts are likely to refuse to intervene. There is no consensus concerning the legality of the legislative veto or of the provision whereby Congress can, by silence or inaction over a specified time, deprive the President of his powers as Commander-in-Chief. However, both Congress and the Presidents have avoided a head-on confrontation on the constitutional issue, as neither has considered that anything would be gained. Not court decisions but political realities have determined the interpretation of the war making powers and the balance between President and Congress, and this will not change. There will be the usual more-or-less cyclical swings. The President's ability to use United States Armed Forces for sustained actions abroad will depend on his ability to mobilise public support for his policies. There is a consensus among critics and defenders alike that, as formulated by *New York Times* in an editorial ten years after the withdrawal of American forces from Vietnam, 'the ultimate lessons of Vietnam for all Americans should be evident. This country will not effectively wage war unless it understands the reason for the pain'.[54] In his book *No More Vietnams*, Richard Nixon concurred.[55] The most serious mistake of the American leaders had been their failure to explain the war to the people and mobilise them behind it. The same, *mutatis mutandis*, might be said about the preconditions for any prolonged deployment of American military forces abroad.

This does not mean that the War Powers Resolution is meaningless. It is a certain constraint on the President's freedom of action, limiting his ability to conduct prolonged military operations, to wage undeclared wars. It does not, however, derive its strength primarily from its legal character, but from being a symbol of congressional involvement and from serving as a tool for congressional oversight and review of Executive actions. It may contribute to the integration of the dispersed powers into a workable government, by emphasizing 'separateness but interdependence'.

Notes

1   Arthur M. Schlesinger, Jr., *The Imperial Presidency*, Boston, 1973, p. 2. Cf. also Schlesinger, 'Congress and the making of American foreign policy', *Foreign Affairs*, 1972, p. 80.

2   Robert S. Hirschfield, 'The problem of presidential power', *Dialogue*, 1974, 3, p. 4.

3   Hugh Gregory Gallagher, *Advise and Obstruct: The Role of the United States Senate in Foreign Policy Decisions*, New York, 1971, p. xi.

4   Louis Henkin, *Foreign Affairs and the Constitution*, Mineola, NY, 1972.

5   Edward S Corwin, *The President: Office and Powers, 1787–1957*, 4th rev. edn., New York, 1957.

6   Amaury de Riencourt, *The American Empire*, New York, 1968, p. xi.

7   Göran Rystad, 'From the "Imperial Presidency" to "Neo-Congressional

Government''? Congress and American foreign policy in the 1970s'; in G. Rystad, ed., *Congress and American Foreign Policy*, Lund, 1981, p. 11ff.

8   Robert S. Hirschfeld, ed., *The Power of the Presidency: Concept and Controversy*, New York, 1968, p. 173; Göran Rystad, 'Invitation to struggle: checks and balances in the American political system', in Arne Axelsson and Elisabeth Herion Sarafidis, eds., *American Power: Direction and Balance in Political Action*, Uppsala, 1987.

9   On Congress, the Presidency and the foreign policy process, see for example Cecil V. Crabb, Jr. and Pat M. Holt, *Invitation to Struggle: Congress, the President and Foreign Policy*, Washington D.C., 1980; Thomas M. Franck and Edward Weisband, *Foreign Policy by Congress*, New York and Oxford, 1979; Cecil V. Crabb, Jr. and Kevin V. Mulcahy, *Presidents and Foreign Policy Making*, Baton Rouge and London, 1986; John Rourke, *Congress and the Presidency in U.S. Foreign Policy-making. A Study of Interaction and Influence, 1945–1982*, Boulder, 1983; John Spanier and Joseph Nogee, eds., *Congress, the Presidency and American Foreign Policy*, New York, 1981.

10   On the background to and enactment of the War Powers Resolution, see for example Alton Frye, *A Responsible Congress: The Politics of National Security*, New York, 1975, and, especially, Robert F. Turner, *The War Powers Resolution: Its Implementation in Theory and Practice*, Philadelphia, 1983; *The War Powers Resolution. A special study of the Committee on Foreign Affairs*, April, 1982 (cit. *WPR Study*). The study has the text of the resolution as an appendix, pp. 287–91. The same has another study of interest in this context, Robert D. Clark, Andrew M. Egeland, Jr. and David B. Sanford, *The War Powers Resolution: Balance of War Powers in the Eighties. A National War College Strategic Study*, Washington, D.C., 1985 (cit. *War College Study*).

11   Cf. *WPR Study*, chapter 7, 'The War Powers Resolution and the fall of Indochina', p. 179ff.

12   *War College Study*, p. 20f., *WPR Study*, p. 197ff.

13   On the Mayaguez incident, Richard G. Head, Frisco W. Short and Robert C. McFarlane, *Crisis Resolution: Presidential Decision Making in the Mayaguez and Korean Confrontations*, Boulder, Col., 1978, *WPR Study*, p. 205ff; *War College Study*, p. 22ff. Also John Rourke, *Congress and the Presidency in U.S. Foreign Policymaking: A Study of Interaction and Influence, 1945–1982*, Boulder, Col., 1983, p. 290ff.

14   Turner, *The War Powers Resolution*, p. 54; Raymond Tatalovich and Byron W. Daynes, *Presidential Power in the United States*, Monterey, CA., p. 332. President Ford's own comments, G. Ford, *A Time to Heal*, New York, 1978, p. 275ff.

15   *WPR Study*, p. 211ff.

16   David M. Abshire, 'Foreign policy makers: Presidents vs Congress', in David M. Abshire and Ralph D. Nurnberger, eds., *The Growing Power of Congress*, Washington, DC., 1981. *WPR Study*, p. 229ff.

17   Turner, *The War Powers Resolution*, pp. 68–9.

18   On the abortive hostage rescue mission, see Paul B. Ryan, *The Iranian Rescue Mission: Why it Failed*, Annapolis, Md., 1985; also Steve Smith, 'Policy preferences and bureaucratic position: the case of the American hostage rescue mission', *International Affairs*, 61:1, Winter 1984/85, p. 9ff. For President Carter's own version of the reasoning, see J. Carter, *Keeping Faith. The Memoirs of a President*, Toronto etc., 1982, p. 511ff. Cf. also Zbigniew Brzezinski, *Power and Principle: Memoirs of the National Security Adviser 1977–1981*, New York, 1983, p. 486ff.

19 *WPR Study*, p. 222ff.

20 *The War Powers Resolution; Relevant Documents, Correspondence, Reports*, Congress, House, Committee on Foreign Affairs, Subcomittee on Security and Scientific Affairs, Committee Prints, Washington, D.C., 1981, p. 49.

21 On the Grenada intervention Hugh O'Shaughnessy, *Grenada: Revolution, Invasion and Aftermath*, London, 1981; *Lessons of Grenada*, US Department of State, February 1986; K. P. Schoenhals and R. Melanson, *Revolution and Intervention in Grenada*, Boulder, 1985.

22 'America's commitment to peace'. Address by Ronald Reagan, 27 October 1983, *Department of State Bulletin*, December 1983, p. 4. *War College Study*, p. 35f.

23 *WPR Study*, p. 225ff. Hearing before the House Committee on International Relations, 1 September 1976, 'Deaths of American Military Personnel in the Korean Demilitarized Zone', Washington, D.C., 1976.

24 *War College Study*, p. 27ff; *WPR Study*, p. 247ff.

25 *International Herald Tribune*, 8–9 August and 28 September 1987; *Time Magazine*, 5 October 1987.

26 *The New York Times*, 18 April 1986. Rystad, *Congress and American Foreign Policy*, p. 42ff.

27 *The New York Times*, 20 April 1986.

28 Anti-Terrorism Act of 1986 (S. 2335 and H.R. 4611) was introduced on 17 April 1986 in the Senate by Robert Dole and Jeremiah Denton and in the House by Joe Barton, Duncan Hunter and Bob Livingston. Hearings were held before the House Foreign Affairs Subcommittee on Arms Control, International Security and Science, *Hearings before the Subcommittee on Arms Control, International Security and Science of the Committee on Foreign Affairs. House of Representatives. Ninety-Ninth Congress, Second session. April 29, May 1 and 15, 1986*, Washington, D.C., 1986 (cit. *Hearings*).

29 *Hearings*, p. 187ff.

30 *Hearings*, Appendix 13, p. 283ff. *The New York Times*, 20 April 1986.

31 *Hearings*, p. 164ff.

32 S. J. Res. 340. The Joint Resolution, co-sponsored by senators Cranston, Inouye, Pell and Eagleton, was an amendment to the War Powers Resolution. *Hearings*, p. 216f.

33 Highlights of the debate in the Senate and the House on 28 September 1983, in *Congressional Digest*, 62:1. November 1983 (cit. *Congr. Digest*).

34 *Congr. Digest*, p. 265.

35 *Congressional Quarterly*, 28 August 1982, p. 2158. *Weekly Compilation of Presidential Documents*, 30 August 1982, p. 1065f.

36 *Congr. Digest*, p. 288.

37 *Congr. Digest*, p. 268.

38 Thomas Eagleton, *War and Presidential Power: A Chronicle of Congressional Surrender*, New York, 1973. The same year Senator Jacob K. Javits published a book on the same subject, *Who Makes War? The President versus Congress*, New York, 1973.

39 *Congr. Digest*, p. 270ff.

40 *Congr. Digest*, p. 271.

41 *Congr. Digest*, p. 276ff.

42 *Congr. Digest*, p. 282.

43 *Congr. Digest*, p. 281.

44 *Congr. Digest*, p. 285ff.

45   Appendix B, *War College Study*, pp. 51–4.

46   *Congressional Quarterly*, 15 October 1983, p. 1963.

47   *WPR Study*, p. 282; *War College Study*, p. 40f.

48   John F. Knoeckel, 'Immigration law: constitutionality of one-house veto of stays of deportation', *Harvard Law Journal*, 22, 1981, p. 423. Cit. from *WPR Study*, p. 282.

49   M. Destler, 'Dateline Washington: Life after the veto?, *Foreign Policy*, 52, 1983, p. 181ff.

50   *Supreme Court of the United States. Syllabus. Immigration and Naturalization Service v. Chadha et al.* Appeal from the United States Court of Appeals for the Ninth Circuit. 103 S.Ct. 2767, 1983.

51   M. Destler, 'Dateline Washington: Congress as Boss?', *Foreign Policy*, 42, 1981, p. 174f. On the Chada decision see also Raymond J. Celada, 'Effect of the legislative veto decision on the two-house disapproval mechanism to terminate a presidential declaration of national emergency' in *The US Supreme Court Decision Concerning the Legislative Veto*, Hearings, Congress, House, Committee on Foreign Affairs, Washington, D.C., 1983, p. 367.

52   President Nixon's Veto of War Powers measure, 'Message from President Nixon, 24 October 1973', *Weekly Compilation of Presidential Documents*, 29 October 1973; *Department of State Bulletin*, 26 November 1973, p. 662ff.

53   *Ibid.*, p. 663. Cf. also R. Nixon, *No More Vietnams*, New York, 1985, p. 225.

54   *New York Times*, 7 April 1985, p. 6.

55   Nixon, *No More Vietnams*, p. 165ff.

Budgetary continuity and change: an assessment of the Congressional budget process

Introduction

The purpose of this chapter is to describe and assess the congressional budget process since enactment of the 1974 Budget and Impoundment Control Act, Public Law 93–344. This requires an understanding of the continuity and change in the budgetary process since enactment of the 1974 congressional budget reform, an understanding of the objectives of the budget act, and the impact of the reform on the way Congress makes decisions about spending and taxing.

Budgeting is central to politics. Budgets tell a great deal about a nation's priorities, problems, and processes of social choice. Decisions about federal government spending, revenues, deficits, and debt all affect the economy, employment, productivity, prices, welfare, and national security of the United States. Historically Congress has played a primary role in making those decisions about what money is to be received and how it is to be spent. Congress is given the 'power of the purse' in the Constitution of the United States as a check on executive power. Through history there has been a struggle between the executive and Congress over that power and recent years have been no exception. The debate over deficits, debt, the size and composition of government taxing and spending goes back to the first Congress and first Secretary of Treasury, Alexander Hamilton. This struggle continues to be at the centre of American politics. Budgeting involves decisions about who pays for programmes and who benefits from expenditures and there is nothing more important in a political system.

Budgeting can be organised into four main stages in the American federal political system: (1) executive branch budget preparation and submission; (2) congressional passage of buget resolutions;

(3) congressional authorisation, appropriation, and (4) budget execution and control. This chapter focuses on the second stage: the congressional budget resolution process, with only tangential reference to the other budgeting stages.

The American economy faces large structural deficits and debt that will not disappear easily even if the economy grows rapidly with full employment, if the trade deficit is reduced, and inflation and interest rates stay low. They also must confront politically wrenching budget adjstments to meet the deficit targets during the next decade under the 1985 Balanced Budget and Emergency Deficit Control Act, Public Law 99–177 (commonly called the Gramm-Rudman-Hollings Act or G-R-H). The projected cuts necessary to balance the budget are seemingly impossible for a pluralistic political system that seems designed to represent specific interests that continually push for governmental subsidies and adoption of new spending programmes. Although congressional budgeting has been highly centralised under the Congressional Budget Act of 1974 and G-R-H, the battle of the budget dominates the congressional agenda and is still an incremental battle of the parts versus the whole, as it was before these reforms.

After a dozen years of the congressional budget act and with the uncertain future of the federal budget under G-R-H, this is an excellent time to examine the major institutions through which the United States must cope with its budgetary dilemmas. After a reasonable test of the budget reforms, what have we learned from implementation of the 1974 congressional budget act? Have the reforms lived up to their sponsors' expectations? What are the institutional and policy consequences of the 1974 and G-R-H budget acts? Is the budget process under G-R-H capable of handling the difficult budgetary and political trade-offs that lie ahead? The primary purpose of this chapter is to answer these questions. The chapter is organised into four parts. The first part briefly describes the congressional budget process and the major institutions associated with it. The second section judges the success and failure of the congressional budget reforms using an evaluation criteria proposed by the sponsors of the two major budget acts. The third part describes several structural and behavioural consequences of the congressional budget process. Part four summarises the continuity and change in the congressional budget process since 1974.

The Congressional budget process

Passage of the Congressional Budget and Impoundment Control Act of 1974 was one of the most significant changes in the way Congress makes budget and spending decisions in the last two hundred years. It was passed by overwhelming majorities in the House and the Senate. Supporters included those who wanted higher defence spending and those who did not; those who wanted more outlays for social programmes and those who did not; those who wanted a balanced budget and those who did not. All shades of political ideology supported the 1974 budget reform. The Congressional Budget Act, consisting of Titles I through IX of P.L. 93–344, established several major congressional institutions and procedures. The act created two standing committees on the budget in the House and the Senate with the responsibility for setting overall tax and spending levels. It also required Congress annually to establish levels of expenditures and revenues and prescribed procedures for arriving at those spending and income totals. The procedures include three important elements: (1) a *timetable* establishing deadlines for action on budget-related legislation intended to ensure completion of the budget plan prior to the start of each new fiscal year (see Table 4.1); (2) a requirement to adopt *concurrent budget resolutions* (not requiring presidential approval) to establish initial targets for total budget authority, budget outlays, and revenues for the upcoming fiscal year and finally a binding resolution with ceilings on budget authority and outlays and a floor under revenues; and (3) a *reconciliation process* to conform revenue, spending, a debt legislation to the levels specified in the final budget resolution.

The 1974 Budget Reform Act also created a Congressional Budget Office (CBO), headed by a director who is jointly appointed by the House and Senate to a four year term, and with over 200 professional, technical, and clerical personnel.[1] It serves as a principal source of information and analysis on the budget, and on spending and revenue legislation, and has a specific mandate to assist the House and Senate Budget Committees and the spending and revenue committees. CBO also responds to requests from other committees and individual members of Congress, provides special reports on budget-related problems and issues, and performs budget forecasting and scorekeeping functions. Another key responsibility of CBO is to submit to the Budget Committees report on fiscal policy,

Table 4.1: Congressional budget process timetable: G-R-H and 1974 Budget Act

Action to be completed	Gramm-Rudman-Hollings	1974 Budget Act
President submits fiscal 1987 budget to Congress	First Monday after 3 January	15 days after Congress reconvenes
CBO submits report on fiscal policy to budget committees	15 February	1 April
Congressional committees submit 'Views and Estimates' to budget committees	25 February	15 March
Senate Budget Committee reports budget resolution	1 April	15 April
Congress completes action on budget resolution	15 April	15 May
Annual appropriation bills may be considered in the House	15 May	15 May
Congressional committees report new authorising legislation	No provision	15 May
House Appropriations Committee reports all appropriations bills	10 June	No provision
Congress completes action on reconciliation legislation	15 June	No provision
House completes action on all appropriations bills	30 June	No provision
'Snapshot' of fiscal deficit taken by CBO and OMB	15 August	No provision
CBO and OMB issue report to GAO on fiscal deficit and initial sequestration order	20 August	No provision
GAO issues fiscal deficit and sequestration report to president (now unconstitutional)	25 August	No provision
President issues initial fiscal 1987 sequestration order based on GAO report	1 September	No provision
Congress completes action on all appropriations bills	No provision	7 days after Labour Day
Congress completes action on second budget resolution	No provision	15 September
Congress completes action on reconciliation legislation from second budget resolution	No provision	25 September
Fiscal sequestration takes effect	1 October	No provision
Fiscal year begins	1 October	1 October
CBO and OMB issue a revised report to GAO reflecting final congressional action	5 October	No provision
GAO issues a revised report to president	10 October	No provision
Final fiscal sequestration order based on revised report becomes effective	15 October	No provision
GAO issues a compliance report on sequestration order	15 November	No provision

including alternative levels of revenue and outlays and a discussion of national priorities.

The 1974 Act created House and Senate Budget Committees responsible for budget formulation but structured them quite differently. To dispel the fears of the members of the House Appropriations and Ways and Means Committee that the House budget panel might gain dominance in the spending and revenue areas, several limitations were written into the act. The House Budget Committee (HBC) must rotate members with no member eligible to serve for more than two out of five successive congresses. This has had the effect of making the committee somewhat weaker and less attractive than its Senate counterpart. Members can not build seniority, expertise, and a long-term career on the committee. The HBC also includes five members each from the House Appropriations and Ways and Means Committee, eleven from other standing committees, and one member each representing the majority and minority leadership. The primary loyalty of HBC members is usually with their parent committee assignments where their House career opportunities lie. Selection for service on the committee is made without regard to seniority in the House generally. These restrictions give the Budget Committee a disadvantage compared to the other House standing committees, especially Appropriations and Ways and Means. However, with the leadership of recent HBC chairs such as Rep. William H. Gray III, it has become a major player in the House.

No such restrictions were written into the Budget Act in the Senate. There is no limitation on length of service and Senate Budget Committee (SBC) members are selected by both parties from the entire Senate. In contrast to the House, SBC members may build seniority, expertise, and long-term careers on the committee. Generally they are more loyal and committed to the SBC and the process than their counterparts in the House. The consequences of the House rules have been to create a weaker and more partisan House Budget Committee and a stronger more prestigious and bipartisan Senate Budget Committee. These differences have been responsible to some degree for the way both committees have operated. From the beginning, the SBC has taken a bipartisan approach and made a strong commitment to the budget process. The chairmen and ranking minority members as well as the rank and file committee members have worked closely together, with the result that Senate budget resolutions have been consensus documents. The influence of the SBC on the floor of the

Senate has been enhanced by this bipartisan approach. In contrast, the HBC has been highly partisan from its creation. The Committee divides sharply along party lines.[2] This partisan division has been carried into the votes and the House floor debate. The HBC also splits along liberal–conservative lines as well as on specific issues such as defence and social spending levels. This has made it difficult to build a majority coalition for House budget resolutions. Frequently there are many amendments to the budget resolution offered on the House floor by the different factions represented on the committee. House budget resolutions are frequently rejected and only intervention by strong party leadership has rescued the process and the resolutions.[3]

The 1974 Budget Act provides a reconciliation process under which the Budget Committees may direct other committees to determine and recommend revenue and/or spending actions deemed necessary to conform to the determinations made in the budget resolution. The reconciliation process allows the budget committees to direct one or more of the legislative committees to make changes in existing laws to achieve the desired budget reductions. The budget committees submit the recommended changes to each house 'without any sub-stantive revision'.

The budget committees were first successful in invoking the reconciliation process for FY 1981 by requiring several congressional committees to reduce spending by about $6.2 billion and for the tax-writing committees to recommend revenue increases of $4.2 billion. The FY 1981 reconciliation bill (Public Law 96–499) established an important precedent and resulted in savings for fiscal years 1981–1985 of more than $50 billion in outlays and $29 billion in additional revenues projected over the same period.[4] David Stockman, Reagan's first OMB Director, used this precedent in his successful strategy to build support for President Reagan's FY 1982 budget.

The reconciliation process as contemplated in the 1974 Budget Act was to be a relatively brief and simple exercise intended to reconcile actual spending and/or taxes to the amounts specified in the second budget resolution. By most interpretations, reconciliation measures were to be in the second concurrent resolution (not the first) and applied to appropriations. However, the House and Senate Budget Committees turned the process around and included reconciliation directions for authorisation and appropriations committees in the first budget resolution for FY 1981. Even though it was clearly the intent of the Budget Act that reconciliation was to be used for the second 'binding' resolution, the strategy of placing ceilings on the first resolution worked.

The reconciliation process has two major steps: reconciliation instructions and a final reconciliation bill. Reconciliation instructions are internal congressional orders requiring certain committees to report on legislation. The budget committees have the option to mandate that House and Senate committees report legislation that will meet budget authority, outlays, and revenue targets.[5]

The Reagan administration and allies on Congress used the reconciliation process for the FY 1982 first concurrent budget resolution using FY 1981 budget committees precedent. The Senate and House instructed committees to report out legislation by 12 June 1981 that would save $36 billion in outlays. To the surprise of many observers, the committees reported out savings in the House of $37.7 billion (H.R. 3982) and in the Senate of $39.6 billion (S. 1377) on 17 June 1981. More than 250 members of Congress met in fifty-eight mini-conferences between 15 July and 29 July to draft a conference committee report which was eventually passed by Congress and signed into law by President Reagan on 13 August 1981. The FY 1982 reconciliation bill, the second stage of the reconciliation process, established major cuts in the budget which became an important element of so-called 'Reaganomics' (President Reagan's cuts in social programmes, increases in defence expenditures, and cuts in taxes).

Title X of Public Law 93–344, includes the impoundment control provisions of the reform. The act sanctions two kinds of presidential impoundments: deferrals and rescissions. However, the President must inform Congress when he impounds funds in these two manners. Deferrals are when the President requests Congress to allow him to postpone or delay spending for a particular program. The funds are withheld immediately. If either House of Congress votes to disapprove the deferral, the funds must be spent. However, because of the problem of severability, it appears that the unconstitutionality of the one House legislative veto may have dragged down the President's deferral authority with it.

Rescissions are when a President takes back all authority to spend for a programme. This changes the law that gave him the legal authority to spend by 'rescinding' the funds. The President withholds funds immediately upon sending a rescission message to Congress. If within forty-five legislative days, the Congress fails to pass a bill approving the rescission, the President must spend the money.

The Balanced Budget and Emergency Deficit Control Act of 1985 (G-R-H), Public Law 99–177, changed the congressional budget process further by establishing a procedure to reduce deficits to annual maximum levels through mandatory sequestration of funds.[6] The law provides for annual reductions in the budget deficits from $171.9 billion in fiscal year 1986 to zero in fiscal year 1991 (see Table 4.2).

Table 4.2: *Statutory and projected deficits, 1986–91 (billions of dollars)*

	G-R-H deficit limits	Projected deficits by OMB	Projected baseline deficits by CBO	Baseline by CBO less targets
Fiscal 1986	172	221 (actual)	221 (actual)	49
Fiscal 1987	144	147	174	30
Fiscal 1988	108	88	169	62
Fiscal 1989	72	74	162	90
Fiscal 1990	36	46	134	98
Fiscal 1991	0	16	109	109

Note: The baseline estimates and deficit target include Social Security, which is off-budget.

Source: EOP, OMB, *Historical Tables: Budget of the U.S. Government, Fiscal Year 1988*, Washington, D.C., U.S. Printing Office, 1987; Congressional Budget Office, *The Economic and Budget Outlook*, Washington, D.C., CBO, January 1987; CBO, *An Analysis of the President's Budget for Fiscal Year 1988*, Washington, D.C., CBO, February 1987.

Originally G-R-H required the Comptroller General of the US General Accounting Office to issue a report (sequestration order) setting forth the amount of reduction to be made in each account on the basis of a joint OMB/CBO report estimating the fiscal year's deficit, expected economic conditions, and the budget base of accounts and programmes. The President was then required to implement, through the sequestration order, the reductions specified by the Comptroller General. However, the sequestration process, using the Comptroller General, was invalidated by the Supreme Court on 7 July 1986.[7] The Supreme Court declared the automatic spending cut procedure unconstitutional because Congress can initiate removal of the Comptroller General by a joint resolution and thus he is subservient to Congress. In the view of the Supreme Court, an agent of Congress may not exercise executive powers of the type given the Comptroller

General under G-R-H. Fallback procedures for making the spending cuts were written into G-R-H. Rather than the Comptroller General ordering the President to make the necessary cuts, G-R-H calls for the OMB/CBO report outlining the automatic cuts to be translated into a joint resolution and reported to the House and Senate floor by the two budget committees acting jointly. If adopted, the resolution then goes to the President for signature or veto. If signed by the President, any cuts it calls for becomes law.

In summary, the 1974 Budget Act and G-R-H have created several major institutions and processes that has centralised consideration of the congressional budget. Budget committees in the House and Senate were established with the responsibility for setting overall tax and spending levels. The act also created a timetable for adopting concurrent budget resolutions and a reconciliation process to conform spending and revenue differences and bring discipline to budgeting. A congressional budget office was created to bring an independent source of budget information and analysis. The act also set an impoundment control mechanism. Finally in 1985 G-R-H set targets for reducing the deficit and established a new budget timetable. What has been the impact of these new institutions and processes?

Judging the Congressional budget process

How the congressional budget process is viewed under the 1974 act and G-R-H depends greatly upon one's expectations.[8] The congressional budget process has experienced thirteen years of turbulence. Since passage of the 1974 Budget Act, no two years have been alike, and Congress faces the difficulty of radically reducing the federal deficit under G-R-H, with a new and shortened decision making process. Members of Congress, presidents, the press, and scholars have continued to express concern about the incessant budgetary warfare on Capitol Hill.

It is useful to re-examine the expectations of the 1974 Act and ask whether they make sense in terms of the historic strengths and weaknesses of Congress, the way budget decisions are actually made on Capitol Hill rather than the way the budget reforms state they should be made. How well did the budget process work under the Congressional Budget and Impoundment Control Act of 1974 and what does it reveal about the future of the process under G-R-H? Did members have unreasonable and conflicting expectations about the budget process reforms? Were there misconceptions about what the congressional budget process could do? Were the goals of the 1974 Act and G-R-H politically unrealistic?

Liberal, conservative, Democratic, and Republican advocates of the 1974 Budget Act argued that it would: (1) curb the growth in federal spending, (2) reduce the amount of uncontrollable spending, (3) complete budgeting on time, (4) change federal budget priorities, (5) allow Congress to control fiscal policy, (6) improve information for budget decisions, and (7) control presidential impoundments. Supporters of G-R-H also argued that the new budget process would reduce deficits, curb federal spending, change budget priorities, allow Congress to control fiscal policy, and force Congress to complete budgeting on time. How successful has Congress been in meeting these goals under the 1974 budget process and G-R-H?

Curbing the growth in federal spending
Federal outlays increased rapidly in the 1960s and early 1970s, more than 64 percent, rising from $340.4 billion in fiscal year 1960 to $528.7 billion in fiscal year 1974 (measured in 1982 constant dollars, see Table 4.3; also see Table 4.4 for budget resolutions and actual budget totals, FY 1976 to FY 1987). During the same ten-year period, the federal government ran a deficit in all but 1969 when it had a $9.0 billion surplus. There has been only two years with a surplus in thirty years (1958 to 1988). The deficit increased from $12.0 billion to $190.2 billion from 1974 to 1985 (in constant 1982 dollars).

There was an overwhelming desire by Congress and the president to reduce the deficit and restrain the growth of spending in 1974 as there was in 1985 when G-R-H became law. Conservatives, joined by significant numbers of moderates and liberals, were alarmed in 1974 (and in 1985) by the rapid growth of federal spending and the size of deficits. Large segments of the public and Congress advocated a new budget process as a means to limit federal spending, which many viewed as out of control.[9] However, even after enactment of the 1974 centralised congressional budgeting process, controlling federal spending continued to be a major concern. As shown in Table 4.3, the deficit dropped sharly from 1976 to 1979 and then shot up to an unprecedented $200.7 billion in fiscal year 1983. Only enactment of G-R-H deficit limits seemed to put a damper on the projected increase in deficits (see Table 4.5 for G-R-H deficit limits). Total outlays have grown 61.8 percent from $609.9 billion in FY 1976 to $866.2 billion

Table 4.3:   *US federal government outlays, deficit, and debt, 1958–88 (billions of dollars)*

	Total outlays in constant 1982 dollars	Total outlays as percent of GNP	Surplus or deficit in constant 1982 dollars	Total gross federal debt	Total gross federal debt as percent of GNP
1958	332.8	18.3	− 10.8	280	62.1
1960	340.4	18.2	1.1	291	57.4
1965	394.9	17.6	− 4.7	323	48.0
1970	509.4	19.8	− 7.4	383	38.6
1974	538.7	19.0	− 12.0	486	34.3
1975	586.0	21.8	− 93.9	544	35.7
1976	609.8	21.9	− 120.9	632	37.2
1977	622.6	21.2	− 81.6	709	36.7
1978	652.2	21.1	− 84.1	780	35.9
1979	660.2	20.6	− 52.7	837	34.1
1980	699.1	22.1	− 87.3	914	34.2
1981	726.5	22.7	− 84.6	1,004	33.6
1982	745.8	23.8	− 128.0	1,147	36.5
1983	777.6	24.4	− 200.7	1,381	41.6
1984	789.9	23.1	− 171.9	1,577	42.8
1985	848.0	24.0	− 190.2	1,827	46.4
1986	866.2	23.8	− 193.2	2,133	51.2
1987 (est.)	862.2	21.7	− 147.0	2,372	53.7
1988 (est.)	839.3	21.1	− 88.3	2,585	54.6

Note: All years referred to in all tables are fiscal years.

Source: Executive Office of the President, Office of Management and Budget, Historical
Tables: Budget of the United States Government, Fiscal Year 1988, Washington, D.C.,
U.S. Printing Office, 1987.

Table 4.4:   *Congressional Budget Resolutions and Actual Budget Totals (billions of dollars)*

Fiscal Year	Revenues	Outlays	Surplus or deficit (−)
Fiscal Year 1976			
First resolution	298.2	367.0	− 68.8
Second resolution	300.8	374¾	− 74.1
Actual	299.2	364.8	− 65.6
Fiscal Year 1977			
First resolution	362.5	413.3	− 50.8
Second resolution	362.5	413.1	− 50.6
Third resolution	347.7	417.5	− 69.8
Third resolution amended	356.6	409.2	− 52.6
Actual	356.9	401.9	− 45.0
Fiscal Year 1978			
First resolution	396.3	461.0	− 64.6
Second resolution	397.0	458.3	− 61.3
Actual	401.1	449.9	− 48.8

Table 4.4 (contd):   *Congressional Budget Resolutions and Actual Budget Totals (billions of dollars)*

Fiscal Year	Revenues	Outlays	Surplus or deficit (−)
Fiscal Year 1979			
First resolution	447.9	498.8	−50.9
Second resolution	448.7	487.5	−38.8
Revised second resolution	461.0	494.5	−33.4
Actual	465.9	493.7	−27.7
Fiscal Year 1980			
First resolution	509.0	532.0	−23.0
Second resolution	517.8	547.6	−29.8
Revised second resolution	525.7	572.7	−47.0
Actual	520.1	579.6	−59.6
Fiscal Year 1981			
First resolution	613.8	613.6	0.2
Second resolution	605.0	632.4	−27.4
Revised second resolution	603.3	661.4	−58.0
Actual	602.6	660.5	−57.9
Fiscal Year 1982			
First resolution	657.8	695.4	−37.6
Revised second resolution	628.4	734.1	−105.7
Actual	617.8	728.4	−110.7
Fiscal Year 1983			
First resolution	665.9	769.8	−103.9
Revised second resolution (a)	604.3	807.4	−203.1
Actual	600.6	796.0	−195.4
Fiscal Year 1984			
First resolution (b)	679.6	851.2	−171.6
Revised second resolution	672.9	845.6	−172.7
Actual	666.5	841.8	−175.3
Fiscal Year 1985			
First resolution (c)	750.9	932.0	−181.2
Revised second resolution (c)	736.5	935.9	−199.4
Revised second resolution (d)	736.5	946.3	−209.8
Actual (c)	734.1	936.8	−202.8
Actual (d)	734.1	946.3	−212.3
Fiscal Year 1986			
First resolution (d)	795.7	967.6	−171.9
Actual	769.1	989.8	−220.7
Fiscal Year 1987			
First resolution (d)	852.4	995.0	−142.6

Note: Actual totals have been adjusted where necessary to agree with the budgetary treatment of various items for the budget resolutions and may, therefore, differ from the totals shown elsewhere in this report. Data for fiscal year 1984 and earlier years exclude outlays primarily Federal Financing Bank, Strategic Petroleum Reserve, and Postal Service) that were considered off-budget before enactment of the Balanced Budget and Emergency Deficit Control Act of 1985.

(a)   Outlays exclude amounts reserved pursuant to Section 2 of the Budget Act.
(b)   Adjusted for enactment of reserve fund programmes.
(c)   On-budget only; see note.
(d)   On- and off-budget combined; see note.

Source: Congressional Budget Office, *The Economic and Budget, Outlook: Fiscal Years 1988–1992* Washington, D.C., Congressional Budge Office, January 1987, pp. 142–3.

Table 4.5: Percent controllability of budget outlays, 1976–88

1976	70.7
1977	70.8
1978	72.2
1979	72.3
1980	73.6
1981	73.8
1982	74.4
1983	74.6
1984	74.1
1985	72.8
1986	75.3
1987	75.9 (est.)
1988	77.5 (est.)

Sources: EOP, OMB, *Historical Tables: Budget of the United States Government, Fiscal Year 1988*, Washington, D.C., U.S. Printing Office, 1987 and *Congressional Quarterly Service, Congressional Quarterly Almanac for 1983 and 1984*, Washington, D.C., Congressional Quarterly, Inc., 1984 and 1985.

in FY 1986 (in constant 1982 dollars). There was little curbing of growth in federal spending during the Reagan years. President Reagan advocated cutting taxes and increasing defence spending in 1981 and Congress went along with it without significantly cutting social expenditures. Reaganomics increased the federal deficit from $84.6 to $193.2 billion and debt from $1,004 to $2,133 billion between 1981 and 1986, and debt as a share of GNP moved from 33.6 percent to 51.2 percent (see Table 4.3).

Fisher argues that a number of procedures associated with the 1974 Act encouraged higher spending, such as the preferred status of entitlements, the greater advocacy from congressional committees and lobbyists through the new access points of the 15 March budget estimates, and the use of inflation factors to increase spending levels from the current services budget.[10] This has not changed significantly under G – R – H. The 1974 Act did not restrain the growth of federal spending. The change in political and fiscal climates under G – R – H is not radically changing spending patterns either.

In the context of the deficit rising from $52.7 billion to $200.7 billion in four years, G – R – H was passed as a desperate act to bring 'automatic' discipline to Congress. G – R – H requires that the deficit be eliminated by 1991 either through conventional congressional budget processes or through unprecendented automatic across-the-board spending cuts.[11] The G – R – H law sets maximum limits on the budget deficit for fiscal 1986 through fiscal 1991, none of which are likely to be met according to both OMB and CBO. The statutory and estimated limits are shown in Table 4.2.

Congress seems politically unwilling or unable to curb federal spending. Budget makers face the unpleasant alternative of raising taxes or freezing prevailing budgetary allocations without satisfying demands for new programmes. Raising taxes, freezing existing budget allocations, and killing all new programmes all cause conflict and electoral problems that members of Congress eventually run away from, even though they are calling for a balanced budget. James C. Miller, Director of the Office of Management and Budget in the Reagan administration argues,

Running deficits is easy because it makes people feel wealthier ... The liability for public debt is dispersed throughout society and is not assigned to anyone in particular. This leads us all to underestimate the costs of deficit financed spending. And as with any activity where the benefits are personal and the costs are social, deficit financing leads to too much spending.[12]

Reducing the amount of uncontrollable expenditures
Curbing growth in the federal budget is but one type of control. Budget control can have another meaning besides the ability to limit or decrease spending. One can speak of the congressional budget process being out of control in the sense that Congress finds itself without the mechanisms to work its budgetary will through the appropriations process, regardless of whether that will is in the direction of decreased or increased federal expenditures. Used in this sense, the lack of congressional control has been evidenced by the increasing percentage of expenditures that could not be altered without changing the basic authorising statute and by the fact that less than half of the budget was subject to annual appropriations.

Before the 1974 reform about 70 percent of the budget was considered 'relatively uncontrollable under existing law' and because of 'backdoor spending' measures (primarily indexed permanently authorised entitlements) only about 44 percent of the budget in fiscal year 1974 could be directly controlled by the Appropriations Committees on an annual basis. Any spending programme is ultimately 'controllable'; however, the nature or degree of controllability differs significantly among programmes. For example, the relatively uncontrollable budget outlays estimated in fiscal year 1988 are estimated to be 77.5 percent with 43.5 percent uncontrollable due to payments for individuals, 15.1 percent for fixed programme costs, and 18.9 percent from outlays from prior-year contracts and obligations (see Table 4.5).[13]

These programmes are 'uncontrollable' primarily because of the political ramifications associated with the proposed cuts. The eligibility for benefit levels is normally established in authorising law rather than through appropriations of budget authority. Efforts by Congress or the president to reduced spending on these entitlement programmes requires changes in the authorising legislation which is politically very difficult to do. In the absence of such legislative changes, the payments will be made automatically, and in many cases such payments are made from the budget authority that is available without appropriations action to finance the programme. The rise in permanent budget authority (resulting in most part from these various forms of backdoor spending) has led to a diminished relationship between congressional budgetary decisions in any given year and the actual outlays of that year. However, the Budget Act prohibited two important forms of backdoor spending: contract and borrowing authority. In addition all new entitlements are subjected to review and possible reduction by the appropriations committees. However, the percentage of the budget that is controllable continues to be a major problem as shown in Table 4.5, increasing from 70.7 percent in 1976 to 77.5 percent uncontrollable in 1988 and is a continuing problem for Congress under $G = R = H$.

One primary reason for this uncontrollability is the failure of Congress to control growth of pre-1975 entitlement expenditures (almost 44 percent of the budget). Entitlements or payments to individuals include such big spending items as social security, disability insurance, railroad retirement, military and civil service retirement, and medicare. All these programmes have permanent indexed authorisations. These are popular programmes with a large number of beneficiaries who pressure members of Congress for full funding.

Most uncontrollables are in the form of entitlements or net interest which are influenced by demographic trends, not through annual legislative appropriations. Entitlements are also indexed to the rate of inflation so that outlays are automatically adjusted to increases in the cost of living without congressional budgetary or appropriations actions. They 'run on automatic'. $G - R - H$ has put increased pressure on Congress to focus on the uncontrollables, but there is little evidence that members of Congress have the political will to reduce spending or increase revenues for these popular big spending programmes. Reagan's O.M.B. Director Miller captures the lack of congressional concern for the uncontrollables as follows: 'Deficits create many winners and few losers ... Every legislator is in a position to try to confer benefits on his or her favorite constituencies, and the incentive for any individual legislator to refrain from such behaviour is virtually nonexistent.'[14]

It is difficult for members of Congress to go against well-organised constituents who want to assure continued funding of a programme that is permanently authorised to do so. One solution is for the formula for spending to be changed in the entitlements, another is to reduce defence spending, and yet another solution is to raise taxes. All are perceived to be politically dangerous if not suicidal options for an electorally sensitive Congress.

Passing budgets on time
Budgetary control can also mean the ability of Congress to meet its own decision-making deadlines. The inability to control large amounts of federal spending caused the delay of budgetary decisions and the delay has contributed to large deficits. Appropriations bills are rarely-completed by the beginning of the fiscal year, causing many federal agencies to operate on continuing resolutions. Before the 1974 budget process, not one appropriation bill since 1968 was enacted before the beginning of the fiscal year. Supporters of the 1974 reform sought to impose deadlines and jurisdictional limitations that would increase the power of the appropriations committees and at the same time force them to meet deadlines for reporting bills. The 1974 Budget Act established an elaborate timetable designed to ensure enactment of all regular appropriation bills by 1 October. The beginning of the fiscal year was extended from the previous 1 July to help meet the appropriations deadlines. Despite the new schedule, Congress has had difficulty in completing its work on regular appropriation bills by the start of the fiscal year (see Table 4.6). As a consequence, again it has been compelled to provide stopgap funding through continuing appropriations (see Table 4.6). Except for fiscal year 1977, when the budget timetable effectively prodded Congress to complete its appropriations work on schedule, it has been necessary to rely on continuing appropriations. In fiscal 1980 only three of the thirteen regular appropriation bills were enacted by the start of the fiscal year; for fiscal 1981

Table 4.6: *Meeting the budget resolution deadlines and supplemental appropriations: Fiscal Years 1975–88*

	1st Con. Resolution		2nd Con. Resolution		Number of Supplemental Appropriations
FY	House	Senate	House	Senate	
1975	On time	On time	Late (12 November)	Late 12 November)	7
1976	On time	On time	On time	On time	5
1977	On time	On time	On time	On time	5
1978	On time	On time	On time	On time	9
1979	On time	On time	Late (28 November)	Late (16 November)	1
1980	On time	On time	Late (18 November)	Late (19 November)	6
1981	On time	On time	Late (10 December)	Late (9 December)	2
1982	Late (10 June)	Late (21 May)	1st res. became binding	4	
1983	On time	On time	2nd res. did not pass		2
1984	On time	None passed	2nd res. did not pass		7
1985	On time	Late (23 May)	2nd res. did not pass		N/A
1975–85	91% On time	73% On time	27% On time	27% On time	
1986	On time under the Gramm-Rudman-Hollings timetable				
1987	Late under the Gramm-Rudman-Hollings timetable				
1988	Late under the Gramm-Rudman-Hollings timetable				

Source: Congressional Budget Office.

only one regular appropriation bill was enacted; none of these bills had been enacted into law when fiscal 1982 began. These delays were similar to the years leading to the 1974 Act. The second concurrent resolution has been passed on time only 27 percent of the time. However, since 1982, the first resolution has taken on many functions of the second. The objective of timeliness has fallen far short of the mark. Fisher concluded that the timetable is 'now far behind what it was before 1974, even with the additional three months gained by changing the fiscal year'.[15]

Both in the 1974 Budget Act and G – R – H, Congress changed the budget deadlines and decision making process but not the motivations and behaviour of its Members. The reforms did not change constituent and interest group pressures to reduce taxes and to fund programmes. Members did not change their tardy budget making because there was no immediate pressure to do so.

Changing federal budget priorities

Advocates of the 1974 Budget Act argued for 'an improved congressional system for determining relative funding priorities'.[16] As political and economic factors eliminated the 'fiscal dividend' that had been promised for the 1970s, it became clear to members of Congress that hard either/or choices would have to be made, choices that could not be avoided by continuing to increase the size of the pie. Those who recognised this prospect felt that congressional budgetary reform was needed in order to unify the disaggregated budgetary process and to create a mechanism for setting budget priorities. However, Schick estimates that Congress did more reordering of budget priorities 'before it had a budget process than it has since'.[17]

The congressional budget process is driven by a highly representative decentralised decision-making system that is organised to make incremental distributive decisions in favour of strong groups, agencies, and congressional committess. Schick reminds us that 'incrementalism's political process is pluralistic with each interest guarding its part of the budget. Claims satisfied in past budgets are accorded preference over new claims, thereby legitimising the role of veto groups in budgetary poltics'.[18] G – R – H forces Congress to reaffirm existing budget priorities rather than allow major shifts in spending. Automatic across-the-board cuts in the sequester base outlays called for in G – R – H by definition to not change budget priorities, they simply set existing programme preferences permanently in place. If change does come it will likely be increment by increment or 'exceptions', not through radical reordering of budget priorities.

Table 4.7:   Change in federal budget priorities, 1974–88

	As percentages of outlays							
	1974	*1976*	*1978*	*1980*	*1982*	*1984*	*1986*	*1988 (est.)*
National defence	29.5	24.1	22.8	22.7	24.9	26.7	28.6	29.0
Human resources	50.4	54.8	52.8	53.0	52.1	50.7	48.7	50.0
Physical resources	9.3	10.5	11.5	11.2	8.3	6.8	5.9	5.0
Net interest	8.0	7.2	7.7	8.9	11.4	13.0	13.7	13.6
Other functions	9.1	7.3	8.6	7.6	6.8	6.5	7.4	6.9
Offsetting receipts	−6.2	−3.9	−3.4	−3.4	−3.5	−3.8	−3.3	−4.4
TOTAL	100.0	100.0	100.0	100.0	100.0	100.0	100.0	100.0
	As percentages of GNP							
	1974	*1976*	*1978*	*1980*	*1982*	*1984*	*1986*	*1988 (est.)*
National defence	5.6	5.3	4.8	5.0	5.9	6.2	6.6	6.3
Human resources	9.6	12.0	11.2	11.7	12.4	11.7	11.6	10.8
Physical resources	1.8	2.3	2.4	2.5	2.0	1.6	1.4	1.1
Net interest	1.5	1.6	1.6	2.0	2.7	3.0	3.3	2.9
Other functions	1.7	1.6	1.8	1.7	1.6	1.5	1.8	1.5
Offsetting receipts	−1.2	−0.8	−0.7	−0.7	−0.8	−0.9	−0.8	−1.0
TOTAL	19.0	21.9	21.1	22.1	23.8	23.1	23.8	21.7

Note: The outlays are organised by superfunction.
Source: Executive Office of the President, Office of Management and Budget, *Historical Tables: Budget of the United States Government, Fiscal Year 1988*, Washington, D.C., U.S. Printing Office, 1987.

Table 4.7, 'Change in federal budget priorities, 1974–1988, reveals only slight change in priorities at the superfunction level in government spending patterns since 1974. As percentage of outlay, the national defence budget went from 29.5 to 29.0 percent of the budget or 5.6 to 6.3 percent of GNP. A very slight incremental shift in human resource outlays also occurred: 50.4 percent of outlays in 1974 to 50.0 percent in 1988, a shift from 9.6 to 10.8 percent of GNP. The most dramatic shift in spending preferences was caused by the interest on the federal government's debt (+ 5.6% from 1974 to 1988) which was not caused by the internal budget making procedures.

Federal budget outlays have grown significantly since 1974 from $538.7 to $839.3 (estimated) billion in 1988 (in 1982 constant dollars) and from 19.0 to 21.7 percent of GNP, in the same time period (see Table 4.3). This real growth in government spending happened primarily through pluralistic incremental decision making with each programme getting its perceived 'fair share' of increase. No major group was significantly disadvantaged. There have been no major shifts in spending priorities as a direct result of the 1974 budget process or G – R – H, as was argued by the advocates of both reforms. The centralised budget process itself did not produce those shifts and probably will not in the future. Presidential or party leadership, change in the economy, and change in member's political will through constituent and special interest pressure helped to cause those shifts, not reform in the budget process.

Controlling fiscal policy
A fifth expectation of budget process reformers was to allow Congress to control fiscal policy. Supporters of the Budget Act argued that federal budget policy could produce major changes in economic growth, inflation, and umemployment. Because the pre-1974 budget making involved a series of isolated, unrelated decisions, Congress had no independent way to set fiscal policy – that is, to set the proper level of economic stimulus or restraint that could be exercised through the federal budget. Some members argued that the 1974 budget reform would allow them to control fiscal policy more easily. Other members, mostly conservatives, felt that if representatives and senators were forced to vote on the deficit or surplus, the tendency toward larger and larger deficits would be reversed. To this extent, they saw the vote not as a way to exercise fiscal policy, but as a means to limit spending. Other members, however, saw a need for a vote on the overall deficit or surplus so that Congress would have the capability to challenge the executive branch's dominance in setting fiscal policy. Nearly everyone has been disappointed. Today many observers feel this was an unrealistic objective and indeed by any measure, Congress (and the President) has been unable independently to control fiscal policy. Without co-operation from the Federal Reserve Board, the international trade arena, the price of oil, weather, and a variety of other factors, controlling fiscal policy by Congress will continue to be an elusive goal.

More often than not the budget resolutions are adjusted to economic changes rather than produced by them. The budget process itself has not been the stimulator or restrainer of economic growth, inflation, or unemployment. Since only incremental changes in tax and spending levels are made annually, the likelihood of major changes in the economy is bound to be slight. Federal tax and spending policy alone is rarely responsible for major changes in the economy. Federal Reserve Board monetary policy, the performance of the industrialised nations, the productivity of the nation's workforce, the trade deficit, and other uncontrollable factors have a collective impact that is more important than the annual changes in revenues and outlays. Control of fiscal policy by Congress is probably an unrealistic objective of the congressional budget process. Those who feel that the budget resolutions should have more than marginal impact on the economy will continue to be disappointed under G – R – H also.

Improving budget information

Another objective of the Budget Act was to overcome congressional dependence upon OMB and executive Branch agencies for budget information and analysis. Congress wanted its own OMB. There was almost unanimous support to create an independent congressional agency to give timely budget information and analysis. 'Information', said Senator Lee Metcalf during the debate of the budget reform act, 'is the name of the game in budget control.'[19] During the years preceding the passage of the Budget Act, Congress felt itself at a great disadvantage to the President's Office of Management and Budget and the thousands of budget experts and policy analysts in the executive branch agencies.

Congress wanted and got an independent source of budgetary knowledge and analysis through the Congressional Budget Office (CBO). CBO supplies timely multi-year budgeting, scorekeeping, economic forecasting, and policy analyses that seem to help Congress to confront budget reality. According to a recent survey of members of Congress and staff, CBO is considered a success and an effective source of budget information and analysis.[20] According to the House Commission on Information and Facilities, it has, 'established itself as a full-fledged, competent, and respected member of the con-gressional support family'.[21] The demand for CBO studies and testimony has grown significantly since its creation. However, its influence has been hard to measure. Allen Schick argues that, when measured against the great expectations of those who hoped that the Congressional Budget Office would turn Congress into an avid cus-tomer for analysis, the record of the first years has been disappointing.

The quality of CBO's analytic work has been quite good in its strong areas, such as welfare policy. Yet the production of solid analyses has not by itself influenced many legislative outcomes or evoked much congressional interest, though 'numbers' work addressed to the immediate concerns of the budget has made an impact.[22]

Improving budget information does not make decision making automatically easier nor does it reduce budgetary uncertainty, an important goal in creating CBO. CBO assumptions are central to establishing a realistic budget plan for each upcoming fiscal year. Under G-R-H the budget resolution is supposed to meet deficit targets so that a balanced budget exists in 1991. The budget resolutions are generally based on economic, legislative, administrative, and technical assumptions made by CBO for Congress. The integrity of these CBO assumptions has a direct impact on the budget. CBO has been unable to reduce all uncertainty in the budget estimates and deficit projections. This uncertainty comes not from the quality of CBO analysis but from fluid economic assumptions and technical re-estimates. Small changes in the economic outlook of the nation can produce major changes in the budget. For example, a sustained increase of one percentage point in all government interest rates (something not controlled by Congress) would have increased the deficit by $11 billion in 1988 and $26 billion in 1992.[23] Changes in the budget and the projected deficit can also occur because of unanticipated legislative actions and technical estimating errors out of the control of CBO.

Since fiscal year 1980, there has been significant uncertainty in the budget resolutions projections. Projections of budget deficits have been consistently over-optimistic. The difference between actual outcomes and estimates in the first budget resolutions can be divided into four major sources: economic, legislative, administrative, and technical. All four of these sources of error have contributed to underestimating the federal deficit, which is a critical problem when trying to reach the deficit targets in G-R-H (see Table 4.8) and reveals unrealistic economic assumption from 1980 to 1986. An unexpectedly weak economy will reduce federal tax revenues and increase spending for unemployment compensation and welfare benefits, thus causing inaccurate budget forecasts.

The blame for misestimates rests with both the executive and congressional branches of government. Inaccurate legislative assumptions were made in all but one year. Senate and House Budget Committees and CBO must make assumptions about the timing and likely effects of pending tax legislation and spending proposals.

Table 4.8 Sources of differences between actual budget totals and first budget resolution estimates for Fiscal Years 1980–6 (billions of dollars)

Differences	1980	1981	1982	1983	1984	1985	1986
Revenues							
Economic assumptions	8.4	5.0	− 51.9	− 58.0	4.5	− 20.0	− 23.0
Legislative assumptions	6.2	− 3.7	13.0	− 4.6	− 13.7	− 0.2	− 1.5
Administrative assumptions	–	–	–	–	–	–	–
Technical assumptions	− 3.5	− 12.6	− 1.1	− 2.7	− 3.9	− 3.3	− 2.1
Total differences	11.1	− 11.2	− 40.0	− 65.3	− 13.1	− 16.8	− 26.6
Outlays							
Economic assumptions	12.4	6.4	24.1	0.5	7.1	− 5.2	− 12.1
Legislative assumptions	12.4	17.9	1.1	15.6	1.6	19.1	11.8
Administrative assumptions	7.2	6.6	0.1	2.0	− 0.1	3.8	2.4
Technical assumptions	15.6	16.0	7.7	8.1	− 18.0	− 12.9	20.1
Total differences	47.6	46.9	32.9	26.2	− 9.4	4.8	22.2
Deficit							
Economic assumptions	4.0	1.4	76.0	58.5	2.7	14.8	10.9
Legislative assumptions	6.2	21.6	− 11.9	20.2	15.3	19.3	13.2
Administrative assumptions	7.2	6.6	0.1	2.0	− 0.1	3.8	2.4
Technical assumptions	19.1	28.6	8.8	10.8	− 14.1	− 16.2	22.2
Total differences	36.6	58.1	73.0	91.5	3.7	21.6	48.8

Source: Congressional Budget Office, *The Economic and Budget Outlook: Fiscal Years 1988–1992*, Washington, D.C., Congressional Budget Office, January 1987, p. 145.

If the laws enacted differ from those assumed, the budget resolution estimates are likely to be inaccurate.

Executive branch administrative assumptions also contributed to underestimating the deficit every year but one for a total of $22 billion outlays from 1980 to 1986. This accounted for $79.5 billion in unanticipated outlays for fiscal years 1980 to 1986. Administrative misestimates come from unanticipated regulatory and other administrative actions or inactions by federal agencies. These can cause unexpected increases or decreases in outlays and revenues. For example, the Reagan Administration has assumed the sale of CON-RAIL (an offsetting receipt) for several consecutive fiscal years but with no sale, thus there was a decrease each year in assumed revenues for the sale.

Technical assumptions caused the deficit to exceed the estimate in all but two years, as revealed by Table 4.8. Technical assumptions are the differences between estimates and outcomes as a result of imprecise estimating methods and other factors that do not fit into the other three categories. For example, CBO cannot predict exactly how many people will apply for Social Security benefits next year or precisely how large payroll tax collections will be, even if the economic assumptions of the budget resolutions are completely borne out. These misestimates cause significant uncertainty in projections of the budget and the deficit for total unanticipated net outlays of $36.6 billion for fiscal year 1980 to 1986. Unexpected increases in the cost of farm price supports, federal health programs, financial deposit insurance programs, and unemployment compensation added $12 billion, for example, to CBO's estimate of the FY 1987 deficit in just five months, between August 1986 and January 1987.[24] In recent years, errors in technical estimating assumptions have caused targets in congressional budget resolutions to differ from actual deficits by an average of $17 billion per year.

According to the CBO, the net effect of using faulty economic, legislative, administrative, and technical assumptions is a consistent tendency to underestimate outlays and overestimate revenues which is shown in Table 4.8. Actual revenues fell short of the budget resolution estimates in six years out of seven. Actual outlays exceeded the estimates with the same frequency. For both revenues and outlays, the outcomes differ from the estimates by an average of 3.5 percent. These errors are magnified in the deficit, which exceeded the estimates by an average of $48 billion.[25]

Controlling presidential impoundments
Another major objective of the Congressional Budget and Impoundment Control Act of 1974 was to control presidential impoundments. Procedures were established in Title X of the Act to review presidential proposals for two kinds of impoundment: deferrals (postpone or delay spending) and rescissions (cancel or take back authority to spend). When a president proposes deferrals for up to twelve months, either the House or the Senate can approve an 'impoundment resolution'

compelling the release of the affected funds. When a president proposes a rescission, Congress has a forty-five day period during which it can pass a bill rescinding the funds (approving the presidential rescission); if Congress fails to act during this period, the president is required to make the funds available for expenditure. The original deferral process called for a one house legislative veto which the *INS vs. Chadha* decision found to be unconstitutional.[26] However, Congress has circumvented the constitutionality issue by voting on deferral decisions in both houses primarily by adding them to supplemental appropriations bills.

The effect of the impoundment provisions has been important. The provisions regularise and set a legal foundation for presidential impoundments while allowing Congress to overturn these cuts when it so desires. The procedures have been a major success for both Congress and presidents. Congress has control over presidential impoundments and presidents can use the procedure to cut back on spending they deem unnecessary. Table 4.9 shows an overall high approval rate for deferrals (almost 83 percent). President Reagan's success through 1985 was almost 90 percent on proposed deferrals. President Ford's was 76 percent and Carter's 82 percent. Over $100 billion in deferrals was saved by presidents from 1975 to 1985. Ford successfully deferred $31 billion, Carter $25 billion and Reagan $45 billion.

Table 4.10 reveals that the use of the rescission process varies sharply from year to year. In 1975 and 1976 President Ford proposed over six billion dollars in rescissions, but Congress rescinded only $529.6 million, around 7 percent of the proposed cuts. During the Carter administration, the rescission rate increased to 38 percent for a $2.6 billion saving. Reagan resorted to rescissions to implement his budget priorities in 1981 and 1982 with great success. Reagan cut almost $16 billion in his first two years in office. His rescission success rate was almost 59.6 percent. From 1975 to 1985 $19 billion was cut through rescissions for a 46.8 percent congressional acceptance rate, as shown in Table 4.10.

In conclusion, the impoundment provisions of the 1974 Budget Act have worked in a predictable process without major confrontations about the role of Congress and the President in the budgetary process. One primary effect of the Act is that it established a routine constitutional procedure for reviewing appropriated budget impoundments by the executive branch. The impoundment provisions have worked well under Republican and Democratic presidents.

Table 4.9: Deferrals under the Impoundment Act of 1974 (millions of dollars)

	Proposed		Accepted			
	Number	*Amount*	*Number*	*Percent*	*Amount*	*Percent*
Ford deferrals						
1975	161	25,333.0	145	90.1	15,954.8	63.0
1976 and TQ	117	8,145.4	93	79.5	7,762.3	95.3
1977	52	7,048.1	52	100.0	7,048.1	100.0
TOTAL	330	40,526.5	290	87.9	30,765.2	75.9
Carter deferrals						
1977	62	5,001.4	59	95.2	4,975.8	99.5
1978	66	4,966.8	61	92.4	4,910.3	98.9
1979	69	4,685.3	67	97.1	4,676.9	99.8
1980	73	10,523.6	68	93.2	5,027.0	47.8
1981	41	5,670.4	41	100.0	5,670.4	100.0
TOTAL	311	30,847.5	296	95.2	25,260.4	81.9
Reagan deferrals						
1981	90	3,814.1	76	84.4	3,452.7	90.5
1982	253	8,215.3	241	95.3	7,853.4	95.6
1983	83	13,608.0	70	84.3	9,624.0	70.7
1984	67	7,935.5	65	97.0	7,919.5	99.8
1985	77	16,783.3	58	75.3	16,044.7	95.6
TOTAL	570	50,356.2	510	89.5	44,894.3	89.2
GRAND TOTAL						
(all deferrals)	1,211	121,730.2	1,096	90.5	100,919.9	82.9

Source: Office of Management and Budget, 29 October 1985.

Consequences of budget process reform

A central question remains. What are the institutional and behavioural consequences of the 1974 congressional budget act and G-R-H deficit reduction procedures? The impact of the budget process since 1974 on the congressional agenda, committees, party leaders, congressional power *vis-à-vis* the President, interest groups, and members' constituency relationships has been remarkable.

Table 4.10:   *Rescissions under the Impoundment Control Act of 1974*
                (millions of dollars)

	Proposed		Accepted			
	Number	Amount	Number	Percent	Amount	Percent
Ford rescissions						
1975	87	2,722.0	39	44.8	391.3	14.4
1976 and TQ	50	3,582.1	7	14.0	138.3	3.9
1977	13	1,100.4	0	0	0	0
TOTAL	150	7,404.5	46	30.7	529.6	7.2
Carter rescissions						
1977	17	1,786.9	6	35.3	711.6	39.8
1978	12	1,290.1	6	50.0	593.7	46.0
1979	11	908.7	9	81.8	723.6	79.6
1980	59	1,618.1	33	55.9	550.8	34.0
1981	33	1,142.4	0	0	0	0
TOTAL	132	6,746.2	54	40.9	2,579.7	38.2
Reagan rescissions						
1981	133	15,361.9	105	78.9	11,715.2	76.3
1982	32	7,907.4	5	15.6	4,364.7	55.2
1983	21	1,569.0	0	0	0	0
1984	9	636.4	3	33.3	55.4	8.7
1985	244	1,854.8	96	39.3	165.6	8.9
TOTAL	439	27,329.5	209	47.6	16,300.9	59.6
GRAND TOTAL						
(all rescissions)	721	41,480.2	309	42.9	19,410.2	46.8

Source: Office of Management and Budget, 29 October 1985.

Congressional agenda and debate

The Budget Act changed the nature of the congressional policy agenda
and the debate over the budget in several major ways. The first
Chairman of the HBC, Representative Brock Adams stated it simply:
'perhaps the most important aspect of the budget resolution is the
fact that it contains the budget of Congress and not that of the
President'.[27] The process forces Congress to create its own budget
which immediately challenges the President's budgetary priorities.

Through this reform, Congress regained its power of the purse which had slowly been taken away by the executive branch through a variety of reforms and agency actions. However, congressional resurgence in budgeting came at a cost. A second impact of the budget process reform has been the dominance of budgeting over the policy agenda and debate in Congress.

Budgeting by definition is a conservative activity in a system of limited and scarce financial resources. Spending and taxing decisions now take up over 60 percent of the time and debate on the floor of the House and Senate. The nature of this debate is focused on cutbacks rather than on new initiatives and dramatic increases in existing programmes. Congress has had to learn to say 'no' and to say it to Presidents, interest groups, and constituents. With the massive debt and continual deficits, the setting of overall revenue and spending limits each year has caused a major change in the floor debate from 'how can we solve new problems?', be they national security or social, to 'how can we save money and reduce the size of government expenditures?' The Budget Act of 1974 and G-R-H are probably the most important reassertion of congressional authority and prerogatives that has taken place in the last fifty years because it gives the means for Congress to compete with the President's policy agenda as expressed in the budget. However, because of the complexity of the process and because of the federal debt Congress has focused primarily on spending cutbacks and budget control rather than dramatically changing long-existing spending priorities.

Impact on committees
Implementation of the 1974 budget process resulted in significant consequences for congressional committees by placing restraints on spending and by openly relating outlays to revenues. In addition to the obvious increased workload for all committees, stemming from both an altered budgetary timetable and the required reports on projected spending and revenues, the gap between authorisations and appropriations was dramatically reduced. The reform also caused some jockeying for jurisdictional turf between the budget committees and the other standing committees, especially appropriations and taxing committees. That competition still exists under G-R-H. The budget committees, for example, have never competed effectively with the tax committees because of a lack of staff expertise on revenue questions as shown most recently with the 1986 Tax Reform Act.

Finally, the authorisation committees have lost significant power because of the appropriation committees' right to cap new 'backdoor spending'. The appropriations committees have also expanded their use of 'backdoor authorisations' by increasing the number and complexity of restrictive programme provisions in appropriations bills and to appropriate without authorisation.

The 1974 Budget Act required all standing committees to submit estimates of their spending authority for programmes within their jurisdiction by 15 March, and by 15 May to submit a final list of spending authorisations to the budget committees. The committees' reports, a primary reason for their increased workload, formed a major ingredient of the targets in the first budget resolution. The committee estimates of authorisations tended to limit their freedom to pass unanticipated new programmes and higher authorisations after 15 May. The budget targets set outer spending limits for committees and forced them to state priorities and to make difficult choices among programmes very early in the process, rather than authorising high levels of funding and new programmes as a result of strong, well-organised, twelfth-hour lobbying shortly before the beginning of the fiscal year. Before the 1974 reform, programme authorisation levels were commonly (and symbolically) double and even triple the final appropriations. The substantive committees would authorise at very high levels to placate strong pressures from outside Congress, knowing full well that the appropriations committees would push the actual funding down to 'reasonable' levels. After 1974 the authorisation committees could no longer play this game as a result of the requirement to estimate total programme funding within each committee's jurisdiction; thus the gap between authorisations and appropriations was frequently less than 5 percent.

Although Senator Sam J. Ervin, Jr., Floor Manager of the Senate's version of the Budget and Impoundment Control Act, argued that the budget committees 'would not infringe on the jurisdiction of the now existing committees', jurisdictional conflicts have occurred in at least four ways as a result of the reform.[28] First, in order to arrive at targets and ceilings for the functional categories of the budget, the budget comittees must look at specific programmes. Thus, there was an inescapable invasion of authorisation and appropriation committee jurisdictions by the budget committees when they build their aggregate targets and ceiling figures. The Senate Budget Committee (SBC) avoided setting line-item limits in the budget resolution or its accompanying report which was not the case in the House; however, the SBC frequently opposed bills from other committees after passage of the first budget resolution. Second, the Ways and Means and Finance Committees lost power as a result of the budget reform. Rudder has shown that the tax committees lost some control over information, expertise, and issue definition in revenue matters.[29] They were forced to react to budget committee proposals, therefore losing the power of initiative. Rudder shows that this is more observable in the Senate than in the House.[30] Third, budget committee 'score-keeping' (comparing the cost of legislation being reported by committees to the functional targets in the first budget resolution) and keeping committees within the targets is a direct infringement upon the authority of the standing committees. Fourth, the successful power-building strategy of the SBC has caused several direct confrontations with other committees on the floor of the Senate. Senators Muskie, Domenici, and Chiles, the first three SBC Chairs, not only opposed legislation on the floor of the Senate (which is not the style of the HBC) that would break the targets of the first budget resolution, but the SBC has also won several critical battles with the Appropriation Committee, including the right to joint jurisdiction over rescission and deferral impoundment resolutions.[31]

Another impact of the 1974 budget reform on committees was the closing of two types of (since 1974) 'backdoor spending' (i.e., contract authority and borrowing authority) by the authorising committees, which was discussed earlier. Although either house may waive this restriction, the elimination of new 'back doors' brought some increased control over spending by the appropriation committees and thus less freedom for the authorisation committees to circumvent the traditional appropriations process.

Impact on party leadership

As a result of the wide-sweeping reforms of the 1970s, power in the House of Representatives shifted from committee chairmen to sub-committee chairmen and concurrently changes in rules and procedures increased the influence of the Democratic caucus and Democratic party leadership.[32] Thus, the 1970s brought both decentralisation and centralisation of power to the House. This was not the case in the Senate. With the resurgence of the speakership, the budget process may be one of his primary tools for co-ordination and centralisation of decision-making in the House. House Democratic leaders are forced through the budget process to mobilise members behind budget resolutions that do not always please committee and subcommittee chairmen, interest groups, agencies of the executive branch, or the President. However, they must build these coalitions and centralise decision-making in a House that is highly decentralised. Power in the Senate is still firmly in the hands of the committee chairmen. House and Senate party leaders have played different roles in the budget process.

The House leadership has been actively involved in setting budget figures and offering refining amendments in order to marshall support for the resolutions on the floor of the House. The primary impact of the budget reform on the House majority leadership (under Speakers Carl Albert, Thomas P. 'Tip' O'Neill and Jim Wright) is that it has forced centralisation, co-ordination, and the construction of a Democratic coalition behind a congressional budget. Speaker Jim Wright, the House Democratic leadership's former long-time member on the HBC, has been a primary force in moulding workable Democratic budget resolutions. When 'Tip' O'Neill was majority leader under Carl Albert, he played a key role building the narrow margins needed to keep the budget process alive and continued that role as speaker.

The House leadership has also helped give the budget process an independence from the President, but not always from the power and expertise of committee and subcommittee chairmen who put pressure on the HBC for higher spending for their pet programmes. Defence spending, highway funding, water project funding are all instances of constituency interests and budget committee priorities confronting each other. The substantive committee chairs seem to win.

The budget process has come close to breaking down in the House several times except for the efforts of the leadership. During 1975, leaders appealed for 'support of the process', but from 1977 on, they based their persuasion on the policy content of the resolution. A crisis in the process occurred in the spring of 1977 when conservatives, claiming too little money was being set for defence, succeeded in increasing the budget target, thus incurring the ire of House liberals. Another confrontation came in President Reagan's first year in office. Conservatives, both Republican and Democratic, coalesced with President Reagan to pass the 1981 and 1982 reconciliation acts which established higher defence spending and reduced social expenditures. This confrontation caused a great deal of strain on the budget process, especially because of the use of the reconciliation process for the first budget resolution. The reconciliation process (discussed earlier) was Reagan's way of reaching reductions in expenditures within the protected jurisdiction of the tax committees and the sacred 'turf' of the appropriations committees. For example, Fisher estimates that over half of the spending reductions in the reconciliation acts were within House Ways and Means and Senate Finance.[33]

Since 1976, voting on budget resolutions has reflected a sharp split in the House between the parties with remarkable Republican cohesion. During the 1976–1981 fiscal years, approximately 95 percent of the House Republicans voted against adoption of the budget resolutions. For the fiscal 1982 and 1983 budgets, however, the Republicans both in the Senate and House (despite their minority status in the House) gained control of the budget process, and most of them voted in favour of budget resolutions supported by Republican President Ronald Reagan

House Democrats have not been as united as the Republicans. At various times Democrats from both the liberal and the conservative wings of the party have opposed the positions taken by most of their colleagues. Nevertheless, during the 1976–1981 fiscal years, House Democrats supplied sufficient votes to pass the budget resolutions, though on two occasions (the first resolution for fiscal 1978 and the second resolution for fiscal 1980) only after the initial version was rejected. In voting on the 1982 and 1983 budget resolutions, most House Democrats opposed the President's position and, when their view was rejected, voted against adoption of the budget resolutions.

From 1976 to 1982 fiscal year, the Senate displayed a different voting pattern, a bipartisan coalition of Republicans and Democrats ensuring passage of the resolutions by a wide margin. The two parties were polarised on the 1982 and 1983 budgets, and in both years a majority of Senate Democrats voted against approval of the budget resolution. Growing Democratic opposition was matched by increasing Republican support for the resolutions. The party split has made it almost as difficult to pass budget resolutions in the Senate as in the House, and in both 1982 and 1984 the margin of approval in the Senate was a single vote. Votes under G-R-H have also proven to be highly partisan in both the House and Senate. House and Senate Democrats and Republicans would like to see stronger party leadership working more actively to build support for the budget resolutions. However, party leaders do not play an important part in Members' decision-making calculus.

Impact on congressional–presidential relations
A major element influencing the resurgence of power to Congress from the presidency during the 1970s was the 1974 Budget Act. Members could no longer hide behind an archaic budgetary process in explaining deficits and expanding expenditures, and the traditional monopoly over the budget was no longer held by the President. President Carter, for example, faced the reality of the congressional budgetary process:

If President Carter wants an immediate tax cut, he must first convince the budget committees of Congress to approve it. If President Carter wants to stimulate the economy through increased federal spending, he must first persuade the budget committees to accept this. If President Carter wants to balance the federal budget by 1980, he will have to work continuously with the budget committees to reach that goal.[34]

How did the 1974 congressional process work with a President of the same party as the majority in Congress? How has it worked with a Republican President and Senate and Democratic House? Budget committee chairman have argued that the process met the challenge of independence by resisting co-option by President Carter. Senator Muskie asserted that 'it has been a helluva job to maintain the independence of the congressional budget this year, but we've done it'.[35] Former House Budget Committee Chairman Giaimo said the process was free of the dominance of a Democratic President: 'the question was whether we were going to be a rubber stamp or work out our own priorities. I think we've answered that question'.[36] Recent chairmen have stressed the independence of the process, but the preliminary evidence suggests a more tempered judgment. Although Presidents Carter and Reagan and their advisors have lost several major policy battles to Congress through the congressional budgetary process, the budget committees seem to be taking their major cues from the President. This was especially true with Reagan's 1981 and 1982 reconciliation acts that shifted spending priorities from domestic to defence programmes. However, there is ample evidence that the 1974 process was independent of President Carter and President Reagan. The dynamic conflicts between the President and Congress over spending programmes for national defence, social programmes, tax policy, and the deficit reveal significant independent congressional budgetary power. For example, after the House recommitted the first budget resolution for fiscal year 1978 and President Carter lost funds for military spending and face with congressional leaders, he apologised for his own and his colleagues' unknowing and unwitting collisions with the congressional process.[37] After losing military funds and the water projects battle, Carter's Director of the Office of Budget and Management, Bert Lance, added, 'I've learned first-hand these last few weeks that this is still a young and tender process and needs to be brought along'.[38]

As discussed earlier, the Budget and Impoundment Control Act stripped the President of much of the impoundment power that President Richard Nixon exercised. By a simple majority vote, either chamber can force the President to spend immediately any funds that he wants to withhold temporarily. Also, the President cannot revoke spending authority permanently without a majority vote in both the House and Senate in his favour. However, viewed from the presidential perspective, Title X (the impoundment control provisions) of the Act gives both Congress and the President new power over spending.

Impact on interest groups and member–constituency relations
There is some evidence that the 1974 budget reform and G-R-H has had an impact on behaviour and attitudes 'outside' of Congress on interest groups and member–consitituency relationships, but it has not helped to reduce the deficit. Through open debate and more visible and co-ordinated votes on deficits, total spending, taxation, and macroeconomic policy, constituents, electoral opponents, and interest groups have new (and probably better) data for evaluating the performance of Senators and Representatives. No-one has been defeated primarily as a result of information from the budget process, but election campaigns since 1976 have revealed wide use of policy stands on the budget by both incumbents and non-incumbents. The primary influence on constituents – beyond a mini-course in macroeconomics – still is not known, but the size of the deficit is increasingly a salient issue both nationally and locally and has become directly related to the re-election outcomes of members.

Constituents appear to support the new budget process – wondering why it cannot do something about the ever-increasing deficits, while many interest groups see it as a threat to their programmes and have opposed it from the beginning. Since the G-R-H reform forces reduction, it guarantees everyone will not always get more. There is a realisation that the budgetary pie is not growing rapidly enough to take care of expanding old programmes and initiating new expensive programmes. Under the G-R-H process, trade-offs between popular programmes are made. Large interest groups such as the AFL–CIO have been major opponents of the new process, and most small specialised interest groups have found it increasingly difficult to influence the spending levels in their functional areas of the budget. The aggregated, centralised, co-ordinated approach to budgeting has tended to reduce the power of the 'iron triangles' or 'clientelism' (i.e., the relationship of congressional subcommittees, executive agencies, and interest groups inthe same policy subsystem) that has been used to successfully push for expanded programmes, more spending, and less oversight in the past.[39]

New broad-based coalitions have also been formed to lobby the major budget participants. Their central objective is – how can we limit the reduction or get more for our functional category in the budget? For example, health, education, welfare, and labour groups joined forces, and have pressured the budget committees to increase spending for social programmes and reduce money for defence programmes. Their language, analysis, and action is at the aggregate level (functional categories of the budget), at the stage of the budget resolution mark-ups and at the programme level within the authorisation and appropriations committees, the traditional approach to congressional lobbying. This is a case of an internal congressional reform influencing the 'external' lobbying environment of Congress.

For a short period of time in 1981 and 1982, President Reagan and his conservative coalition of supporters in Congress overcame the power of special interest groups that have traditionally pushed for new domestic programmes and expanded federal domestic spending. In 1981 Reagan cut federal domestic spending, increased military spending and cut taxes through the exploitation of the economic, political and budgetary conditions in the US. Reagan followed Carter, who was perceived to have produced a failure in economic policy. There was a strong desire by the American people for change. Reagan used the centralised budgetary process to push through his 1981 legislative programme. The 1974 Budget and Impoundment Control Act was a key institution used by David Stockman, then Director of the Office of Management and Budget, and other Reagan staff in their fight to cut both taxes and domestic spending and increase defence outlays. The 1974 act contained the 'reconciliation process' (discussed earlier) that allowed Reagan and Stockman to force a vote on the budget as a whole rather than specific programmes. The debate shifted from the parts to the whole, thus overcoming the desire by members to please special interests and their committee and subcommittee allies in Congress. Members perceived benefits in shifting from specific federal programmes, in which a small group would gain substantially, to the budget as a whole where the general public would gain. Interest groups and their friends in committees and agencies in the executive branch were taken by surprise in 1981 when Stockman and his allies on Capitol Hill locked in spending ceilings in the 1 May concurrent resolution, thus changing the budget debate from line items to a highly centralised reconciliation resolution. For the first year in office President Reagan, OMB, and their congressional supporters overcame the decentralised decision-making which dominates the congressional budget process. In subsequent years the power and force of interest groups, committees, and executive branch agencies have regained their influence and there is the traditional debate over specific programmes without great concern for solving the problems of the structural deficit. O.M.B. Director Miller argues that the only way to reduce the power of interest group is the line-item veto: 'a line-item veto would enable the chief executive to excise some of the most flagrant special-interest spending that all contemporary presidents have been forced to accept in the context of more general spending bills'.[40]

Conclusions

The Congressional Budget and Impoundment Control Act is one of the most important structural and procedural budgetary reforms to be adopted by Congress in the last fifty years. The ultimate impact of the Balanced Budget and Emergency Deficit Control Act of 1985 (G-R-H) may not be known for many years, but it has focused congressional attention on cutting back the deficit, thus putting pressure on members to increase taxes and cut spending. In conclusion, what are the major successes and failures of these budget process reforms since 1974? How successful has Congress been in meeting the goals of these reforms?

Any concluding assessment of the congressional budget process under the 1974 Budget Act and G-R-H must focus on procedural goals and policy expectations. Implementation of the 1974 budget reforms has not met several of the original objectives, probably because they were politically unrealistic. Procedurally and structurally the congressional budget process has achieved many of its objectives, but the behaviour of members has not changed dramatically and the policy expectations of almost everyone have not been acheived.

Several structural and procedural budget reforms have had important consequences. The reforms have:

allowed Congress to make better decisions about the spending and taxing budget as a comprehensive plan rather than only in parts;

highlighted macro-budgetary and macro-economic tradeoffs for Congress;

focused public attention on the debate over the budget;

given Congress more budgetary power *vis-à-vis* the President;

improved a cumbersome decentralised budget-making process;

improved information and analysis for budget decisions;

allowed Congress to control presidential impoundments;

strengthened the congressional role in the budget-making process;

increased the staff support for budget decision-making;

allowed for the gradual tightening of control over the executive spending discretion;

focused the congressional agenda and debate over spending and taxing on deficits and a 'zero sum budgetary game';

redistributed power among the congressional committees, giving more power to the budget committees and taking away from the other committees;

motivated interest groups and constituents to build new 'self protection' coalitions and lobby Congress more intensely for new programmes and for the maintenance of old ones.

Primary structural and procedural goals of the 1974 Budget Act which have been achieved are the creation of the House and Senate Budget Committees, and the Congressional Budget Office giving Congress a strong budgetary position vis-a-vis the President and executive branch. Congress now has independent budget expertise and estimates of revenues and spending to assist it in formulating budget resolutions for each fiscal year. Congress has also established a consistent and rational process for making budget decisions. It monitors compliance and enforces revenue floors and spending ceilings. Congress has been able to focus on tax expenditures, entitlements, backdoor spending, presidential impoundments, and future-year budgets under the congressional budget process.

The independent impact of the 1974 Budget Act on spending decisions is difficult to calculate, considering the complex set of simultaneous 'environmental' factors that occurred during implementation, not the least of which was President Reagan's budget shifts and passage of the Gramm-Rudman-Hollings Balanced Budget Act. Although there were fears that the 1974 reform would primarily help conservatives in opposing spending for social programmes while giving military spending the upper hand, these were not realised, nor is there evidence of a major change in priorities toward more special spending in the budget as a result of the 1974 process. The process was neutral with no preference given to defence or domestic spending. It provided for a neutral budget process permitting budget decisions to be made by a majority. However, some observers believe the 1974 Act forced some priorisation of major new programme initiatives – that is, consideration of trade-offs between programmes of marginal value and new programme initiatives. The reconciliation process in 1981 and 1982 certainly assisted President Reagan in shifting spending priorities to more defence and less social expenditures. However, his success resulted primarily from the change in majority party in the Senate and the conservative coalition in the House, not from the 1974 budget process. Most thoughtful observers argue the 1974 Act made Congress cost-conscious, focusing on the deficit and ways to balance the budget, to the detriment of both defence and social programmes which in turn led to the Deficit Reduction Act of 1985.

The budget reforms have not:

curbed growth of federal spending;

brought an end to the growth in uncontrollable spending;

reduced the deficit;

allowed Congress to complete budgeting on time;

reordered national budget priorities;

allowed Congress to control fiscal policy, or

eliminated the need for continuing resolutions.

If the will of the public and consequently the will of Members of Congress changes, deadlines will be met and reductions made in the deficit. Simple structural and procedural changes by which Congress makes budgetary decisions (such as G-R-H) without change in the incentives of members will not have a major impact on the interest-group-dominated pluralist behaviour of the institution. G-R-H is a major test of constituency and members' will to change deficit spending behaviour. O.M.B.'s Miller has observed that 'one reason Congress complied with the requirements of G-R-H during its first year is that the political pressures to do so were substantial ... as time goes on, however, it is reasonable to expect those pressures to weaken. And, as many have noted, what Congress does, it can undo'.[41] The conflict in Congress between the complex centralised and co-ordinated budget process and the need for a division of labour and a decentralised decision-making system (committees and sub-committees) that is representative of geographic and functional institutions in society will continue to cause delay, deadlock, and even breakdown in congressional budgeting. New reforms such as further centralisation of the committee process, revenue-neutral authorisations, a two-year budget cycle, an omnibus appropriations bill, and the creation of a standard budget data base all require co-operation from the President and an accompanying change in constituent attitudes, interest group behaviour, and member motivations.[42]

Notes

1   See J. A. Thurber, 'Congressional budget reform and new demands for policy analysis', *Policy Analysis*, Spring 1976, pp. 198–214.

2   See J. W. Ellwood and J. A. Thurber, 'The new congressional budget process: the hows and whys of House-Senate differences' in L. C. Dodd and B. Oppenheimer, eds, *Congress Reconsidered*, New York, 1977, pp. 163–92.

3   See J. W. Ellwood, ed., *Reductions in U.S. Domestic Spending*, New Brunswick, NJ, 1982.

4   *Ibid.*

5   See A. Schick, *Reconciliation and the Congressional Budget Process*, Washington, D.C., American Enterprise Institute, 1981, and D. Tate, 'Reconciliation breeds tumult as committees tackle cuts: revolutionary budget tool', *Congressional Quarterly Weekly Report*, 23 May 1981, pp. 887–91.

6   See E. Wehr, 'Congress Enacts Far-Reaching Budget Measure', *Congressional Quarterly Weekly Report*, 14 December 1987, pp. 2604–11.

7   For two articles on Supreme Court case regarding G-R-H, see J. Rauch, 'The thickening fog', *National Journal*, 12 July 1986, pp. 1721–24 and E. Wehr, 'Court strikes down core of Gramm-Rudman', *Congressional Quarterly Weekly Report*, 12 July 1986, pp. 1559–63.

8   See J. A. Thurber, 'Assessing the Congressional budget process under Gramm-Rudman-Hollings and the 1974 Budget Act', presented at the 1986 Annual Meeting of the American Political Science Association.

9   See Ellwood and Thurber, 'The new congressional budget process'.

10   See L. Fisher, 'Ten years of the Budget Act: still searching for controls', *Public Budgeting and Finance*, Autumn 1985, p. 15. Also see J. Ferejohn and K. Krehbiel, 'The budget process and the size of the budget', *American Journal of Political Science*, May 1987, pp. 296–320 and K. A. Shepsle, 'The Congressional budget process: diagnosis, prescription, prognosis', in W. T. Wander, F. T. Hebert, and G. W. Copeland, eds, *Congressional Budgeting: Politics, Process, and Power*, Baltimore, 1984.

11 See J. Rauch, 'The thickening fog'.

12 J. Miller, 'Miller says decifits beget spending', *A.E.I. Memorandum*, Spring 1987, p. 8.

13 Executive Office of the President, Office of Management and Budget, *Historical Tables: Budget of the United States Government/Fiscal Year 1988*, Washington, D.C., U.S. Government Printing Office, 1987, pp. 8.1(1)–8.1(2).

14 Miller, 'Deficits beget spending', p. 8.

15 Fisher, 'Ten years of the Budget Act', p. 230.

16 J. A. Thurber, 'Congressional budget reform'.

17 See A. Schick, *Congress and Money: Budgeting, Spending and Taxing*, Washington, D.C., The Urban Institute, 1980.

18 A. Schick, 'Budgeting as an administrative process' in *Perspectives on Budgeting*, Washington, D.C., American Society for Public Administration, 1980, pp. 9–10.

19 Senator L. Metcalf, *Congressional Record*, 19 March 1974, S3844.

20 See J. A. Thurber, 'Congressional budget reform'.

21 U.S. Congress, House of Representatives, Commission on Information and Facilities, *Final Report*, Washington, D.C., U.S. Printing Office, 1977, p. 5.

22 See Schick, *Congress and Money*.

23 US Congress, Congressional Budget Office, *The Economic and Budget Outlook: Fiscal Years 1988–1992*, January 1987, p. xxiii.

24 *Ibid.*

25 *Ibid.*, p. 144.

26 See W. P. Schaefer and J. A. Thurber, 'The legislative veto and the policy subsystems: its impact on congressional oversight', presented at the 1980 Annual Meeting of the Southern Political Science Association. Also see Louis Fisher, 'Impoundment: here we go again', *Public Budgeting and Finance*, Winter 1986, p. 72.

27 Lance T. LeLoup, *Budgetary Politics: Dollars, Deficits, Decisions*, Brunswick, Ohio, 1977, p. 126.

28 US Congress, Senate, *Congressional Budget and Impoundment Control Act of 1974: Legislative History, S. 1561 – H. R. 7130*, Washington, D.C., U.S. Government Printing Office, 1974.

29 C. Rudder, 'The impact of the Budget and Impoundment Control Act of 1974 on the revenue committees of the U.S. Congress', presented at the 1977 Annual Meeting of the Midwest Political Science Association.

30 *Ibid.*

31 See J. A. Thurber, 'Assessing the congressional budget process under Gramm-Rudman-Hollings and the 1974 Budget Act', presented at the 1986 Annual Meeting of the American Political Science Association.

32 For a case study of the committee reform effort in the US House of Representatives in the 1970s, see R. H. Davidson and W. J. Oleszek, *Congress Against Itself*, Bloomington, Indiana, 1977.

33 Louis Fisher, 'The Budget Act of 1974: reflections after ten years', paper presented at the Annual Meeting of the Midwest Political Science Association, 19 April 1985.

34 M. Russell and D. S. Broder, 'Hill's budget power survives jolts from outside and in'. *Washington Post*, 15 May 1977, p. A 3.

35 *Ibid.*

36   *Ibid.*

37   *Ibid.*

38   *Ibid.*

39   For a further discussion of this see J. A. Thurber, *Public Policy Making in America: The Role of Policy Subsystems*, Washington, D.C., Congressional Quarterly, Inc., forthcoming.

40   Miller, 'Deficits beget spending', p. 8. For an argument against the item veto, see Louis Fisher, 'The item veto – a misconception', *The Washington Post*, 23 February 1987, p. A 11.

41   *Ibid.*

42   For recommended solutions to the crisis of the federal budget deficit see White Paper by Charles W. Dunn, 'The crisis of the federal budget deficit', the Strom Thurmond Institute at Clemson University, May 1987. For a discussion of the linkage between appropriations, constituents, and elections see D. R. Kiewiet and McCubbins, 'Congressional appropriations and congressional voting', *Journal of Politics*, 1985, pp. 59–82.

The Burger Court in Retrospect

On 13 June 1968 Earl Warren met with Lyndon Johnson and offered to resign as Chief Justice of the United States Supreme Court.[1] Warren was seventy-seven, but age was not a significant factor in his decision. He was in full command of his faculties, and indeed, by the standards of the Court, he was not particularly old. Moreover he enjoyed being Chief Justice, he found the Court and his brethren more than congenial. The reason for his resignation lay elsewhere. It lay almost exclusively with his belief and fear that Richard Nixon was going to be elected president later than November. Warren's antipathy towards Nixon was well known and had a long history. They had not been in the same wing of the Republican party in California, at a time of bitter intra-party strife. Warren disapproved of Nixon's rather 'unattractive' campaigns in 1946 and 1950 and was convinced that Nixon had 'double-crossed' him at the 1952 Republican Presidential Convention.[2] But Warren's decision to resign was not due to past enmities, however deeply felt, but to the prospect of what Richard Nixon, as president, would do to the Supreme Court. His concern was understandable, for Nixon had not concealed his hostility to the Warren Court. Nixon had devoted a considerable percentage of the 1968 presidential campaign to running against the Court. He accused it, among other charges, of '... seriously weakening the peace forces and strengthening the criminal forces in our society'. The Nixon solution to this state of affairs was to appoint only 'strict construction-ists ... [who would] interpret, and not try to make laws'.[3] It was the Nixon solution that led to Warren's resignation. He wanted President Johnson to appoint his successor. The plan, however, did not come to fruition. The Republicans in the Senate prevented the confirmation of Johnson's nominee, Justice Fortas, and so on 21 May 1969,

President Nixon announced the nomination of Warren E. Burger. It was the appointment that Earl Warren had hoped to prevent and that Nixon so desired.

Nixon's ability to refashion the Supreme Court was not limited to Burger. He had the good fortune to fill three further vacancies in the Court during his first term, and although two of his original nominees did not receive the approval of the Senate, it was, nevertheless, an historic opportunity to achieve his objective.[4] Chief Justice Burger was joined by Harry Blackmun in 1970, Lewis Powell and William Rehnquist in 1972. Moreover, in 1974, President Ford appointed John Paul Stevens and, in 1981, Sandra Day O'Connor was appointed by President Reagan. So a majority of the Burger Court has been appointed by Nixon and his two Republican successors. Has the Court, then, fulfilled those hopes and fears, that it would roll back the legacy of the Warren Court?

Clearly some of the initial expectations were extravagant. There was always little likelihood that there would be a widespread reversal of the historic decisions made during the Warren years. No Court, however constituted, was going to resurrect the constitutionality of racial segregation.[5] The reapportionment revolution, by the early 1970s was a fact of political life.[6] Nor was the pre-*Escobedo* and *Miranda* position likely to be reinstated.[7] In general, the objectives of those who saw the Warren Court as providing comfort for criminals, succour for pornographers and encouragement for the permissive society, were always going to be disappointed. Indeed the criteria employed by President Nixon and his Justice Department in their search for suitable candidates for judicial appointments placed considerable emphasis on caution and restraint; characteristics which were not about to produce a dramatic counter-revolution, over-throwing a decade of constitutional history. But if the hopes of what was once described as the 'silent majority' were always going to be unfulfilled, there was another category of Warren Court critics, who did not share the public anger to the Court, but were unenthusiastic about the corpus of work that had emerged during the Warren years. They were not hostile to the impact of the Court's judgements. They did not embrace the political antagonism to the Supreme Court or to the consequences of its decisions. Rather, their uneasiness was about the process through which the judicial conclusions were derived.

The list of these critics, who were primarily academic lawyers and political scientists, is extensive and their views are complex and detailed, so it is not easy to provide a distilled version of their diverse beliefs and opinions.[8] However, certain themes do recur. The first, and perhaps the most important of these themes, is that the Warren majority was seduced by a result-oriented jurisprudence. The primary objective of those justices who controlled the Court was the implementation of certain policy goals. The principal drive was the abolition of segregation, of gerrymandered electoral districts or the imposition of new codes of practice on the police in their conduct of criminal investigations. Other considerations were subordinate, including those which are supposedly at the very core of constitutional adjudication. Stability, continuity, historical analysis, were either relegated to a lower division in the hierarchy of values, or dismissed altogether. But, perhaps most disturbing of all, was that legal argument and principles did not appear to be endowed with an intrinsic integrity. They were seen as entirely instrumental, to be used as only the means to an end, and if and when they no longer achieved the desired result, they were discarded. Principles which were introduced and determinative in one case, simply disappeared from view if they were of no further utility in fulfilling the policy agenda of the Court. This attitude to legal argument and its subordination to policy-making led to a further and even more substantial doubt over the Warren Court. Was the Supreme Court arrogating too much authority to itself? Was it substituting it judgment for those of the political branches of government.

These questions, of course, have been raised frequently over the last two centuries and, not least, over the past fifty years. But they seemed to be particularly germane during the late nineteen-fifties and sixties, owing to the fact that several decisions appeared to have been made because the Justices did not feel that the Congress or the state legislatures were capable or willing to take politically difficult decisions. The Court, as it were, was attempting to fill a vacuum created by politicians, and while those with a civilised political sensibility, on the whole, applauded the substance of the Court's judgments, there remained the nagging doubts of all democrats — was not the Court, despite its good intentions, undermining the political process? Were not legislatures, rather than courts, the appropriate location for deciding many of these issues? This sentiment was strengthened when the opinions of the Court did not overwhelm the reader with legal or constitutional scholarship. The Warren Court struck many observers as possessing rather imperial instincts. It was confident of its own values but rather dismissive of a political process which, in its view, too frequently catered to the baser instincts of the electorate. Thus the Warren majority, in most of the conflicts that arose, was predisposed to impose their own more 'enlightened' beliefs. It was a predisposition that, many critics believed, took the Supreme Court down a very dangerous path of a judicial autocracy, however benign.

These were the most substantial doubts over the Warren Court and to some extent they provide the intellectual reference for considering the Burger Court. Did the Burger Court approach the task of adjudication in a dissimilar manner? Were its legal, constitutional and judicial values very different? Has its record been in marked contrast to that of the Warren Court? In one sense, this last question is the easiest to deal with. Philip Kurland, writing about the Warren Court, believed that it had a goal, that of an 'egalitarian society'.[9] Even those who would not agree with Kurland's assessment would at least understand how he arrived at such a conclusion. There was, by the early 1960s, a group of Justices: Brennan, Douglas, Marshall, Goldberg, his replacement Fortas, and Warren who, along with the frequent but unpredictable support of Mr Justice Black, formed a majority on the Supreme Court. These justices shared, at the very least, similar instincts; instincts over the judicial function, the legal process and, to some extent, over a broader, ethical system. But as this majority eroded through resignation and reached a point where it no longer was a majority, it was not replaced, in the sense that the appointees of Nixon, Ford and Reagan, have shown no signs of forging a constitutional cohesive coalition. These latter six justices have not shared a comparable vision.

The absence of such a majority is due to several factors. There is, for instance, no-one on the current Court who is as adept as Warren − at least Warren after the departure of Frankfurter − in the management of his brethren, as skilful in placating colleagues, who all too easily take offense. There is also no distinctive and powerful mind, such as Black or Douglas, who could provide a measure of intellectual leadership. Only Rehnquist, perhaps, possesses the requisite combination of intellectual energy, judicial ability and political skills in order to construct a coherent position on a range of constitutional issues. But few of his brethren have shown any sign of being persuaded by his 'conservatism' − for want of a better word. Blackmun and Powell increasingly have become distanced from Rehnquist and on several major constitutional issues have been more inclined to join with Brennan and Marshall. Stevens has ploughed his own rather idiosyncratic furrow for the past thirteen years and Justice O'Connor, who is still in the process of establishing her presence, betrays what some feel is a refreshing unpredictability. But what of the Chief Justice? He, too, has not shared Rehnquist's views on numerous occasions. Indeed, Burger incorporates within himself the character of the Court over these past sixteen years. No real coherence can be detected in the corpus of his opinions. No rounded, well considered judicial philosophy can be uncovered. The Chief Justice's opinions, to put it rather woundingly, have a random quality about them, they lack an intellectual core and that is also the position collectively. The Burger Court's record is not readily classified. There is no easy description of it, no internal consistency, no sequence of interrelated values that identified the Warren years. Instead the record is diverse, the intellectual thrust diffuse. There is an inchoate quality about the Burger years, but that is not necessarily a weakness.

The absence of consistency does indicate there is no agreed goal but it could also imply that the Court has emphasised the particular, rather than the general, the merits of each case and not wider and overriding considerations. It might even suggest that the Burger Court has been rather solemn and modest, eschewing its predecessors' penchant for the grand constitutional statement, when litigation under consideration could be decided on narrower grounds. However, this has not entirely proved to be the case. Of course, there have been numerous cases, and several areas of constitutional law, where the Burger Court has indeed been circumspect. In the field of criminal procedure, for instance, the Court has moved cautiously, far more so than was initially expected.[10] Interestingly, a leading constitutional scholar, and no particular friend of the Court, Yale Kamisar wrote that '*Miranda* and *Mapp* ... [by] the early 1980s ... appear more secure than they have been for a number of years'.[11] Similarly, in another area, that of freedom of the press, where the evident sympathy that the Warren majority had with those who worked in journalism is no longer obviously present, the Burger Court has nevertheless not significantly reduced, or indeed modified, constitutional protections despite the many opportunities to do so.[12] This attitude of caution and incrementalism is present in several other areas, but it is not universal. In cases on race relations and on reproductive freedoms, the Burger Court cannot be accused of merely marginally altering the constitutional frontiers. The changes they have instituted in these areas were extraordinarily far-reaching. In race relations, the Court extended the constitutional prohibition on *de jure* racial segregation to these school districts which were, in effect, racially separate because of *de facto* segregation. Moreover, the Court imposed a policy of busing school children within a school district, and on occasion even outside of it, in order to achieve a satisfactory racial balance within each school. Somewhat more hesitantly, the Court has, starting with *Regents of the University of California v. Bakke* ventured into the difficult arena of affirmative action.[13] Here the record is less dramatic, but by the end of 1986, the Court has broadly established the constitutional legitimacy of such programmes. Certainly by the time of the Chief Justice's resignation in 1986, the constitutional landscape of race relations had been transformed.

An equally dramatic transformation took place over the question of reproductive freedom, indeed, the change here, if anything, was more startling. Until 1973, the law relating to abortion lay within the jurisdiction of the fifty states; however, in 1972, the Court agreed to hear argument on the status of abortion. In January 1973, the Court ruled in two cases – *Roe v. Wade* and *Doe v. Bolton* – that anti-abortion laws were an unnecessary intrusion by the state into the decision of a woman and her doctor to terminate her pregnancy.[14] A woman had, according to the majority, a constitutional entitlement to decide whether to abort; a right that was circumscribed to some extent only as the pregnancy progressed. It was a development that was as breathtaking as it was unexpected.

The interest in these cases about race and abortion is not conse-quent on this sense of dramatic change. Nor is it dependent on the fact they were intrinsically important decisions, which have had a profound impact on American society, nor that they were politically highly charged. After all, there are other cases that came before the Court, which also fell under the intense gaze of public scrutiny, perhaps none more so that *United States v. Nixon*. This case the Court could not step away from but had to provide an answer, admittedly a rather inadequate one, which once again laid bare the Chief Justice's less than impressive abilities at constructing a majority opinion.[15] But the reason why *United States v. Nixon*, which fulfills the require-ment of having a high profile and impact as well as intellectual inadequacies, is not discussed here is that, unlike the busing, affir-mative action and abortion cases, it does not raise one very substantial issue – that of judicial legitimacy. A recurring question in the race and abortion cases is how did the Burger Court arrive at its conclusion? On what basis did it decide? These are the very same questions that were raised about so many of the Warren Court's decisions. Why then were these questions asked once again about the Burger Court? They were asked because no satisfactory account can be given of these decisions, which does not in the final analysis rely on judicial policy-making. The issue of race relations provides a graphic illustration.

Until 1954, it was constitutionally permissible for a governmental authority to distinguish between its citizens on the basis on their race. All eleven southern states, plus several on the boundaries of the South and the District of Columbia, availed themselves of this constitutional interpretation to provide various services on a racially segregated basis. However, in *Brown v. Board of Education*, the Supreme Court withdrew the authority for that practice; *de jure* segregation was at an end.[16] Chief Justice Warren made it clear that the Court would no longer allow any governmental authority to classify its citizens racially and treat them differently, and that any attempt to do so would violate the protections of the Fourteenth Amendment. *Brown* itself applied only to the public education system, but the Surpeme Court soon extended the principle to the other public services. The decision appeared to endorse Mr Justice Harlan's claim, made some sixty years previously that the Constitution was 'color blind'.[17] It was a claim that had not been fulfilled easily.

Virtually from the moment that *Plessy v. Ferguson* was decided, in 1896, there had been a lengthy and arduous campaign to overturn the separate but equal rule. The Legal Defense Fund of the National Association for the Advancement of Colored People, amongst others, had petitioned the courts repeatedly to overrule *Plessy*, but with no real measure of success.[18] However, *Brown* provided the successful culmination to this long drawn out campaign, which at times had appeared more likely to fail than to achieve its objective of a 'color blind' Constitution. But the triumph of a 'color blind' Constitution proved to be remarkably short lived. Within a few years of *Brown* it was evident that racial separation continued to be the reality for most black Americans. The Constitutional prohibition against *de jure* segregation, however momentous, was insufficient to remedy the position. In the arena of public education the vast majority of black children, both in the South and the North, attended schools that were either exclusively or overwhelmingly black. The cause of this state of affairs was not difficult to uncover.

The legacy of *de jure* segregation in the South and Border states and widespread discrimination virtually everywhere else had led to a pattern of residential occupation that was, by and large, racially exclusive. The absence of legally enforced segregation in the major conurbations of the North East and mid-West, interestingly, had not produced a position markedly dissimilar to that found in the South. Furthermore, one consequence of this racial exclusivity was that it was replicated in the school system, as the principle used by most school boards was to assign children to their neighbourhood school. The result was an educational system in most northern cities that was in effect segregated. *Brown*, of course, did not address the issue of *de facto* segregation and, moreover, the principle of a 'color blind' constitution was not helpful if a *de facto* school system was to be integrated. Indeed, it inhibited the introduction of the most useful device to remedy *de facto* segregation: the busing of school children.

The busing of children between or within school districts in order to achieve a satisfactory racial balance in each school requires the appropriate school board to classify children by race and then assign them to schools on the basis of racial origin. The first major busing case, *Swann v. Charlotte-Mecklenburg Board of Education* came before the Burger Court.[19] Chief Justice Burger, on behalf of a unanimous bench, had no difficulty with these requirements.[20] Although the break with *Brown* was considerable, there was no substantial attempt by Burger to justify his position. To some extent, this was understandable as the court had begun, in earlier cases, particularly *Green v. County School Board of New Kent County*, to indicate that *Brown* was not solely concerned with the abolition of legally enforced segregation but that it also imposed affirmative duties on the states to remedy the legacy of segregation.[21] Although this movement from the abolition of *de jure* segregation to integration, was itself a substantial development, it had come about almost by stealth, by assertion and assumption rather than by reasoned argument. So the Chief Justice in *Swann* continued down this path. He merely incorporated busing into the arsenal of weapons that the Court could now use to ensure a satisfactory − satisfactory, that is, to the judiciary − racial balance within schools. In *Swann*, Chief Justice Burger went to some considerable length to point out that the solution of busing was being used specifically to erase the long history of *de jure* segregation in Charlotte. The Court, as it were, was only succumbing to the use of racial categorisation of children because of these circumstances. This principle of compensation of past official racial discrimination justified the rather drastic measure of busing and the abandonment of the principle of colour blindness, even though the abandonment had been undertaken in silence. This principle of compensation of *de jure* segregation was not germane to the existence of *de facto* segregation in the conurbations outside the South. However, this did not prove to be a substantial difficulty for the Court.

In 1973 the Supreme Court issued its judgment in *Keyes v. School District No. One, Denver, Colorado*, where the facts, on the face of it, did not appear to indicate that there had been a history of legally enforced discrimination.[22] The city of Denver in the State of Colorado possessed one of the better records in race relations. Denver did not suffer, at least comparatively, from racial antagonisms, and had never required racial separation in its schools because such an act was explicitly prohibited by the Colorado Constitution. Moreover in 1895 Colorado had enacted a law making racial discrimination illegal in public accommodations, and extended the prohibition in 1917. The state established an antidiscrimination commission in 1957 and outlawed racial discrimination in housing in 1959. Colorado consequently appeared to offer infertile territory for the principle of compensation for prior legally enforced discrimination. Furthermore, the Denver School Board had already moved away from the principle of racial neutrality in student assignment and was concerned to achieve a racially balanced school system. At one point the School Board had even opted to use busing as a device to achieve this balance, but due to its manifest unpopularity with the voters of Denver had withdrawn the plan to bus children. Nevertheless, even after the decision to rescind the busing plan, the School Board continued their search to improve the racial balance in each school by other means.

However, neither the absence of state sanctioned discrimination nor the apparent desire of the Denver School Board to obtain a satisfactory racial balance, albeit without busing, was sufficient to prevent the Supreme Court from imposing a busing plan on Denver. Justice Brennan, speaking for the majority which included Chief Justice Burger, devised a new standard in *Keyes*. The mere incidence of racial imbalance, which was apparent in Denver, was, according to Brennan, sufficient to indicate a segregative intent on the part of the School Board.[23] Indeed, Brennan went further and suggested that the position in Denver was the consequence of *de jure* segregation or state imposed segregation, practices which, of course, had not occurred in Colorado, at least by the traditional definition of those words. The implication of Brennan's remarks suggested that racial imbalance by itself was now evidence of *de jure* segregation. Although Brennan does not elaborate on this new definition of *de jure* segregation, Justice Douglas, somewhat more frankly in his concurring opinion suggests that the distinction between *de facto* and *de jure* segregation was somewhat meaningless. Racial imbalance, according to Douglas, whatever its cause, is the result of a segregative intent and in that sense is state enforced and state sanctioned. Consequently all racial imbalance must be removed and must be compensated for. Thus the reasoning of *Swann* was all but jettisoned and replaced in *Keyes*.[24] The race relations record of the Burger Court, however inadequate, did not end with these two unfortunate cases. The makeshift principles, the less-than-substantial reasoning, the deliberately brief and concise style of argument was to surface again in the affirmative action cases.

Unfortunately, the Burger Court's decisions in the arena of race relations continued in the vein of *Swann* and *Keyes*. Principles enunciated, however, inadequately, by the Court in one case were simply ignored or in effect reversed *sub silentio* in subsequent cases. Moreover, the quality of the argument left a great deal to be desired, that is, on those occasions where the argument could even be discerned. The justices, at least those of the majority, adopted a terse and elliptical style, frequently making it difficult, if not impossible, to understand what was being said. If one was inclined to be unkind, it could be said that the brevity was an attempt at damage limitation. Given the intellectual shortcomings of *Swann* and *Keyes*, the less said the better. But even the inadequacies of the busing cases did not fully prepare the ground for the intellectual contortions of the affirmative action cases that followed.

The affirmative action or positive discrimination programmes were developed and implemented after the passage of the 1964 Civil Rights Act. The designated agencies of the Federal Government, which were entrusted with the administration of the Act, claimed that the principle of affirmative action was written into Titles VI and VII of the Act. It is a claim that is extraordinarily difficult to justify from the historical record. Indeed the record suggests otherwise. Debate within the House of Representatives and Senate, which was lengthy and substantial, had numerous contributions from supporters of the Act, declaring that the principle of affirmative action or preferential treatment was the last thing on their mind. Nothing, they collectively declared, could be further from the truth. The suggestion that blacks would be preferentially treated was a canard raised by southern opponents of the Bill, desperate to find an argument, however, untruthful, to damage the chances of its passage. The objective of the Act, according to Representative Celler, Chairman of the House Judiciary Committee, who was responsible for introducing the legislation in the lower chamber, was to ensure 'that actual discrimination could be stopped'. Celler continued that there would be no 'power to rectify existing racial or religous imbalance in employment by requiring the hiring of certain people without regard to their qualifications simply because they are of a given race or religion'.[25] Celler's sentiments were written into the Act. For instance, in Title VII the Act states that 'nothing contained in [the Act] shall be interpreted to require any employer ... to grant preferential treatment to any individual or to any group because of the race of such individual or group'.[26] Again, in Title VII the Act declares unlawful any attempt by an employer to classify his employees 'in any way which would deprive or tend to deprive any individual of employment opportunities ... because of each individual's race, color, religion, sex or national origin'.[27] The words of the Act are clear. The meaning is unmistakable; discrimination on the basis of race, colour, religion, sex or national origin, for whatever reason, is unlawful. But regardless of the overwhelming weight of congressional opinion and the apparent meaning of the words on the written page that the principle of affirmative action was not incorporated in the Civil Rights Act, federal agencies began to require such programmes from a wide array of public and private institutions. In part, their insistence arose from sound administrative reasons.

Federal civil servants chose a strategy that did not rely on examining individual allegations of discrimination, but instead shifted the onus of proof to the institutions concerned. There was a *prima facie* case of discrimination if a company failed to employ or a university failed to admit a designated percentage of black or other minority applicants. When such a failure occurred, the burden rested with the organisations to explain the deficiency. Organisations could claim mitigating factors for their failure. A common and traditional excuse would be that there were an insufficient number of minority applicants to meet the standards set by the institutions. However, the federal agencies have become increasingly suspicious of such standards. They are reluctant to approve qualifications or tests which have a disproportionately adverse affect on minorities.[28] Consequently, there are fewer and fewer valid reasons at least in the eyes of the Federal Government for an institution's failure to employ or admit the designated percentage of minorities.

Under pressure from the Federal Government, private and public bodies have thus increasingly used preferential treatment for minorities. Employers, for instance, have established quotas to be filled only by minority applicants and they have accepted that candidates employed under such a procedure may well be less qualified than those normally employed. Indeed, they have recognised that they may well be turning down mainstream applicants who were better qualified than the minority applicants who are chosen. The case of *United Steelworkers of America v. Weber* arose because the Kaiser Aluminum and Chemical Corporation reserved on behalf of black employees 50 percent of the openings in an in-plant training programme designed to enable unskilled workers to learn a craft regardless of the black's seniority or ability in relation to their white colleagues.[29] Universities also established similar procedures and it was just such a scheme of racial quotas and preferential treatment that was the source of the controversy at the very first major affirmative action case, *Regents of the University of California v. Bakke*.[30]

The facts in *Bakke* illuminate the quandary that faced the Supreme Court. In 1971 the Medical School of the University of California at Davis instituted a special admissions programme which reserved 60 percent of the incoming class for minorities. The ethnic group which qualified as minorities were blacks, Chicanos, Asians and American Indians.[31] The process of admission to the Medical School under both the general and special admissions programme was similar. The applicants' overall undergraduate grade averages, their grade averages in science courses, scores in their Medical College Admissions Test, plus interview performances, were taken into account and marked out of a total of five or six hundred. In 1973, Allan Bakke, a white male, applied for admission and was given a mark of 468 out of 500, and in 1974 he achieved a mark of 549 out of 600. In both years Bakke was rejected, even though minority applicants with a lower mark than his were accepted through the special admissions programme. After the second rejection, Bakke filed a suit in the Superior Court of

California, alleging that his rights under the equal protection clause of the Fourteenth Amendment has been violated as well as those under section 601 of Title VI of the 1964 Civil Rights Act. He urged the Superior Court to order his admission to Davis. The University in turn asked for a declaration that its special admissions programme was lawful, but the Superior Court held that the special admissions programme was not lawful because it constituted a racial quota and racial quotas violated the equal protection clause and Section 601 of Title VI. However, the Court refused to order Bakke's admission on the grounds that he failed to prove he would have been admitted but for the existence of the special admissions procedure. Both Bakke and the University appealed to the Supreme Court of California, which upheld the lower Court's verdict that the Davis admissions procedure violated the equal protection clause. The California Supreme Court's judgment did not deal with any possible violation of Title VI.[32] It ordered the University to admit Blake and enjoined it in future not to take into account, in its admissions procedures, the race of any applicant; at which point the University appealed to the United States Supreme Court.

On 28 June 1978, the Supreme Court announced its decision. The opinion of the Court was written by Mr Justice Powell. In it Powell upheld the California Supreme Court in as much as he too ordered the admission of Allan Bakke and found the special admissions programme at Davis to be unconstitutional. However, he did not share the California Court's view that the use of race *per se* invalidated the admissions procedure. Powell went to considerable pains to point out that the constitutionally objectionable element of the Davis special admissions programme was not that racial minorities received preferential treatment, but that the programme used a specific racial quota. It was the mechanical device that Powell found objectionable, not the goal.

Intriguingly, Powell was unable to persuade any of his brethren to support his opinion in its entirety. Instead the court was divided into two groups of four justices with each group only supporting a part of the Powell opinion. Justices Stevens, Stewart, Rehnquist and Chief Justice Burger supported the judgment to admit Bakke and invalidate the Davis special admission programme. The second group of justices, Brennan, White, Marshall and Blackmun agreed with Powell that race could be used as a criterion in a University's admission policy but dissented from his conclusion over Bakke's admission and the constitutionality of the Davis special admission programme. A further complicating factor was that support for Powell's conclusions did not necessarily mean that either group had arrived at the same destination as Powell through a similar route. Stevens *et al* had joined in Powell's conclusion but on different and more limited grounds. Powell had conducted his evaluation of the issues raised in the *Bakke* case within the ambit of the equal protection clause of the Fourteenth Amendment. Stevens, by contrast, deliberately avoided constitutional argument and chose to resolve the litigation within the reference of the 1964 Civil Rights Act. The Brennan group agreed with Powell that *Bakke* raised constitutional questions, although they did not share Powell's interpretation of the constitutional rights guaranteed by the equal protection clause. Thus, only five members of the Court, and they were not in agreement, offered a constitutional evaluation of the Davis special admissions programme, while the other four refrained from doing so.

So the *Bakke* decision was confused. There were a multiplicity of opinions, and the very status of the judgment that can only command the support of one justice must be problematic. Nevertheless something very significant did emerge from *Bakke*; something that was quite extraordinary and which has been sustained in the subsequent affirmative action cases. Racial discrimination was declared constitutional. Five justices, Powell plus the Brennan group, declared that race could be used as a factor in a university's admissions policy; and they did not mean solely as a basis for classifying or admitting students. They meant that students of specific racial or ethnic origins could now be given preference constitutionally to those with different racial or ethnic backgrounds. In other words, the Constitution now permitted racial discrimination. However, it is worth noting that in *Bakke* only five justices declared their support for such a reading of the equal protection clause, and that they themselves were divided only on the mechanics of such a discrimination. Powell felt that specific quotas went too far, although his own preference seemed to suggest that universities should seek a target for minority admissions rather than impose a quota. Of course this does lead one to ask, when does a target become a quota? The other four justices did not show their hand in *Bakke* on this issue. However in *United Steelworkers of America v. Weber*, they had another opportunity.[33]

The heart of the problem in *Weber* was the same as in *Bakke*. Because of the agreement between the Kaiser Aluminum and Chemical

Corporation and the United Steelworkers of America, 50 percent of the vacancies on an in-plant training programme were reserved for blacks. Brian Weber, a white male, applied for one of nine vacancies but was unsuccessful, although two out of the five successful black candidates had less seniority than Weber. Weber thereupon took Kaiser and the United Steelworkers to court alleging that the 50 percent minority quota violated the Civil Rights Act, and in particular Title VII, which deals with employment. Although *Weber* was resolved within the interpretation of the 1964 Act the constitutionality of racial discrimination was at the very heart of the issue. Once again the Court sustained the affirmative action programme and in so doing upheld the constitutionality of racial discrimination, with only Justice Rehnquist firmly declaring his opposition to the notion of racial preference.

In both *Weber* and *Bakke* the institutions concerned were guilty of racial discrimination. They did not seek to conceal this fact, they openly proclaimed it. By endorsing these acts of racial discrimination, the Supreme Court was, in effect, reversing the very heart of *Brown* – that racial discrimination was not only unacceptable, but unconstitutional. The Court was changing the interpretation of the equal protection clause that had stood unchallenged for a generation. Compared to this reversal, the movement away from a 'color blind' constitution was relatively minor. The Court was now willing to sanction racial discrimination over a wide array of social policy-making. It was reversing everything that the judiciary had been saying for the previous three decades. This cannot be said better than by the late Alexander Bickel:

The lessons of the great decisions of the Supreme Court ... [had] been the same for a generation: discrimination on the basis of race is illegal, immoral, unconstitutional, wrong, and destructive of democratic society. Now this is to be unlearned and we are told that this is not a matter of fundamental principle but only a matter of whose ox is gored. Those for whom racial equality was demanded are to be more equal than others. Having found support in the Constitution on equality, they now claim support for inequality under the same Constitution.[34]

It was as Bickel notes, a breathtaking turn of events, and perhaps most breathtaking was the absence of any weight of legal reasoning, historical argument or constitutional development. Rather, what is apparent is the dominant impulse of judicial policy-making. A majority of the Burger Court believed that preferential discrimination was socially beneficial, and that affirmative action policies were required if members of minority groups were to fulfill themselves educationally and economically. Consequently, the Court or at least the majority, was going to permit it. Under the power of this impulse the legal process and constitutional interpretation becomes an instrument, an instrument subordinated to the attainment of a particular set of social arrangements. The meaning of the Constitution, thus, can change at bewildering speed. It can mean racial discrimination is permissible at one moment and impermissible at the next. The Constitution can be 'color blind' today but not tomorrow. Moreover no argument of any great profundity has to be developed and then presented to justify the changes. The Court just imposes that which it believes is good social policy and then says that this is now also the only constitutional policy. The Burger Court behaved in this manner over affirmative action and they also did so on the question of abortion.

In 1973, the Court handed down its judgment in *Roe v. Wade*.[35] It was perhaps the most controversial decision, along with the companion case *Doe v. Bolton*, of the Burger Court and perhaps laid to rest the notion that the Burger Court was the counter-revolution to the Warren Court's revolution.[36] The facts in *Roe* were as follows: the state of Texas, like most but by no means all other states, had very restrictive rules governing abortions. Indeed, abortion was a crime other than for 'the purpose of saving the life of the mother'. As a consequence, Jane Roe, an unmarried, pregnant woman, filed suit against the District Attorney of Dallas County, seeking a judgment that the Texas statute on abortion was unconstitutional. Roe's suit was filed as a class action, and she was joined by several other plaintiffs. The case wended its way through the lower courts and reached the Supreme Court in 1971. Though this was the first case to deal with the constitutionality of state abortion laws to come before the Court, the justices postponed decision and heard re-argument in 1972. In 1973, Mr Justice Blackmun, speaking for all but two of his brethren, held for the plaintiffs, Roe *et al*, and declared that not only was the Texas statute unconstitutional but all other statutes regularing abortion in the first three months of a pregnancy were also unconstitutional. Even a partial victory would have been a surprise to the lawyers representing the plaintiffs, but the scale and the completeness of victory was entirely unexpected.[37]

Justice Blackmun commenced his opinion with a survey of considerable detail on the history of abortion laws and attitudes towards abortion, both within and outside the United States. The principal object of this survey was to show that attitudes towards abortion have not been constant, that polities have not arrived at the same solution to this issue. There has always been a wide range of opinion over abortion both in the past and currently: a fact that was evident by the decision of a few legislatures to remove any substantial restrictions on abortion. Clearly, by 1973, abortion was not seen universally as a crime.[38] But having established persuasively that opinion has not been monolithic over abortion, Blackmun ran into an impasse. How did this continued existence of a diversity of views assist his interpretation of the Constitution? The answer was, on the whole, rather little. If anything, the diversity tends to suggest that, at least until 1973, the Constitution has permitted a variety of legislative solutions. But, of course, variety was not the solution that Blackmun was about to impose.

According to Blackmun, the issue of abortion was to be considered within the doctrine of the right of privacy. This doctrine was first enunciated by Mr Justice Douglas in *Griswold v. Connecticut*, the birth control case.[39] In *Griswold*, the Court had declared unconstitutional a Connecticut statute which made it a crime to use or counsel the use of birth control. Mr Justice Douglas, in his majority opinion, found that Connecticut was intruding on a right of privacy, 'a right of privacy older than the Bill of Rights – older than our political parties, older than our school system'. Nevertheless, was a right of privacy to be found in the Bill of Rights? According to Douglas, it was. The guarantees contained in the First, Third, Fourth, Fifth, and Ninth Amendments to the Constitution have 'penumbras, formed by emanations from those guarantees that help give them life and substance ... [these] guarantees create zones of privacy'.[40] It was not a substantial basis on which to create a major new constitutional doctrine. As a leading critic of the abortion cases has noted ironically, 'emanations are vapours, penumbra a shadow, and we would suggest that's not a very solid basis for a major sweeping constitutional change'.[41] But shadows and vapours notwithstanding, the right of privacy was born. It was strengthened subsequently, during the Burger years, in the case of *Eisenstadt v. Baird* and, of course, was to be put to its most far reaching use in *Roe*.[42]

One of the major characteristics of the right of privacy is its lack of definition, and not only of its origins. There is no standard developed by which certain categories of actions or behaviour are excluded or included. Undoubtedly, this was one of its attractions to Douglas in *Griswold* and presumably, to Blackmun in *Roe*, because there is no significant attempt to account for the inclusion of pregnancy within this right; Blackmun just asserts that pregnancy is a condition that demands the protection of the right of privacy.

Interestingly, Blackmun does not claim that privacy covers the entire nine months of pregnancy. He divides the length of pregnancy into equal trimesters. In the first of these trimesters, the right of privacy is paramount and as a consequence, a pregnant woman has the unfettered decision to choose an abortion. In the second trimester the state can make reasonable regulations concerning abortion, but the regulations have to be governed by the interests of maternal health. In the last three months, when the unborn child is potentially viable outside the womb, the state may, if it so desires, ban abortion. Perhaps a less circumspect Justice than Blackmun, say Douglas, might not have created quite such an elaborate and intricate structure. But in the very fact of his circumspection, of course, Blackmun makes transparent that his judgment is nothing other than a policy decision. There is no constitutional, historical, legal basis for the trimesters and their differing protection under the right of privacy. They are entirely a construction of Blackmun's personal predilection. Even those scholars who are not indisposed to judicial policy-making and believe it to be inevitable and, to some extent, desirable, find the opinion in *Roe* difficult to accommodate.[43] If the *Roe* judgement was a document of social policy, the solution it appears to offer may well be reasonable and acceptable to a wider polity. But as a judicial document it is anything but judicial. There is no authority that can be cited by Blackmun. Indeed, there is nothing or very little that resembles the traditional structure of a legal argument. Perhaps even more than the affirmative action cases, *Roe* is an illustration of those instances when Courts have come to the conclusion that the political process is unable to arrive at a civilised solution and, consequently, the judiciary must impose one on the American polity. This impulse cannot be concealed in the abortion cases. There is no other explanation.

The Burger Court has thus succumbed on several very important occasions to the same ailment that beset the Warren Court. It has done so less consistently and on not as wide a front as its predecessor. Nor has there been a nucleus of Justices who have had a sense of shared objectives. So its policy-making instincts have been more random and less predictable, but they have been present. The Burger years have demonstrated, if it ever needed to be, that Justices appointed by conservative presidents are as susceptible to the heady power of the US Supreme Court. Justices have the authority to vitiate the unattractive political compromises that emerge through the legislative process, and all too frequently they have come to believe that unattractiveness equates unconstitutionality. But a constitutional democracy does not necessarily choose the solutions that are preferred by those with a civilised political sensibility. The Court in the Burger years found it as difficult to reconcile itself to this political fact of life as did the Justices who sat on the Warren Court. Justices on both Courts, conservatives as well as liberals, should have listened to the advice given by Mr Justice Stone some fifty years ago. It is as apposite today as it was in the 1930s. '[W]hile the unconstitutional exercise of power by the executive and legislative branches of the government is subject to judicial restraint, the only check upon our own exercise of power is our own sense of self-restraint.'[44]

Notes

1 Warren's offer to resign was 'to be effective at your [i.e. the president's] pleasure', and not as usual from a specific date. The reason for this unusual procedure was to give President Johnson as much flexibility in making the new appointment. See N. Bowles, *The White House and Capitol Hill*, Oxford, 1987, pp. 152–3.

2 J. D. Weaver, *Warren: The Man, The Court, The Era*, London, 1968, p. 182.2a.

3 B. Schwartz, *Super Chief*, New York and London, 1983, p. 763.

4 The two nominees who were not confirmed were Clement Haynsworth and Harold Carswell.

5 See *Brown v. Board of Education*, 347 U.S. 483 (1954); 349 U.S. 294 (1955); *Bolling v. Sharpe*, 347 U.S. 497 (1954).

6 See *Baker v. Carr*, 369 U.S. 186 (1962); *Reynolds v. Sims*, 377 U.S. 583 (1964).

7 *Escobedo v. Illinois*, 378 U.S. 478 (1964); *Miranda v. Arizona*, 384 U.S. 436 (1966).

8 See in particular, N. Glazer, 'Towards an imperial judiciary?', *The Public Interest*, vol. 41, Fall 1975; R. Berger, *Government by Judiciary*, Cambridge, 1971; D. L. Horowitz, *The Courts and Social Policy*, Washington, 1977; R. A. Maidment, 'Policy in search of law. The Warren Court from *Brown* to *Miranda*', *Journal of American Studies*, vol. 9, 1975.

9 P. B. Kurland, 'Foreword: equal in origin and equal in title to the legislative and executive branches of the government', *Harvard Law Review*, vol. 78, p. 143, 1964.

10 See J. Israel, 'Criminal procedure, the Burger Court and the legacy of the Warren Court', *Michigan Law Review*, vol. 75, 1977.

11 Y. Kamisar, 'The Warren Court (was it really so defense-minded?), the Burger Court (is it really so prosecution-oriented?), and police investigatory practices' in V. Blasi, ed., *The Burger Court*, New Haven and London, 1983, p. 90.

12   See J. Emerson, 'Freedom of the press under the Burger Court' in Blasi, ed., *The Burger Court*, pp. 1−28.

13   438 U.S. 265 (1978).

14   410 U.S. 113 (1973).

15   418 U.S. 683 (1974).

16   347 U.S. 483 (1954).

17   163 U.S. 537 (1896).

18   See Missouri *ex rel. Gaines v. Canada*, 305 U.S. 337 (1938); *Sipuel v. Oklahoma*, 332 U.S. 631 (1948); *McLaurin v. Oklahoma State Regents*, 339 U.S. 637 (1950), *Sweatt v. Painter*, 339 U.S. 629 (1950).

19   402 U.S. 1 (1971).

20   See B. Schwartz, *Swann's Way*, New York, 1986. Schwartz argues that Burger was less than enthusiastic about busing, but only supported it in order to give the appearance to the outside world that he was in control of the Court.

21   391 U.S. 430 (1968).

22   413 U.S. 189 (1973).

23   *Ibid.*, pp. 208−9.

24   *Ibid.*, pp. 214−16.

25   110 *Congressional Record* 1518 (1964). The words of Senator Humphrey, floor manager of the bill in the Senate, should also be noted. 'Contrary to the allegations of some opponents of this title, there is nothing in it that will give any power to the [Equal Employment Opportunities] Commission or to any counts to require hiring, firing or promotion of employees to meet a racial quota or to achieve a certain racial balance. That bugaboo has been brought up a dozen times; but it is non-existent. In fact, the opposite is true.' *Ibid.*, p. 6549.

26   42 U.S.C. 2000e−2(j).

27   42 U.S.C. 2000e−2a(2).

28   L. Smith, 'Equal opportunity rules are getting tougher', *Fortune*, 19 June 1978, pp. 153−4.

29   443 U.S. 193 (1979).

30   438 U.S. 265 (1978). Although the issue of affirmative action had come before the Court in *De Funis v. Odegaard*, 416 U.S. 312 (1974), a majority of the justices avoided the substantive issues by holding the case moot.

31   It is curious that Asians were included within the special admissions programme, because in 1973 and 1974, students of Asian origin gained 10 percent of the admissions under the general admissions programme to the Davis Medical School, while Asians amounted to somewhat less than 3 percent of the population of California. See R. M. O'Neil, 'Bakke in balance: some preliminary thoughts', *California Law Review*, vol. 67, 1979, p. 183.

32   18 Cal. 3d 34 (1976).

33   443 U.S. 193 (1979).

34   A. Bickel, *The Morality of Consent*, New York, 1975, p. 133.

35   410 U.S. 113 (1973).

36   410 U.S. 179 (1973).

37   Interview with R. Weddington, counsel to Jane Roe.

38   The states that had abolished restrictions by 1973 were New York, Washington, Alaska and Hawaii.

39   381 U.S. 479 (1965).

40 *Ibid.*, p. 492.
41 Interview with John C. Wilkke, President, National Right to Life.
42 405 U.S. 438 (1972).
43 See J. Ely, *Democracy and Distrust*, Cambridge and London, 1980.
44 *United States v. Butler et al.*, 297 U.S. 1, 78–9 (1936).

Part 3

Non-governmental adaptations: mass media, parties and pressure groups

Mass media and governance in the United States

'You guys ... All you guys in the media. All of politics has changed because of you.'
President Lyndon B. Johnson, 1971[1]

Political science is centrally concerned with the processes of governance and political communication is highly significant in those processes. Traditionally political scientists concerned themselves little with the importance of mass media in political communication, preferring to give their attention to the core institutions of government and those informal groupings – parties, and groups of all kinds – which were the dynamic of democratic political systems. For a decade or more that situation has been changing rapidly, and political scientists have shown increasing interest in the various roles played by mass media. In part this change is an inevitable consequence of an evolving discipline; but it also reflects rapid changes within mass media and political processes and their effects as seen by politicians, journalists and academics, if not always by reporters and editors.

Perceptions of change in relationships are never easy to assess accurately. Assertions that change *has* occurred are usually accompanied by parallel assertions of approval or disapproval. In the case of the relationships between mass media, especially television, and governance, this relationship is clear since, critics assert, change has been so recent and so far reaching that it entails worrying trends so far as democracy in the United States is concerned. There is, for example, widespread concern that mass media, interacting with tiny primary electorates and weak political parties, have created a formula for serious distortion of the presidential nominating process, and one largely unintended by party reformers in the 1970s. This concern encompasses the seeming inability of presidents to provide leadership except by decreasingly successful appeals to the national electorate and a decreasing willingness to bargain with intermediating groups in Washington. While the Carter administration exemplified this, the Reagan administration has by no means stilled such concerns. If such questions are well founded then the stakes are high, and political science has to concern itself with such matters.

To assess such large questions it is necessary to see that they entail a series of sub-questions, and we may see these as falling into two broad groups. First, are mass media in a changed, or changing, relationship with mobilising activities in the US − with groups, parties, and politicians? Second, are mass media in changed, or changing, relationships with governing institutions and activities − with presidents, bureaucracies, the Congress and the judiciary? Have mass media acquired influence at the expense of other legitimate power-holders, or have they generated influence independent of others and are thus able to be, or seem to be, disproportionately influential? Have they, for example, acquired an agenda-setting capability of their own? Have mass media elbowed their way into the circle of participants or been pulled in by others? Or is it the case that mass media have simply widened the crowd of participants in the democratic process, and that American democracy is better for it?

Mass media have legal access to the political process but no legal power to compel attention or change behaviour. It follows, therefore, that whatever influence or power they have acquired and/or enlarged must be in the realm of persuasion, that is, by changing opinions at both mass and elite levels. Hence before any changes in the relationships between media and institutions may be considered, we need to be clear how media may influence political attitudes and behaviours. Only when this ground is cleared should we proceed further.

This essay then divides into several sections. First, we consider the questions involved in media effects. Second, we look at mass media and mobilising institutions and activities − parties, groups and elections. Third, we turn to questions involved in media relations with the presidency, the Congress and the Supreme Court. Fourth, we look at mass media and the executive agencies of the Federal Government and see how media have affected their relationships with the presidency, Congress, and clientele groups. Finally, we survey the overall picture and attempt conclusions on the whole question of mass media and governance in the US.

Media effects

The question of the *capacity* of mass media to affect the ideas and behaviour of citizens is not new and has to be set in the context of larger theorising about the nature of human society and its varied political arrangements. Knowledge, always being recognised as a kind of power, was usually prized and reluctantly shared by rulers. Hence mass media as the modern equivalents of earlier modes of communication, speeches and writings of all kinds, are heirs to much theorising on their roles and influence and, inevitably, the targets of activities seeking to constrain or mould their outputs.

General theorising on mass communication and mass media in the twentieth century has revealed the complexities of the factors involved.[2] From current perspectives it may be said that scholars began by ascribing too much influence to mass media in the 1930s and 1940s, swung to a position where media influence was viewed as heavily dependent and constrained in the 1950s, and currently is seen as highly influential except when in direct conflict with personal experience or strongly-held beliefs.[3] The agenda-setting school stresses the significance of *information* to citizens and its capacity to alter their perceptual maps, the rules of thumb by which they manage their environment. Doris Graber shows how citizens use such rules of thumb to 'manage the information tide', but stresses how such rules are influenced and adjusted in light of information supplied by mass media on the salience of issues and leaders.[4] Few scholars any longer doubt that media coverage *can* be very influential, and that it is by information (news) and not editorial utterances that mass media primarily achieve their impact.

Mass media impact is measurable in terms of voter cognitions and these, in turn, affect voter attitudes and behaviour.[5] The information mass media offer is therefore important chiefly because of its effects on the electorate. What exactly mass media offer American voters is a product of fewer and fewer ownerships as all media become more concentrated in their patterns of ownership or control. Thirty years ago C. Wright Mills pointed out that the ratio of opinion-givers to opinion-receivers was changing drastically, and to the detriment of democracy in the US.[6] The agenda-setting literature demonstrates that media not only increase issue and candidate salience for voters, but also help frame attitudes toward salient matters by the supply of information. By 1983 Austin Ranney, quoting Michael Robinson with approval, argued that for most Americans 'televised political reality' is 'real reality' and that in its news and entertainment activities television has decreased trust in the US system and voter turnout.[7] Berkman and Kitch in a parallel analysis argued that media coverage legitimates power-holders, makes the less educated voter cynical, confused, and more dependent on the knowledgeable. Since the Federal Communication Commission has promised to remove restrictions on media ownership by 1990, Berkman and Kitch see a future of even greater concentration of ownerships and more mass manipulation. The information gap between rulers and ruled, they argue, will steadily widen.[8] We will return to this later when we discuss government news management.

These are large scale assertions. If mass media, especially television, have indeed become so potent then it can only be by media having developed changed relationships with parts of the political system.

Parties, Political Action Committees and elections

American political parties have rarely been programmatic or strong organisationally, although they have frequently been urged to become so. Their weaknesses in both dimensions, as might be expected, have been a frequent theme in mass media coverage. Progressive literature before 1914, and in the 1920s, dwelt on the 'smoke-filled room' aspects and never failed to stress the personality angle in leaderships.[9] The New Deal political polarisation pleased those who wished for programmatic parties and a clear electoral choice for voters. In 1950 the American Political Science Association voiced the strong feelings of those who urged a more responsible two party system.[10] By the 1960s, the political parties had to contain the strains of the black revolution and Vietnam simultaneously, and the Democratic Party split in 1968. Both convulsions, and new issues such as the environment, helped stimulate the growth of a phenomenon, the Political Action Committee (PAC), which by the 1970s was being reported in the media as possibly ready to administer the *coup de grace* to already weakened parties. 'Single issue' politics, the rise of political consultants and moribund parties became media themes. Conversely, media roles in weakening parties was but a subsidiary theme.

The relationship between PACs, political parties, consultants and the media are complex and not easily encompassed briefly. Nelson Polsby argues that mass media are becoming increasingly important in the American political system as media attention confers legitimacy on some groups and withdraws it from others.[11] He argues that the balance between the three major vehicles of political intermediation available to voters – interest groups, mass media, and political parties – has been changed to the detriment of parties and groups specialising in representing direct and material interest. What has happened, he suggests, is not that single interest groups of all kinds have burgeoned, but that there has been 'a precipitous decline in the capacity of party elites ... to ... limit the demands of these groups for extraordinary influence over the presidential nominating process'.[12]

Polsby is properly concerned about the consequences of this development for presidential–congressional relations, declining expertise in governmental bureaucracies and, above all, for accountability. When presidents are 'loosely attached to their parties',[13] and believe 'a high level of public approval is the central resource needed to govern', then an unwillingness to bargain with Congress and other centres of power becomes routine and dangerous to governance.[14] We shall return to this aspect later.

The history of party–PAC relationships is illuminating. Parties, like government, sought to use the new 'science of public relations' to help sell themselves and their policies. After their defeat in 1928 the Democrats installed Charles Michelson, a former leading campaigner against Prohibition, as chief of the party's new 'publicity bureau' and the Republicans followed suit in 1930.[15] The New Deal intensified party willingness to acquire and use expertise on polls and market survey techniques. Larry Sabato notes that by the 1940s the California firm of Whitaker and Baker was managing campaigns for political candidates and, later, propaganda campaigns for the American Medical Association.[16] The same author notes that, as late as the 1950s, parties were using public relations firms more than individual candidates, sometimes contracting out an entire party campaign.[17] Instead of making use of their new expertise parties then encouraged or allowed candidates to engage their own consultants. For Sabato parties thus helped to sow the seeds of their own decline, 'missing a golden opportunity to develop internally the techniques that would become so pervasive in less than a decade'.[18] In the 1980s, however, the picture seems more multifaceted and hopeful as parties and PACs compete for the same funding, but also generate *more* funding and helpers than ever before. Sabato portrays PACs as having taught the parties lessons about modern campaigning, lessons which first

Republicans and then Democrats proved capable of learning. He argues that currently 'the competition from PACs is one of many factors stimulating a dramatic surge in party organisation, technology, programs and fund raising'.[19]

Sabato argues powerfully that PACs have dominated media coverage but 'parties may be winning the long term battle for political supremacy'.[20] He notes that in 1982 the six national party committees raised $218 million as against the $190 million raised by PACs. Though 87 percent of that money was raised by Republicans, his analysis of the Democratic revival suggests that the margin between party and PAC funds will widen.[21] As important as fund-raising are the consequences of party distribution of such funds. These Sabato sees as helping to 'nationalise candidate recruitment, campaign techniques and, to some degree, nominees' stands on some issues'. Party expenditures are beginning to pull marginal candidates to victory, while candidates are to a degree being homogenised by party training and party stands on issues. Overall 'parties are clearly meeting whatever challenge PACs pose to their authority and predominance in the political system'.[22]

One of the 'lessons' that PACs have taught parties is the use of modern campaign skills. Among these is the use of private polls by candidates, including presidents. While these had been available and used earlier, by John Kennedy for example, not until McGovern in 1972 did they become prominent, and not until 1976 were private polls a decisive factor. Pat Caddell, Carter's pollster, 'rose from the role of pollster to become a full-fledged political advisor and entered the circle of Carter's closest advisors'; by November 1976 only Hamilton Jordan, Rosalyn Carter and Jody Powell had more influence.[23]

Altschuler worries about the consequences of poll reliance, particularly in the context of the combination of not-always-expert pollsters and the willingness of television to take almost any paid advertisements. Jimmy Carter, for example, saw none of his own television advertisements before April 1976.[24] Worries over paid advertisements are reinforced by concerns over the reporting of private polls since reporters are rarely, if ever, given all the raw data, only the conclusions.

The impact of media coverage on presidential nominations and elections, generally, is complex. Thomas Marshall demonstrates how during the seventies, mass media coverage adjusted to the demands of lengthy open competition by concentrating on candidate personality, on dramatic campaign incidents, and on the horse-race aspects of the campaign.[25] F. Christopher Arterton found candidates increasingly explicit in their attempts to orchestrate news coverage, more able to do so for the incumbent in the White House but, even then, more able to do so on the horse-race aspect of the election than on their image and issue stands. The latter grow slowly, are linked to events and non-campaign perceptions in voters' minds, and 'become the filter through which evidence is selected and judgements rendered'.[26] Politicians learn that images, once established among voters, are tenaciously held and not amenable to rapid change. The incumbent or challenger with an image of success can withstand many campaign gaffes and inappropriate policy stands, and the converse is true. Most candidates exhaust their money and organisations during their first contests. To keep in the race they must win favourable media coverage and, with it, poll gains, money and helpers. As Marshall noted, 'candidates who fail to win a favorable early judgement from the media will either be forced to conduct but a limited campaign effort or else will be driven from the contest altogether'.[27]

Presidency, Congress, the Supreme Court and mass media

Once elected, a president comes into an office which is at the very centre of national attention and aspiration. Inevitably it is an office which is both in receipt of change and an agent for further change. The literature on the institution in all its aspects is voluminous and need not be fully analysed here. What can be clearly seen in the most recent literature, however, is a variety of attempts to comprehend changes in the presidency in the light of changes in parties, interest groups, voters, and mass media. Most authors project a sense of real concern that the last decade has seen an important and perhaps decisive shift in the nature of presidential selection and effectiveness, and one full of imponderables for the future.

Bert Rockman sets the institution of the presidency in four dimensions: the constitutional, political, and economic constraints of the office; the cycles of mass and elite moods affecting leadership possibilities; the trends affecting individual and group behaviour; and the impact of private and public presidential personae.[28] Each of these dimensions proffers constraints and opportunities, and each is deeply affected by the capacity of mass media to intrude, focus attention, and amplify messages to the point of distortion. Rockman detects that the presidency, in common with executive leadership in a variety of democratic systems, is participating in a widespread multifaceted problem of leadership in modern, complex industrialised states which have fully mobilised competing interest groups and weakening parties.

Theodore Lowi argues that to cope with this leadership problem, the presidency has been obliged to become a 'personal presidency ... based on the new democratic theory that the presidency with all powers is the necessary condition for governing a large, democratic nation';[29] this despite what he terms the Second Law of Political Dynamics, which holds that 'as presidential success advances arithmetically, public expectations advance geometrically'.[30] The consequences for Lowi are dangerous: escalating rhetoric, upwardly rising popular expectation, and the fuelling of adverturism abroad.

Samuel Kernell diagnoses a situation in which, to try to meet public expectations, presidents have to deny or confront mediating institutions by 'Going Public', by reaching out over such institutions to summon a popular following in the country at large. For Kernell the reason behind this style is not the accessibility of the mass public by means of improved communication and media manipulation capabilities, not weakening parties nor impossibly numerous and voracious groups. It is to be found in the belief that the strategy seems more promising than it did in the past. Politicians in Washington are less tractable than they once were. Weaker leaders, looser coalitions, more individualistic politicians, and stronger public pressure are pushing presidents 'to embrace a strategy of leadership antithetical to that prescribed by theory'.[31]

Kernell cannot fail to note that the phenomenon is not confined to presidents: in Washington congressmen run against Congress, group leaderships denounce the world in which they successfully operate, leaders denounce leadership as such. Each seeks not to bargain with other power-holders or power-seekers but to win, seemingly totally. Atomisation or fragmentation, and at best loose, impermanent coalitions of voters and interests, seem to lie at the base of all three analyses. Such fragmentation, and the burden it places on leaderships, demands skilled use of the mass media. The well documented intrusiveness of mass media in elections, and especially in primaries, may be no greater than their intrusiveness when, later, presidents and members of Congress try to govern or seek to appear to do so.

Relations with Congress are central to any presidential effort to govern, and these relations exemplify the 'new politics and new governance'. The first aspect of Congress to note is the level of change that both houses have undergone in the last twenty years. In 1965 Samuel Huntington could characterise Congress as an 'obstructive ogre to its enemies ... [and] ... the declining despair of its friends'.[32] Huntington accused it of insulation, dispersion, and having too great an interest in oversight at the expense of legislation. Congress, he argued, was incapable of establishing national legislative priorities. In 1978 Samuel Patterson noted that Congress 'has great political power and an enormous capacity to frustrate the legislative ambitions of the President. Congress is semi-sovereign.'[33] Clearly things had changed, but how much and in what ways?

Writing in 1981 Norman Ornstein reviewed a decade of change. He showed how nearly every item of Huntingdon's indictment had been transformed. Congress had come to witness a decline both in tenure and the importance of seniority. Members of Congress aspired to other offices, were not provincial in their experience and outlook and had cosmopolitan staffs which embodied enormous experience, expertise, and ambition. Congress, Ornstein argued, was both legislating and overseeing more than it had earlier and, while it often waited on a president, it reacted aggressively to presidential initiatives. Congress, he noted, was now criticised for being too open, too responsive, particularly to single, narrow interests. Ornstein's judgment was that 'it is more accurate these days to criticise the whole of the citizenry for not coalescing around a set of policy ideas ... than it is to criticise Congress for failing to do so'.[34]

Ornstein argued that Congress has in fact become an excellent mirror. Part of this change relates to improved congressional media capabilities and their prompt exploitation by members. Michael Robinson has shown how Congress responded to the pressures of the 1970s. Whether it is improved technology, Watergate and the demise of the Imperial Presidency; whether it is the rise of public interest groups and the general level of political mobilisation and the weakening of parties; whether it is increased turnover in Congress and more demands for services by constituents; all these factors press members into activities involving increased use of mass media between elections as well as during campaigns. Whether it is newsletters to, or surveys of, constituents, instantly available tapes for local radio and television, assiduous cultivation of local media and avoidance of national media – all are devices used by members to survive in an uncertain political milieu. Congressmen continue, as Robinson notes, to 'spend no more time with information than they ever did. Public relations, after all, has become more and more demanding on members' time. Policy can be more efficiently handled by staff or sub-committee.'[35] Being masters of *local* media, satisfying *local* interests, projecting *personally*: these are the keys to survival for members. Together with changes in congressional procedures they produce a Congress much harder to manage for presidents and for congressional leaderships. They also make it one much harder for reporters to cover adequately.

Media may, or may not, have contributed directly to the current 'state' of the presidency and Congress, but it is certain that television, at least, finds that state far from unacceptable. Network television, of its nature, finds it easier to cover *one* president than 535 members of Congress; *simple* stories of White House 'success' or 'failure' are easier to run than complex stories of bargaining and accommodation; and *short run* stories of presidential decisions are inevitably more immediate than lengthy legislative procedures and frequent decisions to defer action. Little wonder that presidents and White House stories are so prominent in network news and that, even in the *New York Times* and the *Washington Post*, congressional stories at best take only a quarter of news stories on average.[36]

Not only do presidents secure more attention, but they secure more favourable attention, at least most of the time. A 1981 study shows that the *New York Times* and *Time* magazine present two favourable, for every unfavourable, story. Even C.B.S., the most critical television network in the period 1968–78, follows a broadly similar pattern on a year by year basis.[37] Attention from mass media, of course, comes at a price. The same study carefully analyses the standard evolution within the White House-reporter relationship. First there is the alliance phase in which the press and White House staff collaborate to get a new president's message out to the voters. This gives way to what Grossman and Kumar call the competition phase in which each side seeks to manipulate the other. Officials now play favourites among reporters, plant stories and give out scoops. Reporters play groups of officials against each other and go on 'fishing expeditions' in Congress and the bureaucracy, hoping to trawl stories on the president or his aides. Finally, there is the detachment phase in which officials avoid the national media while cultivating the regional media, and reporters more and more look outside the White House, and Washington, for the 'real news'.[38]

These phases, of course, are more ideal-types than they are historical in any sequential sense. Events such as the Camp David Summit for Jimmy Carter in 1978 or the near-assassination of Ronald Reagan in 1981 can transform relationships at least for a while. The consequences of reportorial predispositions, derived in part from reportorial perceptions of 'phase', can be important. In Jimmy Carter's case the president, for long periods, seemed able to do no right[39] while, for his successor, the reverse seems to have obtained until recently. In 1981, during the euphoria and relief after the assassination attempt, President Reagan was able to crush the strike of the federal air traffic controllers in a manner which would clearly have been much more difficult a year later, and even more so presently.[40]

If media coverage of president and Congress may be said to be congruent with their contemporary needs, the same may certainly be said of the coverage of the Supreme Court. First, that coverage is small in aggregate terms: some 5 percent of coverage in leading newspapers and about 3 percent of network television news coverage.[41] Second, media coverage is intermittent, sometimes misleading and, by over-concentration on a few areas such as sex and race, helps give a false impression of the range of the Court's concerns and influence. Such distortions may have contributed to a retreat by the Court from its interventionist posture in the seventies.[42]

Generally, media coverage helps perpetuate the image of judicial efficiency and wisdom and the notion of judicial impartiality, the 'most potent myth in American life' accoring to the legal scholar C. Herman Pritchett.[43] Reporters, who usually take on the ambience of the beats they cover, find the Court beat most seductive or, at least, intimidating. Neither the White House nor Congress is able to generate a comparable degree of deference. From time to time, of course, media coverage will highlight and question a Court ruling or a judge's utterances, but rarely is the tone anything but deferential. The 'legislature of last resort' in the American system is needed, and the media reflect that knowledge. Only the Supreme Court generates awe in Washington and reporters do not escape its spell.

Media and the agencies

Mass media clearly have had a considerable impact on the presidency and congress in the last two decades, conditioning the ways they relate both to each other and to the American voter. Additionally, mass media coverage has impacted on the ways that both president and Congress have struggled to mould and dominate the executive branch in its many parts. In a highly complex government system mass media have been used by the parts of the government to communicate with each other and, even more importantly, to communicate with interests outside Washington.

Mass media have given government agencies opportunities to reach out to, and to an extent mould, the opinions of Americans in ways and to a degree not hitherto possible. The US government has developed a large media relations capability which, since its beginnings, has aroused first congressional and then popular concern. Ironically, it was Congress which began the process in the 1880s by pressing the Department of Agriculture to become the vehicle for systematic extension education among farmers. In the twentieth century, World War I, the 1930s depression, World War II, and the so-called Cold War which also involved Korea and Vietnam have only intensified the desire of Washington to improve its news management operations. Two broad developments have made such desires a possibility. First, in the early twentieth century, there was the development of scientific market research, rooted in Freudian psychology, which led to systematic building of products and markets. In turn this fed the evolution of advertising and public relations skills which readily lent themselves to political propaganda and campaign activities. These were first exemplified after 1917 in George Creel's highly effective Committee on Public Information.[44] Second, there was the development of the mass media which meant that, by the 1970s, television had eclipsed both radio and newspapers as the dominant medium at the national level; while at the sub-national level news technology has made it easier for a prestige news source such as government to manage the news supply both to regional and local media and to clientele groups of agencies and departments.

The development of highly skilled public relations techniques, added to the rise of television, represent a formidable congruence and capability. The news provision and news consumption bureaucracies engage in what Herbert Gans characterised as a tango in which government leads.[45] This does not mean, of course, that a president or an agency head cannot get into occasional difficulties because of media coverage. It does mean, however that such difficulties are the exception and not the norm, and that astute government public relations activity can either minimise or even avoid such traumas.

The very structure of the government/press relationship is one fraught with the dangers of closeness and encapsulation. Thus since the 1930s there have been periodic calls for caution. James McCamy, writing in 1939, reflected on how far government media management had developed during the period of the New Deal.[46] Just over a decade later J. A. R. Pimlott in 1951 looked back on the war and post-war efforts which had seen considerable government/media closeness and media management.[47] In 1959 Douglass Cater published a benchmark study arguing that the Fourth Branch had become dangerously manageable and amenable to administatrations claiming to be fighting foreign enemies of all kinds.[48] In 1964 Dan Nimmo followed this up arguing that the dangers of a managed press were that, *inter alia*, government itself lacked the feedback it needed and tended to believe its own propaganda. Nimmo argued that government became progressively unable to mobilise the support it needed and not infrequently ended by looking foolish or malign.[49]

In the 1960s the Vietnam war created a 'credibility gap' between government, reporters, and voters; while in the 1970's Watergate symbolised the breakdown of trust between all three. David Wise's polemic of 1973 only served to publicise the fears that Cater and Nimmo had expressed earlier.[50] Despite the alleged 'cleansing effect' of the near-impeachment of Richard Nixon, and the healthier distance restored to government/press relations, it is far from clear that an over-closeness has not persisted at agency and department level. President Reagan may or may not have had overly favourable coverage in the mass media, especially by television. Like his predecessors, however, he has had to contend with agencies and departments which have not been content to follow the White House line, but rather have made and marketed policies they perceive as being legal, legitimate and demanded by their clientele groups.

The capacity of such agencies and departments to market themselves is considerable. Estimates vary, but it is likely that a 1979 estimate of 4,926 public information officers (PIOs) actually understated the total number engaged in information activities of all kinds.[51] The Reagan administration since 1981 has been engaged in cutting information budgets and, almost certainly, effected some reduction in personnel and monies spent. Yet it is still the case that PIOs outnumber the regular reporters covering most agencies, sometimes by a fair margin. Ironically, devices such as the Freedom of Information Act of 1966 have had the effect not of decreasing but of increasing information staffs as the need to give out information *about* information increased sharply. Reagan administration attempts to curb both the collection and dissemination of information then had marginal success at best. 'Flacks', as media information offices are colloquially known, are still alive and plentiful in Washington.[52] Their capacities to lead and encapsulate journalists do not rest on the intention to do so, but rather flow from the structured relationship they have with reporters and the need of the latter for official 'news' and access to the bureacracy. By advice on matters such as how and when to release information, which official should brief reporters, and how officials may exploit rivalries between them, PIO's can discreetly sell the 'department view' or limit damage when adverse publicity occurs.[53] By anticipating such damage, where possible, PIO's also act as educators of agencies on presidential, congressional and mass tolerances and, thereby, may serve a potentially manipulative function.

The consequences of mass media coverage on the executive branch, especially the upper reaches, have been considerable. Presidents have tried to dominate media coverage and feel obliged to try to 'run everything' within the US government. Agencies and departments have had to fight to maintain the differing degrees of autonomy they enjoy, or wish to assert. In turn this has forced the White House to try to harmonise most US government news, and the Reagan Administration particularly had sought to centralise news release nationally and internationally. The fact that it has met resistance in many areas has made White House aides, not for the first time, seek to make policy in the White House and 'go around' not only the executive branch but, of course, Congress as well.[54] A string of foreign policy decisions on arms control, the Middle East, and Western Europe all testify to the problems involved. Indeedd the current Iran–Nicaragua debacle exemplifies the point and, almost for the first time, reveals how thin is President Reagan's Teflon veneer.

The interaction of mass media and agencies and departments of the federal government suggests that they are able to manage their own media coverage and protect their independence from White

House 'harmonisation'. Mass media may strengthen agency autonomy and thereby make presidential leadership more difficult. Given the president's problems with a fractionated Congress and a federal system, this unintended media effect is an added and galling burden for recent White House incumbents.[55]

Conclusions

It must be apparent that this discussion can be no more than suggestive on changes, if any, in the complex relationships between mass media and the core institutions of the political process in the US.

First, the electoral process has been affected by the greatly enhanced capabilities of mass media, especially by the rise of television. But parties and voters have surely been moulded at least as much by other factors – the black revolution, Vietnam, feminism, economic uncertainties and rapid change, international crises – as they have by media roles in presidential primaries, debates or image-making in crises. The weakening of parties, which anyway were never strong in the US, has certainly, as Polsby notes, limited their capacity to prioritise and modify group demands. But it can be said that new techniques for fund-raising and electioneering, new issues such as abortion and environment which cut across traditional party attachments, and a limited but still potent revival of ideological attachment among voters, together these would surely have been hard even for a 'strong' party system to manage. Events and politics, rather than media reporting of them, may have delegitimated American institutions. In any event voter cynicism and independence in the 1970s were as hard for parties to cope with as were the demands of voracious groups. The media amplified and sometimes distorted the messages of all participants.

Second, the presidency and Congress could not but be affected by such an electoral milieu. Presidents and members of Congress were elected *despite* party, ran against party, Washington, and the institutions they sought to join. Once elected they found that governing and legislating demanded precisely the bargaining style they had professed to distance themselves from. Members of Congress found it easy to settle into the localism Congress fostered anyway and, except for some Senators, could concentrate on 'bringing home the pork' and re-election. Presidents, however, had to try to overawe opposition by 'Going Public' – by using a volatile level of poll support to overawe or get around oppositional elements in Washington or elsewhere. Thus Congress tended toward fractionation and presidents toward frustration. Once again media did not do much more than make available to candidates and incumbents the *means* of reaching large numbers of voters quickly and often less subtly than hitherto. Media themselves did *not* create a situation in which presidents could win elections but govern much less easily.

Third, if the media contributed to presidential and congressional frustration and impotence, the media failed to illuminate the bureaucracy and improve the intra-governmental policy debate. If anything, media management helped agencies and departments to preserve their authority in face of both Congress and presidential orders and appeals. Like Congress, agencies could retreat into 'localism', could cater for their clientele groups, batten down in face of White House displeasure and, generally, behave in ways which made 'presidential leadership' a less than serious proposition.

Thus mass media, if anything, could be actually said to have reinforced trends making for presidential, congressional, and agency isolation. The prime losers in this process were presidents when they sought to govern, as opposed to seek re-election; the voters who were given less political education than they might need, and government by a federal bureaucracy which never much needed to harmonise its policies.

Ben Ginsberg in 1986 provides one perspective on the effects of this at large. Ginsberg argues that democratic governments reached out to enfranchise classes in the nineteenth century to head off dissent and create marketplaces for their services. But, finding that popular expectations exceeded their capacities to deliver, democratic governments had to engage in opinion management to control the very demands they themselves had largely created. For Ginsberg, carefully managed mass opinion has become a vehicle for promoting state power and a danger to genuine democratic participation.[56] While one need not accept fully his assertion that governments, for example in Britain and the US, *intentionally* created political marketplaces, it is clear that, once those marketplaces existed, central bureaucracies had an interest both in service provision and in managing a supportive public opinion. Further, that governments found their capacities strained, even where resources appeared to exist, seems beyond dispute.

The need for managed opinion in the area of foreign policy has seemed clear since 1945. Latterly, however, the domestic arena has generated just as potent a set of imperatives. For a decade or more democratic governments of a variety of partisan pursuasions have sought to lower popular expectations, not only for service provision by governments but also for the *possibilities* of both public and private sectors. In this context managing opinion becomes more difficult for governments as political polarisation and resource limitation lessens their legitimacy and their capacity to buy off opposition. What Ginsberg took to be an outcome of the aggrandising state may well owe its origins to the 'politics of plenty' in the post-1945 democratic world, and things have changed.

The United States, like other democracies, may be finding its institutional structures barely able to cope with the strains of making hard choices over scarce resources in a political world alive to the dangers of government opinion management. The mass media had little to do with the evolution of the underlying situation but have an obligation to assist those institutions to cope with *their* new relationships and *their* responsibilities. Michael Robinson may have overstated his case when he argued that television was delegitimating American political institutions.[57] Few would doubt, however, that he had a point, and that if media *have* acquired new powers and influence they must use them as responsibly as they demand other power-holders do.

Notes

1   Quoted in Godfrey Hodgson, *All Things to All Men: The False Promise of the Modern American Presidency*, London, 1980, p. 183.

2   For a useful recent bibliography see Denis McQuail, *Mass Communication Theory. A Reader*, London and Beverly Hills, CA, 1983, pp. 227–38.

3   This evolution is seen in the change of emphasis between J. Klapper, *The Effects of Mass Communication*, New York, 1960, and, say, Donald L. Shaw and Maxwell E. McCombs, *The Emergence of American Political Issues. The Agenda Setting Function of the Press*, St. Paul, Minn., 1977, and M. B. McKuen and S. L. Coombs, *More Than News. Media Power in Public Affairs*, Beverly Hills, CA, 1981.

4   Doris Graber, *Processing the News. How People Tame the Information Tide*, New York, 1984.

5   On this see Steven Chaffee, ed., *Political Communication Issues and Strategies for Research*, Beverly Hills, CA, 1975, chs. 1–4.

6   C. Wright Mills, *The Power Elite*, New York, 1959, p. 302.

7   Austin Ranney, *Channels of Power. The Impact of Television on American Politics*, New York, 1983, pp. 30, 75, 85. The Robinson article appears as Michael J.

Robinson, 'American political legitimacy in an era of electronic journalism: reflections on the evening news' in Douglass Cater and Richard Adler, eds, *Television as a Social Force: New Approaches to TV Criticism*, New York, 1975, pp. 97–139.

8   Ronald Berkman and Laura Kitch, *Politics in a Media Age*, New York, 1986, ch. 11.

9   Joseph L. Steffens, *Autobiography of Lincoln Steffens*, New York, 1931, is of course a famous example.

10   'Toward a more responsible two-party system', *American Political Science Review, Supplement* to vol. 44, September 1950.

11   Nelson Polsby, *Consequences of Party Reform*, New York, 1983, p. 135.

12   Polsby, *Consequences*, p. 139.

13   Polsby, *Consequences*, p. 152.

14   Polsby, *Consequences*, p. 156.

15   On this see David Herold, 'Historical perspectives on government communication' in Lewis M. Helm *et al.*, eds, *Informing the People*, New York, 1981, pp. 14–21. See also Stanley Kelley, *Public Relations and Political Power*, Baltimore, MD, 1956.

16   Larry Sabato, *The Rise of Political Consultants. New Ways of Winning Elections*, New York, 1981, chs. 2–4.

17   Sabato, *The Rise*, p. 334.

18   Sabato, *The Rise*, p. 334.

19   Larry Sabato, *PAC Power. Inside the World of Political Action Committees*, New York, 1985, p. 152.

20   Sabato, *PAC Power*, p. 152.

21   Sabato, *PAC Power*, p. 153.

22   Sabato, *PAC Power*, pp. 158–9.

23   Bruce Altschuler, *Keeping a Finger on the Public Pulse. Private Polling and Presidential Elections*, Westport, Conn., 1982, p. 165.

24   Altschuler, *Keeping a finger*, p. 140.

25   Thomas R. Marshall, *Presidential Nominations in a Reform Age*, New York, 1981, p. 86.

26   F. Christopher Arterton, *Media Politics. The New Strategies of Presidential Campaigns*, Lexington, Mass., 1984, p. 196.

27   Marshall, *Presidential Nominations*, p. 114. But for a larger discussion see Michael J. Robinson and Margaret Sheehan, *Over the Wire and on TV. CBS and UPI in Campaign 80*, New York, 1983, especially Part III and Gerald Pomper, *et al.*, *The Election of 1984. Reports and Interpretations*, Chatham, NJ, 1985, especially chs. 1–4.

28   Bert Rockman, *The Leadership Question. The Presidency and the American System*, New York, 1984, chs. 3–6. Rockman carries this analysis further in 'The modern presidency and theories of accountability: old wine in new bottles', paper given at the Conference of the American Political Science Association, Washington, D.C., 28–31 August 1986.

29   Theodore J. Lowi, *The Personal President. Power Invested. Promise Unfulfilled*, Ithaca, N.Y., 1985, p. 20.

30   Lowi, *The Personal President*, p. 20.

31   Samuel Kernell, *Going Public. New Strategies of Presidential Leadership*, Washington, D.C., 1986, p. 10.

32   Samuel P. Huntingdon, 'Congressional responses to the twentieth century' in David Truman, ed., *The Congress and America's Future*, Englewood Cliffs, N.J., 1965.

33   Samuel C. Patterson, 'The semi-sovereign Congress' in Anthony King, ed., *The New American Political System*, Washington, D.C., 1979, pp. 176–7.

34   Norman J. Ornstein, 'The House and Senate' in Thomas Mann and Norman J. Ornstein, eds, *The New Congress*, Washington, D.C., 1981, pp. 378–81, 382.

35   Michael J. Robinson, 'Three faces of congressional media' in Mann and Ornstein, eds, *The New Congress*, pp. 55–96. See also Nelson Polsby, *Congress and the Presidency*, Englewood Cliffs, NJ, 1986, Chaps. 5–7, and M. J. Kumar and M. B. Grossman, 'The best in town. Congress and the media in the 1980s', paper given at the Conference of the American Political Science Association, Washington, D.C., 28–31 August 1986.

36   David Morgan, *The Flacks of Washington. Government Information and the Public Agenda*, Westport, Conn., 1986, p. 30.

37   M. B. Grossman and M. J. Kumar, *Portraying the President, The White House and the News Media*, Baltimore, MD, 1981, p. 253 *et. seq*. See also Richard Davis, 'News coverage of American political institutions', paper given at the Conference of the American Political Science Association, Washington, D.C., 28–31 August 1986.

38   Grossman and Kumar, *Portraying the President*, ch. XI.

39   Morgan, *The Flacks*, ch. 6.

40   Morgan, *The Flacks*, ch. 7.

41   Morgan, *The Flacks*, p. 30.

42   Berkman and Kitch, *Politics*, ch. 9.

43   Quoted in David L. Paletz and Robert M. Entman, *Media. Power. Politics*, New York, 1981, pp. 102–3.

44   See Herold, 'Historical perspectives', fn. 15.

45   Herbert Gans, *Deciding What's News. A Study of CBS Evening News, NBC Nightly News, Newsweek and Time*, New York, 1979, p. 116.

46   James L. McCamy, *Government and Publicity. Its Practice in Federal Administration*, Chicago, 1939.

47   J. A. R. Pimlott, *Public Relations in American Democracy*, Princeton, 1951.

48   Douglass Cater, *The Fourth Branch of Government*, Boston, 1959.

49   Dan Nimmo, *Newsgathering in Washington*, New York, 1964.

50   David Wise, *The Politics of Lying: Government Deception, Secrecy and Power*, New York, 1973.

51   John S. Lang, 'The great American propaganda machine', *US News and World Report*, 27 August 1979, p. 43.

52   See Dean L. Yarwood and Ben M. Enis, 'Advertising and publicity programs in the executive branch of the national government: hustling or helping the people', *Public Administration Review*, 4, 2, 1, January–February 1982, pp. 37–46.

53   Morgan, *The Flacks*, chs. 3–5.

54   Morgan, *The Flacks*, ch. 8.

55   Morgan, *The Flacks*, chs. 6–9.

56   Benjamin Ginsberg, *The Captive Public: How Mass Opinion Promotes State Power*, New York, 1986.

57   Robinson, 'American political legitimacy', fn. 7.

The end of party reform

The process of choosing a presidential candidate has not been an easy one for the Democratic party since it nominated Lyndon Johnson by acclamation in 1964. Each of the subsequent contests was, to a greater or lesser degree, divisive and those of 1968, 1972 and 1980 were particularly damaging to the party's image and electoral prospects. Democratic candidates have lost four of the last five presidential elections – three of them by landslides – and have failed to prevent a significant number of Democratic identifiers defecting to Republican or independent candidates.[1] The reasons for this poor performance are complex and go beyond the difficulties that the party has had with its nomination process, but the nomination process has been singled out as the principal battleground for reformers and party leaders in their response to the perceived problems of the Democratic party. For the last twenty years a succession of commissions have reviewed and revised the rules of the nomination game – a quadrennial reform exercise that has almost become institutionalised within the Democratic party.

The first, and the most radical, of these rules-review panels, the McGovern–Fraser Commission, emerged from the shambles of the 1968 convention in Chicago. McGovern–Fraser became the mouthpiece of those demanding reform within the party and it re-wrote completely the delegate-selection rules for the 1972 party convention. The effect of this exercise was to democratise the Democratic party by reducing the influence of party leaders in the choice of presidential candidate, by making the nomination dependent upon an amorphous mass electorate participating in an increasing number of primary elections, by turning the party convention into nothing more than a device for ratifying decisions made by primary and caucus participants, and by almost destroying the federal nature of the Democratic party.[2] That, in turn created another shambles at the 1972 convention and, subsequently, the demand for a second rules-review commission.

The McGovern–Fraser reforms most offended those whom they excluded from the process of selecting a presidential candidate. Party leaders and officeholders, who had hitherto been pivotal in the choice of the party's nominee, were frozen out after 1968 because the new rules prohibited ex-officio delegates and established a more rigid relationship between candidate preferences expressed in primaries and caucuses and delegates selected to go to the convention. Those party leaders and officeholders who wanted to participate in the nomination process were thus forced to compete for delegate status through the primaries or caucuses with their candidate preference or uncommitted status announced publicly in advance. Few chose to do so.

The hope of party regulars was that the second rules-review commission, headed by Barbara Mikulski, would check the reforming ardour of McGovern–Fraser and restore some degree of party control over its own presidential nomination process. But that was not to be. While Mikulski did, indeed, modify some of the more heavily criticised features of the McGovern–Fraser reforms, particularly the quotas for blacks, women and young people in the composition of state delegations, it broadly endorsed the direction of reform taken by McGovern–Fraser and, in some instances, extended it.[3] Thus Mikulski ensured another wide-open, participatory nomination process in 1976 which party regulars would find difficult, if not impossible to control.

The most important extension of the McGovern–Fraser guidelines implemented by Mikulski was the requirement that delegates to the convention be chosen in a manner which fairly reflected the division of preferences amongst those who participate in the primaries and caucuses. The purpose of the 'fair reflection' rule was to ensure that candidates for the nomination would win convention delegates in proportion to the votes won in the primary and caucus contests. Although proportional representation had been a major concern of McGovern–Fraser, the Commission felt able only to *urge* state parties to adopt 'fair reflection' procedures, not to *require* proportionality.[4] Mikulski did require it for 1976 and the 'fair reflection' provision has been retained for each subsequent nomination contest. In the Democratic party's delegate selection rules for 1988 it appears as Rule 12: 'Delegates shall be allocated in a fashion that fairly reflects the expressed presidential preference or uncommitted status of the primary voters, or if there is no binding primary, the convention and caucus participants'.

By 1976, the combined efforts of McGovern–Fraser and Mikulski had significantly altered the nomination process within the Democratic party. As Nelson Polsby has argued, the changed rules changed the incentives for political actors which, in time, changed political behaviour and, ultimately, changed political institutions.[5] While many Democratic party regulars may not have fully comprehended the sequence of changes that led to what Polsby calls a 'transformation' of the nomination process, few could have been unaware that the new rules had changed the outcome and that neither George McGovern nor Jimmy Carter would have been viable candidates, let alone eventual victors, had they fought the 1972 and 1976 contests under the same rules that gave John F. Kennedy the nomination in 1960. McGovern's debacle against Richard Nixon in 1972 and the nomination of a rank outsider in 1976, notwithstanding Carter's victory in the election proper, convinced many party regulars of the urgent need to bring the party back into the nomination process and to modify, or even reverse, some of the McGovern–Fraser and Mikulski reforms. Commenting on the defeat of McGovern in 1972, the former Governor of North Carolina, Terry Sanford, typified the view of many party leaders. 'The seriousness of the situation is not that the Democrats lost, but that the loss demonstrated with a vengeance the flaw of the philosophy embodied in the new rules, an abandonment of the need of consensus in order to gain the nomination.'[6]

Sanford believed that delegates elected to the convention as a representative of a candidate, instead of a constituency within the party, would only have a secondary or short-term interest in maintaining the party, and he feared that conventions made up of candidate-centred delegates would erode party strength little by little until 'in due time there is no party and no continuing structure for politics'.[7] That fear, or variations of it, was shared by enough party regulars to ensure that the delegate-selection rules became the object of a struggle between the party reformers, who were demanding wider participation, openness and fairness in the choice of presidential candidate, and party regulars, like Sanford, who attributed many of the Democratic party's problems to the impact of the reformers and their reforms.

Three further rules commissions followed Mikulski. The Winograd Commission was established in 1975 with limited terms of reference, but its mandate was extended at the 1976 convention and it subsequently revised the delegate-selection rules for the 1980 nomination contest. Winograd was followed by the Hunt Commission, which began work after the 1980 convention and re-wrote the rules for 1984, and Hunt, in turn, was followed by the Fowler Commission, better known as the Fairness Commission, established at the San Francisco convention to review the rules for 1988.

The combined product of Winograd, Hunt and Fowler represent a substantial victory for party regulars over reformers. They did not succeed in undoing completely the work of McGovern–Fraser and Mikulski, nor did they attempt to do so, but they did resist further demands for reform and began to reverse the direction of change fixed by the earlier reform commissions. Winograd, Hunt and Fowler constitute a second and distinct phase of the Democratic party's post-1968 quadrennial rules-review exercise. In essence, they were concerned with reforming the reforms and have succeeded in doing so with little opposition from the reformers whose cause was taken up by McGovern–Fraser and Mikulski. By the time that the Fowler Commission reported in 1986, the reform movement's agenda had effectively been squashed and party regulars had been given the opportunity to get back into the nomination process and assert the interests of party over those of candidates and causes. This was achieved through a number a measures introduced, or extended, by the last three reform commissions which effectively compromised the spirit, if not the letter, of the 'fair reflection' rule such that the reform movement's pressure for fairness and proportional representation in the delegate-selection process was successfully negated.

Jimmy Carter's election victory in 1976 was an important catalyst in the process of diluting the 'fair reflection' rule. It gave a new lease on life to the Winograd Commission, a panel established the previous year by the Democratic National Committee Chairman to examine the implications of the proliferation of primaries since 1968. Winograd's mandate and membership were expanded by the 1976 Democratic convention and it was afforded the opportunity to re-write the rules for 1980, which it did. But, as Winograd was the first of the post-1968 reform commissions to operate with a Democrat in the White House, its report, understandably, reflected the concerns of an incumbent President seeking renomination rather more heavily than it responded to pressures for the further reform.[8] After 1976 it was in Jimmy Carter's interest to lessen the openness of the reformed Democratic presidential nomination process, even though it was that openness that got him the nomination in the first place. Notwithstanding the one or two crusts given to reformers by the Winograd Commission, its work, in the words of commission member Donald Fraser, 'was diverted to rewriting the rules in order to protect the incumbent'.[9] In this effort, President Carter and Democratic party leaders were in rare harmony. His renomination was likely to be more certain than it would have been had the Mikulski rules gone unrevised and, for the first time since 1968, state delegations were encouraged to include public and party officials amongst their number.

Two proposals in particular were advanced by the Winograd Commission which had an effect on the 'fair reflection' rule. Of immediate impact was the proposal to increase the threshold of votes that a candidate needed in any state before he could be awarded delegates from that state. Mikulski had fixed a 10 percent threshold, later amended by the DNC from 10 to 15 percent at the discretion of the state party. The level of the threshold for 1980 was one of the most contentious issues considered by Winograd. Carter's forces on the commission had proposed a sliding threshold, increasing from 15 to 25 percent as the delegate-selection season progressed. Combined with other recommendations, the Carter plan was designed to make it more difficult for an opponent to sustain any challenge to Carter throughout the duration of the contest.[10] The proposal was adopted by Winograd, but later changed by the DNC to an even more complex rule that permitted thresholds of up to 25 percent in primary states and between 15 and 20 percent in caucus states.[11]

The threshold distorts proportionality more than any other provision in the Democratic party's delegate-selection rules because it not only denies delegates to any candidate finishing below the threshold, no matter how close to it he comes, but it also redistributes those delegates to candidates above the threshold, thus exaggerating their primary performance. A threshold fixed at 25 percent has the capacity to exaggerate significantly, as it did in one or two instances in 1980. The worst case was Louisiana which applied a 20 percent threshold in four of the eight congressional districts in which voting was based and 25 percent in the other four.[12] As a consequence, Edward Kennedy's 22.5 percent of the primary voted yielded only 0.5 percent of the delegates whereas Jimmy Carter won all but one of the fifty-one delegates with 55.7 percent of the primary vote.[13]

The second feature of the Winograd proposals that affected the 'fair reflection' rule was the recommendation that each state party be given additional seats of the convention, equal to 10 percent of its delegation, to encourage the inclusion of party leaders and elected officials. The commission insisted that these 'add-on' delegates were to be elected (by elected convention delegates or by a state party convention), would have to designate their presidential or uncommitted status, and should reflect the division of preferences expressed by those who participate in the nominating process, so this particular innovation should have done little to upset the proportional representation idea embodied in the 'fair reflection' rule. Indeed, its immediate impact in 1980 was not very significant,[14] but the add-on provision did, in the words of Crotty and Jackson, provide 'a safe seat for high-ranking officials who might need to use it'[15] and, although it did not breach the McGovern–Fraser rule banning ex-officio delegates, it certainly paved the way for the Hunt Commission's creation of a more exalted category of add-ons, the 'superdelegates', whose presence at the 1984 convention had an important effect on the 'fair reflection' rule.

The creation of superdelegates was one of the four changes made by the Hunt Commision that contributed significantly towards diluting proportionality in delegate selection. In the aftermath of the Carter–Kennedy clash in the 1980 nomination contest and the defeat of Carter in the November election, the Hunt Commision undertook a complete review of the nomination process and, from the outset, its Chairman, Governor James B. Hunt of North Carolina, and the Chairman of the Democratic National Committee, Charles Manatt, stressed that their first priority was to give party leaders and elected officials a greater role in the selection of the party's presidential nominee.[16] The superdelegate provision was Hunt's principal means of achieving this end. An additional 568 delegate slots for the 1984 convention were created to be filled by party leaders and elected officials. These were automatic, ex-officio places for the Chairman and Vice Chairman of each state Democratic party, for three-fifths of the Democratic membership of the House of Representatives and the Senate, and for state elected officials and party leaders not previously selected as delegates. Furthermore, these superdelegates were not required to be pledged to any candidate prior to their selection. Indeed, their unpledged status was an important factor in the Hunt Commission's hope that they 'would restore to the convention flexibility and an ability to respond to changed circumstances'.[17] The superdelegates accounted for 14 percent of the total number of delegates at the 1984 convention and offered an important bloc of votes to the candidate who appealed most to the party establishment. Moreover, although not explicitly stated in the delegate-selection rules for 1984, superdelegates were, by virtue of their unpledged status, exempt from the 'fair reflection' rule and were free to vote for the nominee of their choice quite independently of the views expressed by primary and caucus participants in their state. This is precisely what they did do in 1984. Walter Mondale, who had 38.7 percent of the primary vote and 41.7 percent of the caucus vote, took 79.4 percent of the unpledged superdelegate vote.[18]

The other Hunt Commission innovations that diluted proportionality were not so obviously concerned with expanding the presence of party leaders and elected officials at the convention, but more with enhancing the position of the front-runner, predicated on the theory that the party establishment would coalesce around a likely winner and thus reduce the disunity caused by public intra-party conflict over candidates locked in a long, drawn-out nomination contest. From the perspective of party leaders, any measure which enhanced the capacity of the winner to win more easily and for losers to lose as quickly as possible would be welcome. The superdelegate provision was also quite consistent with rules designed to enhance the position of the front-runner. The expectation was that superdelegates, representing the interests of party rather than candidate, would also coalesce behind the front-runner as, indeed, they did do in 1984.

Hunt made further changes to the threshold rule, fixing the level in caucus states at 20 percent. (Winograd had given caucus states the flexibility to fix thresholds between 15 and 20 percent. The 25 percent maximum threshold in primary states was retained by Hunt, but the Commission permitted those states adopting the 'bonus primary' to impose a threshold of up to 30 percent. The bonus or 'winner-take-more primary' was a Hunt Commission innovation, adopted at the behest of the AFL – CIO,[19] which awarded a bonus delegate to the winner in each congressional district, thus further diluting the proportionality requirement. Finally, Hunt put another nail in the coffin of proportional representation by permitting states to elect delegates at the congressional district level. This device was better known as the 'loophole primary' because it permitted a winner-take-all result at the district level and made possible a statewide winner-take-all result, quite contrary to the McGovern – Fraser rules. In this respect, Hunt also reversed Winograd which had tried to outlaw loophole primaries but had been overriden by the Compliance Review Commission. In one of the two states that did operate loophole primaries in 1980, Illinois, there was a massive deviation from proportionality in the ratio of primary votes to delegates, to the advantage of the front-runner, Jimmy Carter.[20]

Winner-take-all and winner-take-more primaries worked to the advantage of the front-runner in 1984.[21] Walter Mondale won ten out of twelve of these contests, each of which gave him proportionally more delegates than votes won, whereas Gary Hart tended to win in the proportional representation primary states which offered no such bonus.[22] A recent study estimates that about 30 percent of the variance in Mondale's vote share is explained by the winner-take-all and winner-take-more rules.[23]

The rules changes initiated by the Winograd and Hunt Commission and adopted by the Democratic National Committee were a significant factor in the complaints about the unfairness of the nomination process that Gary Hart and Jesse Jackson threatened to take to the floor of the 1984 convention in San Francisco. The general effect of the Winograd and Hunt rules was to deny Hart and Jackson delegates they ought to have won had there been the sort of relationship between votes and delegates that the 'fair reflection' rule suggested there ought to be. For example, from the twenty-nine primary states in 1984, Gary Hart had 135 fewer delegates than he would have won in a strictly proportional system, whereas Walter Mondale had 428 more than strict proportionality would have given him. In some of the states where Hart had supposedly won primaries, he actually ended up with less delegates than Mondale. In New Hampshire, for example, Hart's ten-point victory over Mondale yielded him two fewer delegates. In Massachusetts, Mondale's 25 percent of the vote gave him 51 percent of the delegates from that state – ten more than Hart who 'won' the primary – and, in Florida, Mondale took nearly 60 percent of the delegates with less than one-third of the vote even though Gary Hart 'won' the primary quite comfortably. Taking primary and caucus states together, Mondale finished with 470 more delegates than he would have gained under a hypothetical statewide proportional representation plan, Hart had fifty-nine fewer and Jesse Jackson, who suffered most through the threshold provision, was denied 261 delegates.[24]

Deviations from proportionality occurred in every primary state in 1984, although the District of Columbia came close to achieving a proportional distribution of all categories of delegates. The fact that the votes of superdelegates were counted in the state totals often explains the discrepancy between a candidate's primary or caucus vote and the delegates won in each state, but superdelegates were not the only cause of disproportional representation in 1984. Because of thresholds, bonus delegates and loophole primaries, there was also disproportionality in the distribution of district and statewide (ordinary) delegates and add-on delegates. In New Hampshire, for example, a 10 percent margin of victory in primary votes for Gary Hart over Walter Mondale resulted in both candidates gaining exactly the same number of ordinary and add-on delegates. In Massachusetts, Hart won only one more ordinary delegate than Mondale despite his 13.5 percent margin of primary votes over Mondale and, in Connecticut, where Hart won a majority of primary votes, he was allocated one less add-on delegate than Mondale. In Illinois, the loophole primary gave Mondale a significantly greater share of ordinary and add-on delegates than his share of the primary vote, at the expense of Hart who received 11 percent fewer ordinary delegates and 10 percent fewer add-ons than strict proportionality would have entitled him to. In California, the loophole primary worked in the same way, but, in this case, disproportionately advantaging Gary Hart and disadvantaging Walter Mondale. In Pennsylvania, the loophole primary almost did result in a statewide winner-take-all result. Mondale finished with 90 percent of Pennsylvania delegates and Gary Hart with none, despite winning one-third of the primary vote. The threshold, bonus delegates, loophole primaries and superdelegate provisions cost Jesse Jackson delegates in virtually every contest except in the District of Columbia where his vote share was slightly exaggerated in each delegate category.

To head off potential disruption to the 1984 convention, Walter Mondale agreed to support the creation of yet another rules-review commission to examine the charges of unfairness made by Hart and Jackson. The reason why Mondale concurred was related to another complaint made by Hart and directed against Mondale personally. During the course of the primaries, it was revealed that Mondale had developed an innovative, creative and possibly illegal interpretation of the campaign finance laws that had allowed him to get around spending limitations by establishing 'delegate committees' to receive

Political Action Committee donations.[25] The revelation was a major embarrassment to the Mondale campaign which Hart exploited successfully by forcing Mondale to return the tainted money.[26] But Hart did not stop there. He claimed that Mondale had won 600 delegates with the help of these questionable contributions and announced his intention to challenge the credentials of those delegates at the convention. Mondale, who was in no position to risk a challenge to so many of his delegates, was also intent on minimising any display of disunity at the convention and, once his forces on the convention's rules committee agreed to Hart's proposal then Hart withdrew his threat to the tainted delegates.[27]

Not only did Gary Hart secure a new rules-review commission, but he also got Mondale's agreement that the commission be mandated to make a number of specific revisions to the rules for 1988, and most of these were directed towards aspects of the 1984 rules that had worked to Hart's disadvantage. Included in the Hart reform package were proposals for a sharp reduction in the number of unpledged superdelegates so that they constituted no more than 5 percent of the next convention and were not to be selected until April; increased use of proportional representation by banning winner-take-all and winner-take-more primaries during the first half of the primary season; the establishment of more liberal filing deadlines, and a lowering of the threshold to 15 percent. Jesse Jackson supported the move for a new rules-review commission, but took a tougher stand than Hart on the changes to be made. Jackson wanted the commission to abolish thresholds, bonus primaries, loophole primaries and caucuses altogether.[28]

By pressing for what was to become known as the Fairness Commission, Gary Hart appeared to be taking up the cause of party reform in a counter-attack on the efforts of Winograd and Hunt to dilute the work of McGovern – Fraser and Mikulski. That did not please the Democratic party establishment who were unsympathetic to another rules-review, particularly the kind of review that Hart had forced on it, and were not prepared to let it go unchallenged notwithstanding Mondale's agreement to the Hart reform package. Party leaders hit back almost immediately. The terms of the Hart – Mondale agreement were renegotiated at the convention and the appointment of the commission was put off until after the election.[29] That proved to be crucial because the delay enabled the new Democratic National Committee Chairman,

Paul Kirk, to take control of the Fairness Commission, which he did very successfully.

Kirk wanted a quick, low-key review that involved minimal tampering with the rules and the least possible threat to party unity by accommodating interests wherever possible. He stacked the commission with party regulars — forty-six of the fifty-one members were also members of the Democratic National Committee — and he installed his own choice, Donald Fowler, as chairman, ignoring an understanding that the previous DNC Chairman, Charles Mannatt, had reached with Jesse Jackson that a Jackson nominee would get the job.[30]

The Fairness Commission completed its work quickly, taking a mere six months between its first meeting and completion of its report in November 1985. Its recommendations reflected the views of Paul Kirk and the party leadership and were adopted by the Democratic National Committee on 8 March 1986. The commission did not propose to alter the rules in any radical way: rather it consolidated the changes made by Winograd and Hunt and rejected most of the demands that Gary Hart had made in his deal with Walter Mondale prior to the San Francisco convention.

Neither Gary Hart nor Jesse Jackson had much influence on the deliberations of the Commission and, by virtue of its membership, the commission was insulated from the pressures of the party reform movement. Jesse Jackson pressed the case for reform at one of the commission's public hearings in New Orleans, claiming that the existing rules 'enhance the power of the front runner' and favour 'big shots over long shots and slingshots',[31] but he met with little support among the commissioners. Gary Hart was almost as low-key as the commission itself. It has been suggested that Hart's commitment to his own reform package was lessened following Mondale's defeat in the November election and Senator Kennedy's announcement that he would not be a candidate in 1988. That left Hart as the front-runner for 1988 and, thus, if Jackson's claim was correct, as the major beneficiary of the rules that he tried to change in 1984.[32]

Jackson's claim is supported by a number of academic observers. David E. Price anticipated the bias inherent in the Hunt Commission's provisions that qualified proportional representation. '[They] should make it easier for the party to consolidate around front-running candidates', he wrote in his assessment of the Hunt Commission's work.[33] Gary Orren was even more emphatic after the event.

'Mondale, the pary establishment candidate, found salvation in the new delegate selection rules. Nearly all of the Hunt Commission reforms worked to Mondale's benefit, and their cumulative effect was crucial to his victory.'[34] Abramson, Aldrich and Rohde were somewhat more qualified in their explanation of Mondale's success, but they also put it down to the fact that Mondale's 'capitalized on his assets and the new rules of the nomination for 1984'.[35]

Because the Fairness Commission generally consolidated the Winograd and Hunt rules revision and did nothing to reverse the direction taken by those bodies, it would be reasonable to assume that the 1988 delegate-selection rules will have a similar propensity to distort the proportionality provision and so display the same bias towards the front-runner that was evident in 1984.

It is possible, but by no means certain, that the distortion caused by the threshold may be less in 1988 than it was in 1984. In one respect, at least, the Fairness Commission responded to the complaints made by Hart and Jackson and recommended lowering the threshold level, although it did not go along with Jackson's request that thresholds be eliminated altogether. For 1988 a mandatory threshold of 15 percent, below which candidates shall not be awarded any delegates, has been imposed in all primaries and state convention systems.[36] This, however, may be less of a victory for reformers than it would appear. The extent of the deviation from proportionality caused by the threshold provision in 1988 will depend not so much on the fact that the threshold is 5 to 10 percent lower than it was in 1984, but rather on how many candidates stay in the 1988 nomination contest and for how long. If the primaries and caucuses are fought out by just two candidates then there would be less expectation of either failing to gain 15 percent of the vote in any state than there would be if the nomination contest turned out to be a three or four, or more, horse race. The lower threshold in 1988 will have exactly the same effect as did the higher threshold in 1984 and that is to deny delegates to candidates who fail to reach the threshold and make those delegates available to candidates who do. In a relatively large field of candidates, with perhaps one or two narrowly clearing the threshold and three or four finishing just below it, then the deviation from proportionality consequent upon the threshold provision could be very significant despite the lower level fixed for the 1988 contest.

In other respects the Fairness Commission took the opposite approach to that advocated by Hart and Jackson. For example, it recommended an increase, rather than a reduction, in the number of delegate slots for party leaders and elected officials which will heighten the importance of the add-on delegates, first introduced by Winograd, and the superdelegates created by the Hunt Commission. The Fairness Commission raised the number of add-ons from 10 to 15 percent of a state's base delegation at the convention, the effect of which is that add-ons will constitute approximately 11 percent of the total number of convention delegates in 1988, up from 7.7 percent in 1984. The number of superdelegates should increase by about seventy-five over the 1984 figure. Superdelegate status will be given to four-fifths of the Democratic membership of the House and Senate respectively, all state party chairmen and vice chairmen, all Democratic state gover-nors and all 372 members of the Democratic National Committee. In 1988, the add-on and superdelegates will constitute 27 percent of the convention membership.[37] If they behave in 1988 as they did in 1984, then one might expect an even greater distortion of fair reflec-tion than was evident four years ago, although this will depend on the number of candidates, the nature of the nomination contest and whether or not the front-runner is one who appeals to party leaders.

Finally, the Fairness Commission retained the loophole and the bonus primary, both of which distort proportionality. In 1988, eight states will use the bonus primary, including Florida, Massachusetts, New York and Ohio, and five, among them Illinois, New Jersey and Pennsylvania, have opted for the loophole primary which makes a winner-take-all outcome possible.[38]

The movement for reform of the presidential nominating process within the Democratic party has been concerned with the two different facets of representation. The first, which has not been the subject of this paper, is demographic representation. The goal of the reform movement in this respect has been to make the national convention mirror the social composition of the public in terms of gender, race and age. Despite the fuss over the supposed 'quotas' fixed by the McGovern – Fraser Commission, affirmative action guidelines have worked successfully since 1968 and this particular goal of the reform movement has now been achieved. In 1984, for example, 50 percent of Democratic convention delegates were female, 18 percent were black, and 8 percent were under thirty years of age.[39] The second facet, the subject of this paper, is the representation of the opinions and views of party supporters about presidential candidates by delegates at the convention. The aim of the reform movement in this regard was encapsulated in the 'fair reflection' rule, but the movement's success with 'fair reflection' has been somewhat less enduring than its success in changing the demographic representation at national conventions. The 'fair reflection' provision has been so qualified and so diluted by the last three rules-review commissions that there is no longer any guarantee that delegates will be 'allocated in a fashion that fairly reflects the expressed presidential preference of primary voters'.

'Fair reflection' means, in effect, proportional representation; and Democratic party leaders have shown a decreasing tolerance for this mode of delegate selection as the experience of the 1970s and 1980s has convinced them that the party's electoral misfortunes may have had something to do with the rules of the nominating process. Proportional representation encourages more candidates to contest the nomination, it prolongs the race by enticing candidates to stay in the contest longer, it inhibits consensus and coalition building, it makes it more difficult for a front-runner to remain the front-runner throughout the nomination period, and it increases the possibility of an inconclusive outcome at the convention. The Winograd, Hunt and Fowler Commissions launched a counter-attack on the reform movement's 'fair reflection' goal through such devices as add-on delegates, superdelegates, thresholds, bonus primaries and loophole primaries. The principal effect of these provisions has been the dilution of proportional representation in the selection of convention delegates such that there is good reason to assume that outcomes might be different under a truly proportional system. Orren has shown that, under a hypothetical state-wide proportional representation plan, all else being the same, Walter Mondale would have finished 376 votes short of a first ballot victory in 1984.[40] Yet, without resorting to what might be considered an unrealistically strict measure of fair reflection, it is still possible to quantify some of the distorting impact of the devices introduced by Winograd, Hunt and Fowler. Southwell, for example, has shown that, without the unpledged superdelegates, Mondale would have received only fifty-seven more votes than necessary for victory on the first ballot.[41] That would have meant a much tighter race for nomination and one might reasonably conclude that, in anticipation of a close result, candidate strategies and delegate behaviour at the convention would have been different to what it actually was and one could not rule out the possibility that, under these circumstances, Mondale might have been denied a first-ballot victory. As the rules in 1988 are much the same as they were in 1984, there is every possibility that a close contest in 1988 could produce a difference between the result of the balloting for the presidential candidate at the convention and the expressed presidential preference of primary voters and caucus participants.

In some respects the events of 1984 are a measure of how far the party establishment has succeeded in controlling the zeal of the reform movement and mitigating the worse effects of the McGovern – Fraser and Mikulski rules. By incrementally diluting proportional representation through the last three reform commissions, party regulars have made the quadrennial rules review an exercise in helping winners to win more easily and encouraging losers to lose as quickly as possible, rather than ensuring a fair reflection of the decisions made by primary voters and caucus participants. Given the seriousness and intensity with which the reform crusade was launched in Chicago twenty years ago it is remarkable, although not without parallel, that the party establishment has managed to regain some control over the nomination process. It is also remarkable, and again not without parallel, how quiescent and ineffective the reform movement has been since McGovern – Fraser and Mikulski in defending the early gains it made.

The parallel between the fate of the reform movement in the 1970s and that begun by the Progressives in the second decade of this century has not gone unnoticed.[42] Both movements attempted to broaden the base of the party's electorate and to establish a form of direct democracy in the choice of the party's presidential candidate, and in both cases the party establishment demonstrated that it was able to live with what were seen as anti-party initiatives and manipulate those initiatives to serve the interests of party rather than candidates and causes. The reformism that began with McGovern – Fraser came to an end in the mid-1970s, just as the reformism launched in 1912 had faded out by the mid-1920s, although there the parallel ends. The demise of party reform in the 1920s was brought about by factors unique to that period.[43]

Much has been written on the origins of the McGovern – Fraser wave of reformism within the Democratic party, but very little about its demise. Most contemporary commentators have, quite understandably, been more concerned with assessing the impact of rules on the last election and anticipating the consequences of further changes on the next. In any case, it is perhaps still too early to speculate about the lack of reformist ardour in the post-Mikulski period, particularly about why there was so little support behind the Hart – Jackson pressure at the 1984 convention for further change and why the Fairness Commission was able to turn its back on what remained of the reform movement. If one did speculate, a variety of explanations might be advanced. It might be argued that the reform movement was weakened by its own success and was not able to counter the powerful criticism of the consequences of party reform that emerged in the late 1970s and early 1980s. It might be something to do with the nature, organisation and leadership of the reform movement itself. It might be explained in terms of the reform movement being lulled into a false sense of security after having gained most of what it wanted via McGovern – Fraser and Mikulski. Then, again, it might be more to do with the behaviour of party regulars like James Hunt, and latterly, Democratic National Committee Chairman Paul Kirk, who so skilfully managed the rules review process after the 1984 convention to protect the interests of the party establishment and consolidate the changes made by Winograd and Hunt.

Whilst not suggesting that any of these explanations be discarded, some attention ought also to be focused on the rules themselves as a factor explaining the end of this most recent period of party reform. The existing delegate-selection rules are technically complex and deceptive. Technical complexity makes them difficult both to comprehend and to anticipate the way each provision might work. Richard Stearns, an experienced campaign organiser for both George McGovern and Edward Kennedy, once remarked that he was 'fully confident that there aren't more than 100 people in the country who fully understand the rules',[44] and, while that may be an exaggeration, there is no doubt that mastery of the delegate-selection rules is now a highly specialised activity requiring not only knowledge of the rules themselves, but also familiarity with how they are implemented in each of fifty different states, the District of Columbia, and in the other geographical entities that have representation at the Democratic convention.

Moreover, technical complexity makes it hard to translate dissatisfaction with the rules into a political issue which will generate debate and around which support for reform will be mobilised. The 1968 convention in Chicago did generate a major reform of the rules, but the arguments in Chicago were not so much about the rules, but rather about controversial issues, particularly the Vietnam war, and about the choice of a nominee who had supported the war and who became the nominee through a process that few anti-war activists could understand. When Gary Hart protested in San Francisco about superdelegates, bonus and loophole primaries, and threshold levels, it did not have the same immediacy and reality that the 1968 protest had.

The delegate-selection rules are deceptive in two respects. Firstly, the provisions introduced by Winograd, Hunt and Fowler, designed to counter the effects of McGovern – Fraser and Mikulski, did not, for the most part, replace the McGovern – Fraser and Mikulski rules, but were cleverly superimposed on them so that, in appearance at least, the original victories of the reform movement are still in place. This is especially so with the 'fair reflection' rule, which stands as one of the pillars of the reform movement. Those reformers who urged this particular change on the Democratic party in the late 1960s can now see the principle of 'fair reflection' enshrined in plain English at the beginning of Rule 12. But it is the technical detail about the actual method of allocating delegates (the product of Winograd, Hunt and Fowler) which follows the statement of principle (the legacy of Mikulski) that has the potential to distort quite seriously the principle of 'fair reflection'. As always, general principles are easier to grasp than technical details, which is partly why the last three rules-review commissions have been so successful in moderating the reforming initiatives of the first two.

The other deceptive aspect of the delegate-selection rules is time. State delegations are not selected at one particular moment and often a considerable amount of time can elaspe between the visible part of the selection process (the primary or the first round of caucuses) and the less visible (for example, the meeting of state executive committees) where the composition of the delegations is completed. This is almost always so in caucus states. In Iowa, for example, a four-stage selection process was held in 1984 which began in a blaze of publicity on 20 February and finished in near-obscurity on 9 June. When the Iowa delegation voted at the Democratic convention in July, only then was it readily apparent that Gary Hart had won almost one-third of Iowa's delegates despite winning only 15 percent of the first-round caucus vote five months earlier. There can also be a long drawn-out process in primary states as well, as in the case of Florida in 1984. Despite the national attention given to the Florida primary on 18 March, only just over half of the state delegation was selected on that day with the remainder being selected by the state executive committee some eight weeks later. Thus, state delegations are often topped-up after the primary when much less national, or even local, attention is focused on the finer points of the selection process. This makes it very difficult to see just what is happening to 'fair reflection' until it has actually happened, and then it it too late to do much about it.

Complaints made about the unfairness of the delegate-selection rules by the losing candidates in 1984 may well set a pattern for the future, particularly when the nomination contest has been a close one. So long as the 'fair reflection' principle stands alongside a series of devices designed to counter the effects of that principle, losing candidates may well have cause for complaint. But they will be complaining to a party establishment which has been gradually recovering some of the ground lost to McGovern – Fraser and Mikulski and has deliberately diluted 'fair reflection' in the interests of party over those of candidates and causes. Complaints by losing candidates may well be dealt with by further rules review commissions, but recent experience, particularly with the Fairness Commission, has shown that these bodies can equally well operate as a vehicle for party regulars attempting to reform the reforms, just as they were used as the tool of the reformers some twenty years ago.

Notes

1   In 1984, for example, a CBS/New York Times exit poll estimated that 26 per cent of Democratic identifiers voted for Ronald Reagan, while an ABC/Washington Post poll put the figure at 24 per cent. See Nelson W. Polsby, 'The Democratic nomination and the evolution of the party system' in Austin Ranney, ed., *The American Elections of 1984*, Durham, NC, 1985, p. 60.

2   For the definitive account of the work of the McGovern–Fraser Commission see Byron E. Shafer, *Quiet Revolution: The Struggle for the Democratic Party and the Shaping of Post-Reform Politics*, New York, 1983.

3   For an account of the work of the Mikulski Commission see William J. Crotty, *Decision for the Democrats: Reforming the Party Structure*, Baltimore, 1978, pp. 231–9.

4   See Shafer, *Quiet Revolution*, p. 498.

5   Nelson W. Polsby, *Consequences of Party Reform*, New York, 1983.

6   Terry Sanford, *A Danger of Democracy: The Presidential Nominating Process*, Boulder, 1981, p. 24.

7   Sanford, *A Danger of Democracy*, p. 91.

8   For an account of the work of the Winograd Commission see William Crotty, *Party Reform*, New York, 1983, ch. 8.

9   Quoted in David E. Price, *Bringing Back the Parties*, Washington, D.C., Congressional Quarterly Press, 1984, p. 154.

10   See James I. Lengle, 'Democratic Party reforms: the past as prologue to the 1988 campaign,' *Journal of Law and Politics*, vol. IV, No. 2, Fall 1987, p. 242.

11   See Crotty, *Party Reform*, pp. 81–6 for a detailed explanation of the threshold provision.

12   See Thomas M. Durbin and Michael V. Seitzinger, *Nomination and Election of the President and Vice President of the United States*, Washington, D.C., U.S. Government Printing Office, 1980, p. 234.

13   Voting statistics and delegate totals taken from *Congressional Quarterly's Guide to U.S. Elections* (Second Edition), Washington, D.C., Congressional Quarterly Inc., 1985.

14   See Price, *Bringing Back the Parties*, pp. 201–3.

15   William Crotty and John S. Jackson III, *Presidential Primaries and Nominations*, Washington, D.C., Congressional Quarterly Press, 1985, p. 34.

16   See Price, *Bringing Back the Parties*, p. 160. While it is undeniable that the number of party officials at Democratic party conventions declined as a result of the McGovern–Fraser and Mikulski reforms, it should also be pointed out that party officials were not entirely absent from conventions after 1968. In fact, in 1980, 64 per cent (2186) of all delegates were party officials or elected officeholders and, of these, only 288 were accounted for by the 10 per cent 'add on' provision. See Price, *Bringing Back the Parties*, p. 203.

17   Commission on Presidential Nomination, *Report of the Commission on Presidential Nomination*, Washington, D.C., Democratic National Committee, 1982, p. 7.

18   See Priscilla L. Southwell, 'The 1984 Democratic nomination process: the significance of unpledged superdelegates', *American Politics Quarterly*, vol. 14, Nos. 1–2, January–April 1986, pp. 80–82.

19   See Price, *Bringing Back the Parties*, p. 173.

20   See Crotty and Jackson, *Presidential Primaries and Nominations*, p. 38. The 'loophole primary' gave Carter 91.6 per cent of the delegates from Illinois for 65 per cent of the vote. Kennedy, with 30 per cent of the vote, gained only 9 per cent of the delegates.

21   There were other elements of the Hunt Commission's rules that also worked to the advantage of the front-runner, e.g. the shortening of the primary season (window) and the subsequent 'front-loading' of primaries (see Crotty and Jackson, *Presidential Primaries and Nominations*, pp. 66–7), but this analysis focuses only on those provisions that diluted proportionality.

22   See Gary Orren, 'The nomination process: vicissitudes of candidate selection' in Michael Nelson, ed., *The Elections of 1984*, Washington, D.C., Congressional Quarterly Press, 1985, pp. 36–8.

23   T. Wayne Parent, Calvin C. Jillson and Ronald E. Weber, 'Voting outcomes in the 1984 Democratic party primaries and caucuses', *American Political Science Review*, vol. 81, No. 1, March 1987, p. 76.

24   See Orren, 'The nomination process: vicissitudes of candidate selection', p. 41.

25   See Brooks Jackson, 'Money for Mondale may be illegal', *The Wall Street Journal*, 20 April 1984, p. 46; David Shribman, 'How delegate committees aided Mondale drive', *The New York Times*, 26 April 1984, p. 8; Thomas B. Edsall, 'Delegate units help Mondale raise spending', *The Washington Post*, 29 March 1984, p. A1.

26   See Dan Balz, 'Hart urges Mondale to repay PAC funds', *The Washington Post*, 26 April 1984, p. A 8; David Hoffman and Dan Balz, 'Mondale agrees to return disputed funds', *The Washington Post*, 28 April 1984, p. A 1.

27   See Rhodes Cook, 'Democratic nominating rules: back to the drawing board for 1988', *Congressional Quarterly Weekly Report*, 30 June 1984, p. 1568.

28   See Cook, 'Democratic nominating rules', pp. 1568–9; Lengle, 'Democratic Party Reforms', p. 253. Thomas E. Mann, 'Elected officials and the politics of presidential selection' in Austin Ranney, ed., *The American Elections of 1984*, Durham, NC, 1985, p. 117.

29   See Mann, 'Elected officials and the politics of presidential selection', pp. 117–18.

30   See Rhodes Cook, 'Many democrats cool to redoing party rules', *Congressional Quarterly Weekly Report*, 24 August 1985, pp. 1687–9; Phil Gailey, 'Democratic chief urges quick rules review', *The New York Times*, 27 June 1985, p. A 21.

31   Quoted in Frances Frank Marcus, 'Jackson assails Democrats on rules', *The New York Times*, 25 August 1985, p. 19.

32   See Cook, 'Many Democrats cool to redoing rules', p. 1688.

33   Price, *Bringing Back the Parties*, p. 223.

34   Orren, 'The nomination process: vicissitudes of candidate selection', p. 36.

35   Paul R. Abramson, John H. Aldrich and David W. Rohde, *Change and Continuity in the 1984 Elections*, Washington, D.C., Congressional Quarterly Press, 1986, p. 26.

36   The exception is where no candidate reaches the applicable threshold and then the theshold is fixed at 10 per cent less than the vote received by the leading candidate.

37   See Lengle, 'Democratic Party reforms', p. 259.

38   See Rhodes Cook, 'The game is the same, but not so the rules', *Congressional Quarterly Weekly Report*, 29 August 1987, p. 1988.

39   See Crotty and Jackson, *Presidential Primaries and Nominations*, p. 108.

40   Orren, 'The nomination process: vicissitudes of candidate selection', p. 41.

41   Southwell, 'The 1984 Democratic nomination process: the significance of unpledged superdelegates', p. 85.

42   See especially James W. Ceaser, *Reforming the Reforms: A Critical Analysis of the Presidential Selection Process*, Cambridge, 1982, pp. 24–6.

43   See Ceasar, *Reforming the Reforms*, p. 24.

44   Quoted by Michael Nelson, 'The case for the current presidential nominating process' in George Grassmuck, ed., *Before Nomination: Our Primary Problems*, Washington, D.C., American Enterprise Institution, 1985, p. 32.

Understanding interest group activity in the American states

Unlike most parliamentary systems where special interest groups have their access and influence fettered by strong political parties and a dominant executive branch, the constitutional and political framework in the United States furnishes a multitude of ways and means for interest groups to influence public policy. Perhaps the three most important factors that contribute to this group influence are: the separation of powers system, relatively weak political parties, and the arrangements of federalism. With the fragmented policy-making system which results, America is a Shangri-la for interest groups and lobbyists. In fact, the prominence, visibility and the overall impact of interest groups contribute towards the unique flavour and characteristics of American government and politics at the federal, state and local level as well as in the relationship between various levels and types of governments.

Even before Madison so cogently identified the role and impact of groups (or what he termed 'factions') in *Federalist* No. 10, American politicians were well aware of the importance and power of interest groups. More recently, in the last decade or so, public officials of all types have more than ever become aware of the significance of groups as these developed new techniques of influence and helped fill the void of power and representation left by the decline of political parties, heralding the age of the so-called 'new politics'. Political scientists, however, were much slower in grasping the political significance of groups; and even since their crucial role has been accepted, the attention paid to them in terms of serious research has gone through some peaks and valleys. As a consequence, there is much less hard research available in the interest groups subfield of the discipline than in most other areas such as political parties, voting behaviour, public opinion or legislative politics.

In recent years it has become fashionable to bemoan this lack of information, and particularly the lack of empirical data, on interest groups.[1] This lack of information and hard data has been particularly acute in the area of interest group activity at the state level. Most, perhaps as much as three-quarters, of the research produced on interest groups focuses on national groups and on their activities in Washington, D.C. The 1980s, however, have seen a resurgence of research and publications on interest groups at all levels of government including the state level. In this vein, this chapter draws upon information and data from the Hrebenar–Thomas study which is certainly the most extensive study of state interest group activity conducted to date.

This study involved research on interest groups in all fifty states, and over seventy political scientists were involved in the project. The results are being published in a series of four books, each one focusing on a region of the nation.[2] The two purposes of this chapter are: first, to describe and analyse in comparative perspective the trends and developments that these state studies have revealed. And, second, and more importantly, to present a conceptual framework for understanding and analysing interest group activity in the states. The framework we develop here combines existing ideas with findings from the Hrebenar–Thomas study.

In pursuing this two-fold purpose we first define exactly how we are using the terms *interest group* and *lobby* in this chapter. Then we outline the status of existing research to provide a context for understanding the nature and results of this latest research. Next we move to the core of the chapter and present a conceptual framework for understanding the environmental influences on interest groups in the states. Then we relate the most important of recent trends in the following subject areas: changes in the kinds of groups active in state politics; the role of government as a lobbying force; lobbyists; group and lobbying tactics; and changes in the configuration of group power. Finally, we assess the implications of these findings for modifying existing theories and for developing new ones, and make some brief comments on directions for further research.

1 Two key definitions

Over the years several methodological problems have inhibited the advancement of knowledge on interest groups. Of these, two of the major factors have been disagreement and problems revolving around the definition of the terms *interest group* and *lobby* and the definition and assessment of *group power*. Here we concentrate on the first two terms and leave power for a later section.

Just a cursory reading of the literature will reveal that researchers' have used a variety of operational definitions of *interest group*. Most commonly they have used the legal or regulatory definition. That is to say, they have made their focus of study those groups required to register under federal and state laws and excluded those not required to do so. In certain limited cases such a definition may be adequate; but for most research on state interest groups and particularly that with a comparative focus or component, it has some serious shortcomings.

The major problem with this legal or regulatory definition is that the fifty states vary considerably in what groups and organisations they require to register as lobbying entities. Some states like Oregon have relatively broad rules requiring even state agencies to register. Others, like Georgia, have very narrow regulations.[3] Common sense would lead us to surmise, and research on Georgia demonstrates, that most of the types of groups and lobbies that appear on the Oregon registration lists but are not required to register in Georgia are, in fact, also very active in the Georgia public policy-making process. Therefore, to ignore these non-registered or 'hidden' groups and lobbies, and especially state government agencies, would provide a very distorted understanding of the role in, and impact of, interest groups on Georgia's public policy-making process. For these reasons, using group registration lists as the basis for comparative state interest group research is largely unsatisfactory.

In an attempt to overcome these problems and embrace these non-registered or 'hidden' lobbying forces, Hrebenar−Thomas used the following definition in their fifty-state study: 'An interest group is: any association of individuals, whether formally organised or not, which attempts to influence public policy.'

This, of course, is a variation of what is probably the most widely used definition of interest group, that of David Truman. However, this new definition is shorter and more concrete, embraces, by implication, the various concepts that Truman included and, at the same time eliminates some of the shortcomings of his definition.[4] Obviously, as with all definitions of interest group this new one has its problems. It is a very broad definition and creates some methodological problems of its own; and as most of the contributors to the Hrebenar–Thomas study discovered, it creates some problems in securing data. However, the research results from this project demonstrates that this definition produces a much more comprehensive and balanced view of interest group activity in the states, including many aspects previously unnoticed or only superficially treated, than many previous studies.

Turning to the definition of *a lobby*, used in this way as a noun, it has a much broader connotation than the term interest group and is used as a collective term as follows: 'A lobby is: one or more individuals, groups or organisations concerned with the same general area of public policy, but who may or may not be in agreement on specific issues.'

One example will suffice. The education lobby in most states consists of: public school teachers' unions, the school boards association, the state Parent Teacher Assocaition (PTA) and groups for gifted and handicapped children and the like, the state department of education or public instruction, and the state's higher educational institutions. All of these have a general interest in promoting funding and legislation for educational purposes. However, on specific issues members of this lobby may be on opposite sides. A case in point is binding arbitration for teachers, with the unions usually being for and the school boards association against.

2 The status of existing research

Some aspects of research on national interest groups does, of course, have relevance for state groups, especially that relating to group origins and maintenance and certain aspects of group tactics.[5] Here, however, we concentrate on studies specific to state groups.

The studies that have been conducted to date in this area can be divided into four types. First, there are chapters that deal specifically with interest groups in books on the government and politics of individual states. About thirty states have books containing such a chapter. These, however, display a wide variety of approaches from the purely anecdotal to the highly conceptual and empirical. They also vary in scope and depth of treatment. And most are now quite outdated. Second, there is a small body of literature that has taken what might be termed a micro approach to the study of state interest groups by looking at specific aspects of group organisation and activity. William Browne's and Mark Hyde's and Richard Alsfeld's work on lobbyists' styles and Clyde Brown's work on group membership, are examples.[6] A third category has been concerned with how state groups affect certain policies or specific aspects of the political system. Examples are: Harmon Zeigler and Michael Baer's, and Paul Brace's work on groups and state legislatures; and work by Bell, Wiggins and Hamm on groups and policy making.[7]

The fourth category of literature has taken what we might term a macro approach by attempting to understand interest groups in the context of the state as a whole and particularly in relation to its political and governmental system. The most notable work in this regard has been conducted by Belle Zeller, Zeigler and Hendrik van Dalen and by Sarah McCally Morehouse.[8] The Hrebenar–Thomas project is primarily akin to this category of the literature, though it contains major components of all four categories. Consequently, like these previous macro approaches it provides a synthesis of existing knowledge in an attempt to provide a comprehensive understanding of interest groups in state politics.

However, in contrast to the Hrebenar–Thomas study, previous attempts at comprehensive analysis were based upon original data from only a few states and drew upon other information that varied in its methodology from the impressionistic to the empirical, a divergency that was not ideal for comparative analysis. Therefore, the theories and propositions developed from these studies were arrived at by extrapolation, or by reliance on secondary sources, and sometimes, in the absence of data, by speculation.

Yet these comments should not be interpreted as to understate the significant contribution of these studies. Each was a major source for the evaluation of interest groups at the sub-national level at a time when little other data existed. Zeller was the first to categorise states into strong, moderate or weak interest group systems. Zeigler, and Zeigler and van Dalen developed several theories and propositions about how the economic, social and political system in a state influences the composition, operation and power of that state's interest group system. Most notably they developed a four-category classification of group power within strong interest group states;

and advanced knowledge on the relationship between party strength and group power. More recently Morehouse has built on this work. In particular she expanded on the relationship of parties and groups, and refined the threefold classification system of interest group power vis-a-vis a state's political system (strong, moderate, or weak). She also developed the first listing of the most 'significant' groups in all fifty states. All this has acted as a kind of benchmark to scholars conducting subsequent research. It certainly provided the Hrebenar – Thomas study with an important point of departure.[9]

3   The environment: factors influencing interest group activity at the state level

As a basis on which to build an understanding of trends in group activity in the states, it will be instructive to first consider what are the basic factors that influence that activity. That is to say, what determines: (1) the types of groups that are active in the states; (2) the methods that they use in pursuing their goals; and (3) the role that groups play within state political systems and, in particular, the power that they exert within those systems.

Existing research in this area is rather sketchy. Scholars agree that the answers lie in a complex set of economic, social, cultural, legal, political, governmental and even geographical variables, and that these will vary in their combinations from state to state, giving each state a unique interest group system. However, we can identify five specific sets of factors which appear to be of particular importance in all states. These we develop here into a conceptual framework. The first of these factors relates to the constitutional – legal authority or policy jurisdiction of the states; the second is concerned with political attitudes, especially political culture. The third relates to the level of integration and professionalisation of the policy-making system; the fourth factor is that of socio-economic development. The final one relates to state public disclosure laws that directly affect interest groups.

Policy jurisdiction
Obviously, the constitutional – legal authority or area over which the states have jurisdiction to enact public policy, is of crucial importance in determining what types of groups will be active in state politics. For no group is likely to expend scarce resources in a state capital

if the state government has no authority to help advance its objectives. They will direct their efforts at the level or levels of government that can benefit them. As semi-sovereign governments within a federal system, the American states share in the exercise of certain policy jurisdictions with the federal government. Broadly defined, the policy domain of the federal government falls into six categories: foreign affairs; defence; the police power, maintaining law and order; the provision of human services, education, housing, health and the like; regulation, especially of the economy and of business; and taxation to pay for the cost of government, but more importantly these days, for purposes of redistributing income.

The states are excluded by the Constitution from conducting foreign relations, and with some minor exceptions they play only a small role in the nation's defence. Consequently, the halls of government in state capitals are not jammed by hordes of lobbyists for defence contractors, military personnel and the agents of foreign governments, as is the case in Washington. By far the majority policy concern of the states − at least in terms of their budgets − is human services and especially education, welfare, health, and highways and transportation. Education alone accounts for about a third of state expenditures.[10] In addition, the states perform important regulatory functions. They regulate certain business practices including insurance, occupational standards, banking, and liquor sales; they regulate public utilities; and share with the federal government in regulating environmental protection and labour practices. State tax and redistributive policies − in the form of unemployment pay, business loans, and particularly aid to local governments − is also an important area of policy.

The groups that are active in state government are, as a consequence, education groups, local government organisations, farm groups, labour groups, and, most of all, business and professional groups of all types, including individual businesses, trade associations, and professional associations. These categories of groups have been and remain the major interests active in state capitals. But as we shall see in section four, the types of groups within these categories have undergone some changes in recent years, and other types of groups have become active in the states.

Just because a state has jurisdiction in certain policy areas does not by itself determine the level of group activity; nor, indeed, does it guarantee the level or degree to which any particular policy area will be exercised, if at all; or the extent to which policy in general is formulated in an integrated fashion. As to the first point, Zeigler has argued that the level of group activity is partly determined by the degree of centralisation or decentralisation of the spending system. If spending in a state is decentralised, giving local governments more spending powers, as groups tend to follow spending, there will be less group activity in the state capital.[11] As regards the second and third points, the extent to which a state will exercise a particular policy area, and develop policy in an integrated fashion, will depend, in large part, upon the dominant political attitudes in the state, especially its dominant political sub-culture.

Political attitudes

Political attitudes, namely the political culture and political ideology which predominate in a state, are important determinants of group activity in four major ways. First, these attitudes have an influence upon which policies a particular state government will or will not perform within its allocated policy jurisdiction, and the way in which it performs the policies that it does exercise. Secondly, attitudes will also affect the level of integration or co-ordination and professionalisation of the policy-making process. Third, they set parameters to the methods that groups and lobbyists can use in attempting to secure their goals. And fourth, and a related point, these attitudes appear to have an influence on the types of laws that are passed by the states regarding public disclosure, including lobby laws, and the degree to which these laws are enforced.

Political culture is one element of the general culture of a nation, state or locality. This element embodies a shared set of knowledge, attitudes and symbols which help to define the procedures and goals of politics. The classic treatment of state political cultures is, of course, that of Daniel Elazar. He identifies three types of political sub-cultures for the states – individualistic, moralistic and traditionalistic.[12] In the individualistic sub-culture, politics is seen as essentially utilitarian and a form of business, a process to enhance the economic, social and political well-being of individuals. There is a de-emphasis of communal concerns. In contrast, the moralistic sub-culture places emphasis on the public good: a quest to create a good society for all citizens, which is a principal responsibility of government. The third sub-culture, traditionalistic, has a paternalistic and elitist element to it. 'The purpose of government is to maintain the

social order, and, hence, power is confined to a small elite group based on family and social ties.'[13]

No state has a pure sub-culture of any one of these types. But Elazar argues that one type or a combination of two types will predominate in each state.[14] There is also a close correlation between these sub-cultures and political ideologies based on a conservative—liberal continuum. Traditionalistic states are more conservative and have less activist governments. These also tend to allow more freedom of action to groups in achieving their goals which may extend to bribery and corruption. For this reason such states, which include most of the old South, have less stringent public disclosure laws. At the other end of the scale, predominantly moralistic states like Minnesota, Oregon and Michigan will have more activist governments, place strictures on what are and what are not acceptable group tactics, and have more extensive and more stringently enforced public disclosure laws. Predominantly individualistic states, like Nevada, Illinois and Pennsylvania, fall somewhere in between in these elements.

While the relationship is less clear-cut than with these other factors, political culture and political ideology also influence the degree to which the policy process in the states is co-ordinated or integrated and the extent to which policy-makers — especially elected ones — are allowed to become professionals.

Level of integration and professionalisation of the policy-making system

The purpose of interest groups is to affect public policy in their favour. They attempt to achieve this by first obtaining access to policy-makers (legislators, the governor and his staff, bureaucrats) and then by attempting to influence their decisions. One of the most important weapons in their arsenal of influence is expert knowledge about their interest area. Patterns of access and influence will very much be determined by the extent to which the policy-making system is integrated or centralised within a state and the level of professionalisation of the policy-makers. In short, the more integrated and professionalised the system is, the fewer are the options available to groups in terms of points of access and methods of influence. Conversely, the more fragmented and less professionalised the system, the larger the number of access points and the available methods of influence.

The level of policy integration will depend upon the organisational arrangements and strength of political and governmental institutions. Most important of these is the strength or weakness of political parties and their role in the political system. Two other significant factors are: the number of high level executive offices that are filled by election; and the degree of professionalisation of both elected and appointed state officials.

With regard to political parties, Morehouse has written: 'The single most important actor in state politics is the political party because it is the only organization that can moderate the demands of organized groups.'[15] She goes on to say that it is in large part the strength of the party system that defines the activities of interest groups within a state.[16] Generally, but not in all cases, there will be an inverse relationship between party strength and group strength.

In strong party states, where parties can determine who stands for election, where they provide much of the campaign funds, and where the party can enforce discipline in the legislature, interest groups tend to be weak. Or more precisely, they have fewer access points open to them. They will be forced to work through the party and its leadership and perhaps even ally themselves with one party. Most strong party states are located in the industrial Northeast, Rhode Island, and Connecticut for example, or the upper Midwest – Michigan, Wisconsin, Minnesota and North Dakota. In weak party states, which include almost all the Southern and Western states, there is a more or less fragmented policy-making system. Not being fettered by strong parties, groups have many more points of access and become the major actors in the political process. In some states parties are moderately strong such as Delaware, Illinois and Kansas. In these states the structure of government will be a major determinant of the avenues of access open to groups.[17]

The policy-making process is likely to be more fragmented if several high level executive positions (attorney general, secretary of state and heads of state departments) are elected rather than appointed. Election will give these officials a power base which may enable them to be independent of party or governor, thus undermining the policy co-ordination capability of both. This will increase the access points and the strategy options available to interest groups, both of which will tend to enhance their power.[18]

Group power or influence will also be enhanced when legislatures and bureaucracies are less professionalised. The crucial factor here is sources of information, information itself being a key to governmental decision-making. Where legislatures are part-time and low paid and have minimal staff support, as in Montana, South Dakota and Idaho, they will rely more heavily on groups for the provision of information. The same is true of bureaucracies in states where departmental staffs are small and research facilities are minimal. But in states with more professional legislatures and bureaucracies such as California, New York and Illinois, there will be many more sources from which public officials can obtain important technical information. Thus the effectiveness of this weapon in the arsenal of groups in such states will be reduced.[19]

Socio-economic development

As we noted in section two, several scholars have persuasively argued that socio-economic conditions in a state will influence the type, operating techniques, and the power of groups within that state. These theories have several dimensions to them, many of which need more extensive development or modification. In essence what they argue is that as a state's economic and social system develops it will affect the nature of the interest group system by making it more pluralistic and by reducing its impact on the political system as a whole.

Economic development here is defined as an increase in non-agricultural employment and an increase in the industrial and service sectors; and a decrease in disparities in the distribution of income and wealth. Social development is defined in terms of: an increase in urbanisation; an increase in the percentage of middle-class residents; and an increase in the number of professionals in the population. The consequences of economic development are to increase economic diversity; social development increases the number of people joining groups, as urban dwellers and the middle and upper class are more likely to join groups than rural residents and the working class. Hence, the more econmically and socially developed states have a more diversified and richer group life.[20] Massachusetts, for instance, with its diversified economy, large urban, middle class, and professional and racially heterogeneous population has such a diversified group life. By contrast, North Dakota has a much less diversified interest group system. For here the economy is dominated by agriculture, agribusiness and the rural electric co-operatives. And the population is much less urbanised, less middle class and professional, and much less racially diverse.

Public disclosure provisions

The fifth environmental factor affecting the activity of groups is statutory provisions relating to public disclosure of information that directly affects group operations. These provisions fall into three categories. First are laws requiring group and lobbyist registration and reporting of expenditures. Then there are laws relating to disclosure of campaign contributions; and often laws imposing limits on the extent of such contributions. In this regard, of particular significance in recent years have been laws relating to Political Action Committees (PACs). These are organisations set up by interest groups for the primary, and often the sole, purpose of contributing money to campaigns. Often PACs are formed as a device for circumventing campaign contribution limits. The third category of public disclosure provisions relate to financial conflict of interest of public officials. These laws are intended to disclose which public officials have financial connections with which individuals, groups, organisations and businesses. Sometimes these laws prohibit certain types of financial relations or dealings. Evidence suggests that the extent of public disclosure provisions will have an affect on the way in which groups go about trying to achieve their goals. It may also affect the power of certain groups and lobbyists. Here we will confine our comments to state lobby laws.

By 1976 all fifty states had some form of statutory regulation of lobbying. Watergate was the main impetus for passage of such statutes in states where they had not previously existed and for other states to strengthen their laws. In all cases this regulation takes the form of registration of interest groups and their representatives and in most instances reporting of lobbying expenditures.[21] The thrust of state lobby laws is to provide public information and throw light on group activities rather than to restrict or attempt to control their activities. Indeed, because of the provisions relating to the right to 'petition government' in the First Amendment to the US Constitution and similar provisions in many state constitutions, attempts to restrict lobbying would run into some serious constitutional problems.

As we have noted state lobby laws, however, vary considerably in their inclusiveness, their reporting requirements and in the stringency with which they are enforced. Once again, there appears to be a correlation between a state's political culture and the strength (or weakness) of such laws.[22] As Morehouse has pointed out, however stringently written and enforced, a lobby law cannot reveal the extent of lobbying or the influence of a particular interest group.[23] Access and influence, the most vitally important things to groups, cannot be reduced to statistics.

Like laws regulating campaign expenditures and conflict of interest of public officials, state lobby laws do, however, appear to have contributed to a change in group tactics. Although virtually no data exists from the past upon which to make comparisons, in the last ten or fifteen years, public disclosure has made old-style lobbying methods less attractive to both groups and public officials. No figures exist, of course, on bribery, corruption and other legally questionable activities; but it is reasonable to assume that these have declined since the expansion of public disclosure provisions. Backroom dealings and corruption will probably always be with us in politics. But the credibility of a group and its representatives is an increasingly important weapon of influence as public officials become increasingly sensitive to public scrutiny. Public disclosure has affected group tactics and methods of influence by, among other things: heralding the decline of the wheeler-dealer lobbyist; by making groups much more aware of their public image; and generally by increasing the openness of their dealings with public officials.

As a long-time and prominent feature of state politics, interest groups have proven to be very resilient and adaptable to changes in their political environment, such as in regard to public disclosure laws and restrictions on campaign spending. In fact, placing limits on campaign expenditures largely precipitated one of the most prominent recent developments in interest group tractics – the rise of Political Action Committees. We will explore the extent of this development in section seven.

The utility of this five-factor framework

This conceptual framework for understanding the environmental influences on group activity in the states is a synthesis of previous research and of findings from the Hrebenar–Thomas study. While all five factors and their various elements are not new, what is original is the way that many of these elements have been used here, and the integration of the five factors into a single conceptual framework. Application of this framework can tell us much about the types of groups that will be active in a particular state, as well as the particular methods that they will use, and the impact that groups as a whole will have on the state's political system. It also facilitates comparisons, allowing us to account for similarities and differences between states.[24]

In particular, this framework integrates the various elements that determine whether an interest group system in a particular state will be strong, moderate or weak in relation to other influences on state public policy-making. As we have seen, strong systems tend to have a narrower range of groups, relatively weak political parties, a less integrated policy-making system, a less diverse economy, and are less urbanised than weak group systems. Strong systems also tend to have traditionalistic or individualistic political cultures. Moderate group systems tend to fall between the strong and weak systems in regards to these elements. They also tend to have individualistic or moralistic political cultures or a combination of both. Weak systems tend to have a political culture that is predominantly moralistic.

Strong interest group states also tend to be dominated by business and often there are a few prominent interests in state politics. Groups here have many points of access open to them and need not align themselves with any one political party. But as the state develops economically and socially, the power of business declines as the number of groups expands. Also, the narrow range of prominent interests will be challenged by new groups and the avenues of access will be narrowed. The system will move towards the moderate and, eventually, into the weak group system category.[25] At least, that is what the present status of this theoretical framework predicts.

In actual fact, this is an oversimplification of the transition process in practice. Unique circumstances in a state may inhibit the transition; or they may produce other exceptions. What all this means is that this five-factor framework is still rather crude and needs more development and refining. We will point out some of these needed changes at the end of this chapter. But even in its present form, this framework can throw considerable light upon the nature of state group systems and help us comprehend more fully the recent changes in these systems.

4 Changes in the number and kinds of groups active in state politics

One of the major aspects of the expansion of political pluralism that has taken place in the United States since World War II and especially since the mid-1960s, has been a considerable expansion in both the number and kinds of groups active in state politics. While many have questioned the extent of this expansion, claiming that it does not approach the increase in Washington, D.C., there is no doubt that considerable change has taken place.[26] As a result, the range of groups lobbying in state capitals is much less narrow than Zeigler described a few short years ago.[27] In addition, there has been a change in the make-up of traditional lobbies, namely, business, labour, farmers, education and local governments.

There are three explanations most often given for these changes. First, there is the rise of non-economic and social issue groups such as: minority groups including women's organisations; environmentalists; good government, individual rights and morality groups; and public interest and citizen groups of all types. This would include many so-called single issue groups about which much has been written. Second, as government has increased its role, and particularly its regulatory function, many groups have been forced to become politically active for both self-protective and for promotional purposes. A third and related explanation is the so-called reaction formation theory. As certain groups become politically active, others, especially opposing groups, also do so for purposes of protection. The findings from the Hrebenar–Thomas study certainly corroborate these explanations. In addition, this study has identified three related, but much less well-documented, reasons for this expansion in the numbers and kinds of groups.

First, there has been a fragmentation of traditional interests especially among business groups, but also professional and labour groups and local government organisations. What has happened in the business sector is that umbrella organisations, such as trade associations, have seen many of their members branch out and lobby for themselves when these member groups no longer see the trade association as effective, or see it pursuing policies contrary to their interests. Or, when the latter situation is the case, a rival trade association may be established. The banking industry in the states presents a good example of such fragmentation. In Missouri, for instance, federal deregulation of financial institutions began to undermine the power and representative function of the Missouri Bankers' Association as it received challenges from bank holding companies and the Missouri Independent Bankers' Association. While the Hrebenar–Thomas research confirms previous work by Zeigler that business interests constitute the bulk of groups in each state, this fragmentation process is an important part of the explanation for recent changes in the range of groups active in the states.

The second of these factors is the rise of public employee unions, in particular public school teachers and state employees' associations. As traditional blue collar unions decline, public employee unions are becoming the new face of labour in state capitals.

The current rise of public employee unions began with the founding of the American Federation of State, County and Municipal Employees (AFSCME) in Wisconsin in 1936. In 1959, the Wisconsin legislature passed legislation allowing local governments to bargain with their employees if the employees organised. In 1967, Wisconsin state employees became the first state level employees with the right to bargain collectively with the state government.[28] By 1982, thirty-seven states allowed their state-level public employees the right to bargain. In the meantime, AFSCME has grown to have 2,500 locals within the AFL–CIO totaling over 725,000 members. Several other unions represent governmental employees on the state and local level such as the Civil Service Employees Association with its 124,000 state employees and 88,000 local government employees.[29] The potential for future growth is enormous for by 1986–7, state and local governments employed over 12 million people.

One of the major unions representing public employees is the National Education Association (NEA) which represents hundreds of thousands of public school teachers as a 'guild–labour union' in jurisdictions across the nation. Founded in 1857, by the early 1980s, NEA had 1,600,800 members, sub-organisations in all fifty states, and over 9,000 local sub-units.[30] In many respects, NEA represents the perfect organisational structure for interest group activities on the state and local levels. It is a true national force with sub-units capable of influencing politics in every state and almost every community in the nation. Its more 'union-structured' competitor, the American Federation of Teachers, was founded in 1916, is a member of the AFL–CIO, and has more than 475,000 members within its 2,100 union locals.

The third factor that the Hrebenar–Thomas research has revealed regarding the expansion in group activity is the increasing role of government, particularly state agencies and local government units as a lobbying force in the states. This is of such importance that we devote the following section to the major aspects of this development.

5   Government agencies as a lobbying force in the states

Scholars have long been aware of the significance, in many cases the crucial role, that government agencies play in the complex world of interest group activity and lobbying. Terms such as 'iron triangles', 'cozy triangles' and 'agency–client relationships' have been coined to describe various aspects of the role of government in this regard. And the 'lobbying' prowess of several federal agencies, particularly the military services, in securing their budgets is well known. However, most research on the role of government agencies in the lobbying process has focused on the federal level; very little has dealt with this role at the state level. This is in part, of course, the product of using a narrow definition of interest group; and also because of the methodological problems of gathering data on this subject. Consequently, prior to the Hrebenar–Thomas project very little information was available on the role of government agencies as a lobbying force in state politics.

By government agencies we are referring to federal bureaus, agencies and departments active in state capitals, local governments which lobby, and state government departments, boards and commissions. The political reality is that these agencies at the three levels of government are as much interest groups and lobbying forces to be reckoned with as many private 'traditional' vested interests. All government agencies represent a particular perspective and have a vested interest in protecting their position and the numerous people whose livelihood depends on the agency's continued existence. But because of their 'hidden lobby' status – not being required to register in most states – their role and impact is difficult to assess. Findings from the Hrebenar–Thomas research, however, enables us to identify some key elements of the role of state and local governmental agencies and units.

As we might expect, it is state government agencies which have the most comprehensive role of these three in the lobbying life of state politics. While they are interrelated, we can discern four major aspects of this lobbying role, a role similar to that played by agencies at the federal level. First, there are the ongoing symbiotic relationships between agencies and client groups. Second, there is a constant need to lobby the legislature and the governor's office to protect themselves from *ad hoc* proposals by groups, individuals, legislators and other government agencies that would adversely affect them, either directly or indirectly, by reducing their budget or areas of responsibility, or by adding unwanted responsibilities. Third, there is an advocacy function resulting from the need to promote legislation and changes in regulations to better perform their mandated responsibilities. Finally, and as far as most agencies are concerned probably their key lobbying function, they must work to secure the approval of their annual or bi-annual budget by the governor and the legislature.[31]

Several aspects of this role of state agencies in the lobbying process stand out from this latest research. First, almost all major departments and agencies have a person or persons known as a legislative liaison whose job it is to act as a conduit between their deparment, the legislature and the governor's office. Research indicates that as many as 20 percent of those lobbying the legislature and the governor's office in any given session represent state agencies. And, of course, agency heads, commissioners and the like are intimately involved in the legislative process. Sometimes these agency heads, with their automatic access and the resources of their bureaucracy behind them, are among the most effective lobbyists in the capital city. A good example is Stephen E. Reynolds, the long-serving state engineer in New Mexico. His power base comes from his department's jurisdiction over the distribution of water rights in a state with vast deserts.[32]

A second factor relates to this automatic access and technical expertise that departments and agencies possess. As government becomes more and more complex, as Zeigler and Morehouse point out, more and more responsibility, and thus power, will be placed with state agencies.[33] Recent research certainly bears this out. But even today legislators very much rely upon the expertise and advice of state agencies; and this is even more the case in the so-called citizen legislatures such as Montana, Alabama and New Hampshire, where sessions are short, legislators' pay is low and support staffs are small. Because of this, it is difficult for a group or lobby to enact or repeal a piece of public policy if the agency or agencies affected oppose the measure. Legislators tell a myriad of stories of how lobbying efforts have failed because a group failed to work with the affected agency or were unable to overcome its opposition.

One propositon that emerged from the Hrebenar–Thomas research project is that the impact and lobbying 'clout' of state agencies tends to be greater in states where state and local government employment is the highest. In several western states, for example, Alaska, New Mexico and Hawaii, government is the largest employer.[34] In Hawaii almost half of the forty-eight lobbyists listed as most effective were employees of state and local government (because of Hawaii's lobby law none of these were required to register).[35] But with very few exceptions there is one state agency that has been seen as influential in almost all states. This is the state department of education or public instruction. Because of the large proportion of state expenditure that goes to education, this is not surprising. And when allied with other education groups – teachers, school boards associations, PTAs, etc., – they can be a formidable power. As to local governments, as their budgets have increased their lobbying role at the state level has also expanded. Their status and responsibilities give them a built-in advantage of access with legislators, bureaucrats and the governor's office. One noticeable development here is that local governments have contributed towards the process of interest group fragmentation that we noted in the last section. While still belonging to their state municipal leagues or league of cities or counties, many cities and local jurisdictions, particularly school districts, are hiring their own contract lobbyists to represent them in their state capital.

Some of the changes in the configuration of group power resulting from the points explained in this and the last section, are considered in section 8 below.

6 Lobbyists

Several factors have wrought change in recent years in the types and backgrounds of the people who make up the lobbying community in the fifty state capitals. Of these, the five most important appear to be: the expansion in the kinds and number of groups; the increasing professionalisation of elected and appointed officials; government's increased need for technical information; the development of new techniques of lobbying, especially those made possible by the application of new technologies; and the passage of public disclosure and more stringent lobby registration laws.

As appears to be the situation with most trends in state interest group activity, this change in the nature of the lobbying community began on the east and west coast, worked its way into the middle of the country and is now trickling into the South. Though the truth of the matter is that there is not much detailed information prior to the mid-1970s on state level lobbyists with which to make comparisons. The Zeigler and Baer study is the only major piece of research available.[36] So our comparisons here will be based primarily upon their findings. As the result of the Hrebenar–Thomas research we are in much better shape, however, when it comes to presenting a picture of today's typical state capital lobbying community.

Perhaps the best way to sum up the recent changes in this lobbying community is that it is becoming much more professionalised. In this sense lobbyists in Sacramento, Des Moines, Baton Rouge, Richmond and the other state capitals are becoming more and more like their counterparts in Washington, D.C. Social lobbying – wining and dining and the like – is becoming much less important, and with it the old wheeler-dealer is giving way to a new breed of lobbyist able to meet the new needs of policy-makers and the new political realities. This new breed, while possessing many of the attributes of the wheeler-dealer, tend to be better educated and skilled in the provision of technical information. While former government officials still appear to be the major source for contract lobbyists (those hired for a fee specifically to lobby), attorneys and public relations specialists, skilled in media presentations and information packaging, are very much on the increase. Jim Joyce in Nevada and George Soares in California are examples of this new breed.[37] This trend in the more technically and information oriented lobbyist is likely to continue as government becomes more complex, and more and more responsibility is placed with bureaucrats who tend to emphasise the technical, rather than the political.

Furthermore, while the lone lobbyist is still a prominent feature of state capitals, more and more contract lobbying is being done by lobbying firms. Once again this trend reflects the situation in Washington, D.C. Law firms, public relations firms and the multi-service lobbying firms – offering promotional, legal and other services as well as lobbying – have become important in this regard. The entry of some capital law firms into the lobbying (though most prefer the term advocacy) business is an indication of the growing legal complexity of many areas of public policy, especially the regulatory area. This trend is discernable in states of all sizes of population, from New York to Virginia to Alaska.

So what does a typical state capital lobbying community look like today? First, we should emphasise once again that the chances are that we will not get an accurate picture of this simply by consulting lobby registration lists, as these do not include the so-called 'hidden lobbies'.

In all state capitals we can identify five more or less distinct categories of lobbyists. First, there are the contract lobbyists, those who are hired specifically to lobby by a client for a fee. These we referred to above. They predominantly represent business and economic interests. With some very minor exceptions these will be required to register with their state's lobby registration agency. Next there are the in-house lobbyists. These are presidents, executive directors, government relations directors, and the like, of organisations ranging from the state chamber of commerce to the girl scouts to representatives of individual businesses, who as part of their job description represent their organisation or company to the legislative and the administrative branch. Most of these are required to register in most states, though once again there is a wide variation.

The third category is that of legislative liaisons which we mentioned in the last section. These primarily represent state agencies but some are from federal bureaus, agencies and departments. This category would also include the scores of elected and appointed officials who represent local governments. We also noted above the fact that, because most states do not require this category to register, it is difficult to assess their numbers and their impact. The fourth category is rather an amorphous one that we might term volunteer lobbyists: these represent various civic and community groups and are reimbursed for expenses only, if that. Finally, there are individuals who lobby for personal or 'pet' projects. Most state laws do not require these last two categories to register.

Because of the varying registration requirements, it is difficult accurately to estimate the proportion of total lobbyists that each of these categories constitutes. However, recent research reveals that in terms of their contacts with legislators the first three categories would each have about 30 percent, and the remaining two, 10 percent between them. Even allowing for the loose nature of this estimate, this means that between 30 percent and 50 percent of those persons lobbying legislators do not, in most states, appear on any lobby registration lists. And this percentage is likely to be higher in the case of administrative lobbying where state registration laws are more lax.

One final point about lobbyists: this concerns the view that legislators have of them and the role that they perform. Unlike the common public perception, without exception the Hrebenar−Thomas research results indicate that legislators view lobbyists very positively and see them as essential components of the legislative process, though this does not mean that legislators are unaware of the negative effects that lobbyists and their organisations can sometimes have. With very few exceptions, legislators see the provision of information as the major function of lobbyists. In this regard these findings confirm earlier work by Zeigler.

7 Group and lobbying tactics

As we noted earlier, interest groups enter the political arena for one primary purpose – to affect public policy in their favour. And they achieve this by gaining access to those who make that policy; and then by exerting influence upon those policy-makers. Securing access and achieving influence is the essence of group tactics.

The four major avenues of access and influence are election campaigns, the legislature, the administrative branch and the courts. Public relations and media campaigns provide the major indirect avenue of access and influence, the ultimate purpose of which is to effect direct access and influence. Probably the most common of group tactics is the use of one or more lobbyists. In fact, until the late 1960s this was the *only* tactical method used by most state lobby groups. In recent years increased competition among groups, as their numbers expanded, and the changing needs of elected and appointed officials, have nurtured other tactical devices. These include: mobilising grass-roots support through networking (sophisticated member-contact systems); public relations and media campaigns referred to above; coalition building with other groups; using the courts; and contributing workers and money to election campaigns. The Hrebenar–Thomas study has gathered extensive information on these and other tactical methods, and as a result will be able to describe the nature of state group tactics in detail and discern trends. Here, however, we will briefly deal with what appears to be the most significant development in state group tactics in recent years – the rise of Political Action Committees (PACs).

PACs have proliferated across the nation and have become significant political actors in all fifty states. One reason for this proliferation is the federal system and the need to organise within each of the states rather than just utilise a national level PAC or interest group. Each state has very different rules regarding whether a corporation, labour union, Political Action Committee, or regulated industry can give money in the form of campaign contributions directly to a political campaign. The states have more frequently prohibited corporate contributions than union contributions. Twenty states prohibit direct corporate campaign contributions while only eight prohibit such contributions from labour unions. Conversely, twenty-five states have no limitations on union contributions, while only seventeen impose no limitations on corporate campaign contributions.

All states allow PACs to contribute to political campaigns in one form or another. Thirty allow PACs to contribute without any limitations, while twenty states and the District of Columbia impose some type of restrictions such as dollar limits on certain level campaigns. Michigan, for example, limits PACs to a total $1,700 for a state-wide office; $450 for state senate races; and $250 for state representative campaigns. Connecticut limits labour union PACs to an aggregate of $50,000 per election and corporate PACs to an aggregate of $1 million per election. Utah and Nevada are the only states that have no laws governing the legality of Political Action Committees or how political organisations can give money to state-level political campaigns.[38]

In his study of PACs, Larry Sabato concluded that the 'growth of PACs on the national level has been matched, and in some cases exceeded, by the increase in PAC number and size recorded in states and localities across the country'.[39] The data collected by the Hrebenar–Thomas study confirms the tremendous growth in the number and the impact of PACs on the state level. In Idaho, for example, there were seventeen PACs registered in 1976, but by 1980 over fifty existed. Oregon PACs during the 1970s went from 57 to 410. By 1980, there were well over a hundred PACs operating in Montana politics.[40]

However, it is not so much the number of PACs operating on the state level which is significant, but their impact upon the form and substance of politics. In Arizona between 1974 and 1982, PAC contributions increased by 1,526 percent and accounted for approximately 50 percent of state legislative campaign contributions. Montana's PACs accounted for 19 percent of state legislative campaign contributions in the 1980 elections. Oregon's PAC explosion during the 1970s was accompanied by an increase in campaign expenditures from $200,000 in 1970 to $2.4 million in 1982. Finally, in recent Wyoming gubernatorial elections, PAC money has accounted for about 15 percent of the campaign war chests.[41]

8   Changes in the configuration of individual group and lobby power

The concept of interest group power can denote two separate though interrelated notions. It may refer to the ability of an individual group, coalition or lobby to achieve its policy goals. Alternatively, it may be used to refer to the strength of interest groups as a whole within a state's political and governmental systems, or the strength of groups relative to other organisations or institutions, particularly political parties. Here we will confine our comments to individual group power.

This is not the place to detail the problems involved in defining and assessing individual group and lobby power. Suffice it to say that the problems relate much less to the question of definition than they do to the method of assessment. There are so many variables affecting both long- and short-term group power that it is difficult to develop a methodology to assess and predict it in more than a general way. Three methods have been used for assessing individual group power: the use of purely objective criteria; the perceptual method, relying on the perception of politicians, bureaucrats and political observers; and a combination of the two. The Hrebenar—Thomas study involved this latter methodology. That project's definition of individual group power, which also incorporates its method of assessment was as follows: 'The power of any particular interest group or lobby is: its ability to achieve its goals as it defines them, and as perceived by the various people directly involved in and who observe the public policy-making process (e.g., both present and former legislators, aides, bureaucrats, other lobbyists, journalists, etc.).'

All the changes and developments noted in the previous sections have had their effect upon the kinds of groups that are effective at the state level. Perhaps an obvious, but nevertheless important point, is that there are now more groups sharing power at the state level than was the case up until the 1960s. This has had some important consequences for the power of individual groups and lobbies.

One significant consequence of this appears to be the decline of *dominant* interests in state politics. The days of the dominance by states of one or a few interests – sugar in Hawaii, the Anaconda Company in Montana, the 'big three' in Maine (electric power, timber, textile and shoe manufacture), the Farm Bureau in many rural states – appears to be gone forever. True, some states still have a *prominent* interest operating within their borders – gambling in Nevada, oil in Texas, agriculture in the Dakotas, the Mormon Church in Utah. But the continuing expansion of political pluralism will in all probability work to prevent one or an oligarchy of interests from controlling a vast array of policy decisions.

As to traditional groups and lobbies in state politics, one of these long-term interests, agriculture, has seen an attrition of its power in recent years. This is partly a result of the massive reapportionments of state legislatures that took place after the mid-1960s; but it is also due to changes in the structure of that sector. Agri-business, such as the California wine industry has, however, become politically important.

Business and labour have also gone through some interesting transitions. We noted earlier the fragmentation of the business lobby. But business as a whole is still the most prevalent interest in all states and overall the most influential in most. Labour has seen the decline of traditional union lobbies, especially in the West. These have been replaced by public employee unions, especially public school teachers and state employees.

It is interesting to note the rise of these public employee groups to the very pinnacle of political influence and power within the states. When compared with the findings of Zeigler and Morehouse from previous decades, in state after state, public employee unions are now listed among the most powerful and influential interest groups. In twelve of the thirteen Western states, for example, education associations are listed as powerful interest groups (Hawaii being the only exception). In four states (Alaska, Montana, Nevada and Washington), the rise of education groups has occurred since the Morehouse assessment.

Somewhat less expected was the emergence of state employee associations to such a position of influence. In six of the thirteen western states (Alaska, California, Hawaii, Nevada, Utah and Washington), public employee unions were listed among the most influential. In several states, such as Hawaii and Alaska, interestingly, the two newest states, the public employee unions are perhaps the most powerful lobby groups in their respective states. In five of these six states (Washington excepted), the rise of public employee unions has occurred since the Morehouse assessment.[42]

There has also been a rise in power of local government groups and state agencies. In most Western states and in states as diverse as Pennsylvania, Nebraska and Alabama, these rank among the most effective interests. Somewhat less widely influential, but nevertheless important in several states, are environmentalists. Their strength lies in the West, but states like Michigan, Maine and Ohio are included.

Then there are the interests which, unlike the previously mentioned groups, only become active in state politics on specific issues and do not maintain a constant high profile in state capitals. Such an example is the trial lawyers. The subject of tort reform, which has been a major issue in the states in the last few years, forced this group into the political arena in most states. The issue revolves around rising insurance rates resulting from high awards by the courts in damage suits. The insurance companies have sought caps and other limitations on such awards. However, the well-financed and well-organised trial lawyers have been successful in preventing extensive reforms in this area.

While several other interests are active in state politics, the Hrebenar–Thomas research indicates those mentioned above as being the ones with the most influence in the states as a whole. Hence the range of interests with influence in state politics is far broader than was the case twenty-five or even ten years ago.

9 Conclusion: existing research and suggestions for modifications and new directions

As has been indicated in various points in this chapter, recent research suggests several modifications of existing theories and propositions on interest groups in state politics. Here, however, we will simply mention some of what the Hrebenar–Thomas study revealed as the most important.

Of greatest importance is to develop and modify the conceptual framework for understanding the activities of groups. The problem with the present five-factor framework is that each factor has so many variables, many of which have not been fully explored, or their relationship with other variables is only partially understood. Therefore, in its present form the framework has only limited value as an analytical and predictive model of group behaviour. For example, diversified economies are not always associated with weak group systems, as California and Illinois demonstrate. Second, a similar reconsideration is needed regarding political variables, such as the relationship between the group system and the strength of the governor. Zeigler argues that strong governors are associated with weak interest group systems. But in several cases, such as Hawaii, Alaska and Montana, strong interest group systems exist side by side with strong governors. Most important, strong party systems are not always associated with weak interest group systems as Illinois also demonstrates.[43] In other words, the whole area of the overall impact of groups in states needs refining.

Three other areas that the Hrebenar–Thomas research would suggest need re-thinking are: what constitutes the changing role and the overall effectiveness of lobbyists; the effect that professional-isation of elected and appointed officials has on overall and individual group power; and the role played by money, especially campaign con-tributions by PACs, in access and, particularly, influence. Zeigler and Baer saw campaign contributions as of minor importance.[44] The Hrebenar–Thomas research reveals quite the contrary.

Finally, there are some areas that need propositions developed on them. Most important of these are the factors affecting individual group power, the role of government agencies as lobbyists, and the role of the courts as venues of lobby tactics.

Notes

1   See Douglas Arnold, 'Overtilled and undertilled fields in American politics', *Political Science Quarterly*, 97, 1982, p. 97; Charles W. Wiggins and William P. Browne, 'Interest groups and public policy within a legislative setting', *Polity*, 14, 1982, p. 548; and Ronald G. Shaiko's review article, 'Interest group research: cultivating an "Unsettled Plot" ', *Polity*, 18, 1986, 720–21, which quotes the above two articles.

2   This book series is being co-edited by the author and Ronald J. Hrebenar, professor of political science at the University of Utah. The author would like to thank Dr. Hrebenar for his comments on this chapter and his willingness to allow use here of papers and publications that were co-authored by himself and the author.

The books in this series are: Ronald J. Hrebenar and Clive S. Thomas, eds, *Interest Group Politics in the American West*, Salt Lake City, 1987; *Interest Group Politics in the Midwestern States*, forthcoming 1988; *Interest Group Politics in the Southern States*, forthcoming 1989; and *Interest Group Politics in the Northeastern States*, forthcoming, 1989.

3   William H. Hedrick and L. Harmon Zeigler, 'Oregon: the politics of power', in Hrebenar and Thomas, eds, *Interest Group Politics in the American West*, p. 107; and Eleanor Main, Lee Epstein and Debra L. Elovich, 'Interest groups in Georgia: business as usual', first draft manuscript. Unless otherwise referenced, all information presented

in this paper is taken from first draft manuscripts of the Hrebenar—Thomas book chapters.

4 Truman's definition is: 'An interest group is any group that is based on one or more shared attitudes and makes certain claims on other groups or organizations in the society for the establishment, maintenance or enhancement of forms of behavior that are implied by the shared attitudes,' David B. Truman, *The Governmental Process*, New York, 1951, p. 33.

Despite its insightfulness, the Truman definition has been criticised on the basis of its emphasis on 'shared attitudes' and the modes of political behaviour that result from this. Subsequent work, especially that by Clark and Wilson and by Olson, persuasively challenge the notion that group members share common reasons for joining or maintaining membership in a group; or that all members are concerned or aware of the political goals of the group. See Peter B. Clark and James Q. Wilson, 'Incentive systems: a theory of organizations', *Administrative Science Quarterly*, 6, 1961, pp. 219—66; Mancur Olson, *The Logic of Collective Action*, Public Goods and the Theory of Groups, Cambridge, Mass., 1965; also see Terry M. Moe, *The Organization of Interests*, Chicago, 1980.

5 The four leading texts on American national interests groups in the author's opinion are: Kay Lehman Schlozman and John T. Tierney, *Organized Interests and American Democracy*, New York, 1986; Ronald J. Hrebenar and Ruth K. Scott, *Interest Group Politics in America*, Englewood Cliffs, NJ, 1982; Allan J. Cigler and Burdett A. Loomis, eds, *Interest Group Politics*, 2nd edn, Washington, D.C., 1986; and Jeffrey M. Berry, *The Interest Group Society*, Boston, 1989. This latter book contains an extensive bibliography on American national and state interest groups, see pages 221—31.

6 William P. Browne, 'Variations in the behavior and style of state lobbyists and interest groups', *The Journal of Politics*, 47, 1985, pp. 450—68; Mark S. Hyde and Richard W. Alsfeld, 'Role orientations of lobbyists in a state setting: a comparative analysis', paper presented at the American Political Science Association meeting, August/September 1985; Clyde Brown, 'Explanations of political interest group membership: the case of state level farm bureaus', paper presented at the Southern Political Science Association meeting, November 1986.

7 L. Harmon Zeigler and Michael Baer, *Lobbying: Interaction and Influence in American State Legislatures*, Belmont, Calif., 1969; Paul Brace, 'The effects of organized interests on state legislatures', paper presented at the American Political Science Association meeting, August/September 1985; Charles G. Bell, Keith E. Hamm and Charles W. Wiggins, 'The pluralistic model reconsidered: a comparartive analysis of interest group policy involvement in three states', paper presented at the American Political Science Association meeting, August/September 1985.

8 Belle Zeller, *American State Legislatures*, 2nd edn, New York, 1954, pp. 190—91 and ch. 13; L. Harmon Zeigler, 'Interest groups in the states', ch. 4 in Virginia Gray, Herbert Jacob and Kenneth N. Vines, eds, *Politics in the American States: A Comparative Analysis*, 4th edn, Boston, 1983; L. Harmon Zeigler and Hendrik van Dalen, 'Interest groups in state politics', ch. 4 in Herbert Jacob and Kenneth N. Vines, *Politics in the American States: A Comparative Analysis*, 3rd edn, Boston, 1976; and ch. 3 in Sarah McCally Morehouse, *State Politics, Parties and Policy*, New York, 1981.

9 Both Zeigler and Morehouse are participating in the Hrebenar—Thomas project: Zeigler co-authored the chapter on Oregon, and Morehouse is authoring the chapter on Connecticut.

10   See Robert S. Lorch, *State and Local Politics: The Great Entanglement*, 2nd edn, *Englewood Cliffs, NJ, 1986, ch. 11, esp. pp. 300–304.*

11   Zeigler in Gray, Jacob and Vines, *Politics in the American States*, pp. 114–15.

12   Daniel J. Elazar, *American Federalism: A View from the States*, 3rd edn, New York, 1986, ch. 5, esp. pp. 114–22.

13   Hyde and Alsfeld, 'Role orientations', pp. 10–11.

14   Elazar, *American Federalism*, pp. 134–7.

15   Morehouse, *State Politics*, p. 95.

16   *Ibid.*, p. 119.

17   *Ibid.*, p. 127.

18   *Ibid.*, pp. 135–7; Zeigler in Gray, Jacob and Vines, *Politics in the American States*, p. 122.

19   Morehouse, *State Politics*, p. 100; Zeigler in Gray, Jacob and Vines, *Politics in the American States*, pp. 120–2.

20   For a more extensive consideration of the influence of socio-economic development see, Morehouse, *State Politics*, pp. 107–17, Zeigler and van Dalen, in Jacob and Vines, *Politics in the American States*, pp. 94–109, and Zeigler, in Gray, Jacob and Vines, *Politics in the American States*, pp. 111–13.

21   For the provisions of the lobby laws in the fifty states, see *The Book of the States*, 1986–87, Lexington, KY, 1986, pp. 140–43.

22   Morehouse, *State Politics*, pp. 130–31.

23   *Ibid.*, p. 130.

24   In fact, this conceptual framework can be used to analyse the interest group system at the national level or at the local government level in any country. In addition, by adding a sixth factor, that of regime type (pluralistic, totalitarian, dictatorship, etc.) this framework can be used to compare interest group systems between countries.

25   See Morehouse, *State Politics*, pp. 107–32; Zeigler and van Dalen in Jacob and Vines, *Politics in the American States*, pp. 111–17.

26   See Virginia Gray, 'Fundamental changes in group life at the state level', paper presented at the American Political Science Association meeting, August/September 1984.

27   Zeigler in Gray, Jacob and Vines, *Politics in the American States*, p. 99.

28   Dennis L. Dresang, *Public Personnel Management and Public Policy*, Boston, 1984, p. 303.

29   Gale Research, *Encyclopedia of Associations*, Detroit, 1980.

30   *Ibid.*

31   To varying degrees state agencies will also, of course, engage in lobbying the federal government and local governments in the course of intergovernmental relations. This aspect of lobbying is beyond the scope of this chapter, however.

32   Hrebenar and Thomas, *Interest Group Politics in the American West*, p. 101.

33   Zeigler in Gray, Jacob and Vines, *Politics in the American States*, pp. 119–27; and Morehouse, *State Politics*, p. 135.

34   Hrebenar and Thomas, *Interest Group Politics in the American West*, p. 144.

35   *Ibid.*, p. 65, p. 145.

36   Zeigler and Baer, *Lobbying*, esp. chs. 4–8.

37   Hrebenar and Thomas, *Interest Group Politics in the American West*, p. 146.

38   James A. Palmer and E. D. Fergenbaum, *Campaign Finance Law, 1986, Washington, D.C., Federal Election Commission, 1986.*

39   Larry J. Sabato, *PAC Power: Inside the World of Political Action Committees*, New York, 1985, p. 117.

40   Hrebenar and Thomas, *Interest Group Politics in the American West*, pp. 72–3, 81, 109–11.

41   *Ibid.*, pp. 28, 81, 109–11, 140–1.

42   *Ibid.*, pp. 149–52.

43   Zeigler, in Gray, Jacob and Vines, *Politics in the American States*, pp. 99–122, Zeigler and van Dalen, in Jacob and Vines, *Politics in the American States*, pp. 93–4 and Morehouse, *State Politics*, pp. 137–9 sets out these major theories and propositions on interest groups in the states. A fuller analysis of suggested modifications resulting from work on the Western states is provided in Hrebenar and Thomas, *Interest Group Politics in the American West*, pp. 147–52.

44   Zeigler and Baer, *Lobbying*.

Postscript

Postscript

Nelson W. Polsby

American democracy in world perspective and what to do about it

For those scholars centrally concerned with studying American politics and government from outside the United States, the year 1986 contained two significant landmarks: the 150th anniversary of Alexis de Tocqueville's ever green classic, *Democracy in America*,[1] and the untimely death in his fiftieth year of John David Lees, who did so much to invigorate and sustain American political studies in the United Kingdom. This essay, dedicated to the memory of John Lees, is a meditation upon a theme that occupied him, and de Tocqueville, and all the other students from abroad that the American political system has attracted since its beginning two hundred years ago. It recognises the fundamental tendency of observers to seek analogies between their foreign object of study and the more familiar domestic life around them, and attempts to explore obstacles that the American political system as a foreign object of study places in the path of analogical thinking about its politics.[2] This is, therefore, in part a discussion of ways in which modern American politics is distinctive and, because of its distinctiveness, troublesome to foreign analysts. And not only can it pose problems for analysts; political leaders abroad, friends, adversaries, clients and allies of the United States must somehow reckon with the American political system and live with the consequences of its often mysterious behaviour.

I

I begin with an anecdote. During a friendly encounter with one of the most successful leaders of a Western European political party in the spring of 1985 I was asked to name the person 'in charge of foreign affairs' for the American Democratic Party. This Western European leader remarked that he had known the man with this job – international relations – at the Democratic National Committee during the recent chairmanship of Charles Manatt, but since Manatt's departure as Democratic National Committee Chairman, the Western European leader assumed that a new person had come on board to head up foreign policy for the Democrats.

This was, to me, a most illuminating question. I should say at once that it came from a political leader who was – and is – well educated, well informed about American politics in general, indeed a frequent and a welcome visitor to America, and favourably disposed to the United States. I have no doubt at all that as non-American politicians go, this leader's sympathetic acquaintance with American politics and political figures is very good indeed. Yet the question and the conversation surrounding it also left no doubt that there were structural features of the American political system that either had not come to his attention or that he had misunderstood. It may or may not be a well known feature of political science textbooks the world around to say that American political parties are different from European parties, and separation of powers regimes different from parliamentary regimes. No person of practical affairs has time, even if he or she has at one point read and grasped the texts, to draw each and every warrantable inference from these differences, especially in light of all that we have been hearing in the meantime about changes in the American parties – even an inference as commonplace to Americans as that the Democratic National Committee has no standing whatever as an influence on Democratic policy in foreign affairs.

So this was far from a silly question: it was a diagnostically valuable communication about how very difficult it is to understand American politics for someone embedded in a different political system.

In studying two bad moments in modern Anglo-American relations – Skybolt and Suez – Richard E. Neustadt came to much the same conclusion. Leaders in each country had misunderstood leaders in the other, he found. The bases for the misunderstandings were certainly not ill-will or suspicion or all the difficulties that cloud adversarial misperceptions, but rather false analogies on the part of the leaders on both sides. He reported, 'these men dredged their perceptions of the other side's constraints out of their own heads. They reasoned by analogy and drew conclusions for the other side, and thereupon perceived what they projected.'[3]

I offer a final set of observations – these more casual – in aid of the proposition that American politics poses great difficulties for foreign observers. Among the de Tocqueville sesquicentennial celebrations at American universities a few included foreign commentators – usually persons of very great distinction – who were asked to follow in de Tocqueville's footsteps and to give their observations about democracy in America today. I was present at two of these panels on opposite sides of the country and was impressed by the frequency with which our friends from abroad expressed annoyance with fundamental features of our constitutional order – especially the separation of powers and consequent policy differences between Congress and President. 'It is representative government', I heard a Canadian panelist say, summing up much that had been said by others around him, 'but is it a government?'

I came away from this meeting wondering whether our friendly outside commentators had understood that changes required to meet their objections would not be cosmetic in character, but would attack the very foundations of a political system they also professed in some respects to admire. It would seem that they did not grasp this point, though we must bear in mind that Americans who speak in the same vein seldom do much better.[4] But Americans have readily to hand most of what it takes to inform themselves about the complexities and the routines of the American political system. Foreigners, reasoning so frequently from analogies about what constitutes 'a government' or 'a party programme' in the democratic systems with which they are most familiar, have far greater obstacles to overcome.

II

So it will be my purpose here to catalogue some of these obstacles and to show, if possible, how some of the more obvious differences between the American and other political systems, differences with which school children are, we hope, familiar, lead onward to subtler and less obvious differences. It is a commonplace to remark on the extent to which the constitutional form of the American government departs from the global norm for liberal democracies, but it may nevertheless not be fully appreciated that formal differences have cumulative as well as individual effects.

I begin, therefore, with the separation of powers. Foreign observers are familiar enough with the fact that before international treaties are binding upon the United States they must be ratified by the US

Senate. This scarcely tells them enough of what they need to know about the US Senate, or indeed about the Congress of the United States. It does not disclose, for example, that the American Congress has no counterpart anywhere in the world in the autonomous power that it exercises as a collective entity. For those observers who have grasped that Congress is an institution of enormous power, there is still difficulty in measuring the influence on that genuinely bicameral body of any particular member thereof. And so, frequently enough, overseas observers oscillate between weighing too heavily the public statements of a single Senator or Member of Congress, and dismissing too readily the rumblings they may discern from Capitol Hill.

Only detailed knowledge of the wiring diagramme of the American national legislature can possibly resolve uncertainty about how to weigh any particular Congressional manifestation of opinion. For unlike the parliaments with which so many observers are familiar, the Congress has a highly consequential internal structure. And this is true, but true in different ways, for both the House and the Senate. Thus it matters very much – but differently for each entity – who sits on which relevant subcommittee, and not only substantive subcommittees but also appropriations subcommittees. Each of these units of the whole has its own political configuration. In some the members are dominated by staff and in some vice versa; or the chairman counts for more or less than usual; or the most significant alliance runs between the chairman and the ranking minority member, rather than between the chairman and members of his own party. Distributions of members on committees and subcommittees by age, by ideology, and by constituency, whether homogeneous or diverse in each dimension, will yield up different patterns of policy-making and indeed different substantive policies from subcommittee to subcommittee and from year to year as these features of the membership evolve and change.

Everyone reads the tea leaves of electoral trends after each biennial Congressional election, but seldom is the analysis carried downward far enough into the committees and subcommittees of Congress so that the running balance sheets of overseas observers are well informed and up to date, whether they are interested in acid rain or short range nuclear missiles, or trade protection, or tourism, or whatever. Those observers who succeed in doing the necessary analyses are most emphatically not reasoning from analogies with their own system and have understood the singular and significant point that the American Congress is uniquely important among the legislatures of the world.[5]

It is useful that this realisation be at the centre rather than at the periphery of the consciousness of foreign observers. Those who are only peripherally aware of Congress and hence of the system of separation of powers tend to see Congress as a nuisance rather than as a legitimate actor in American policy making, as a factor, therefore, to be taken account of only after the main lines of policy are understood from the perspective of the lead agencies of the executive branch. Given the fact that the executive branch is itself so frequently divided — even irreconcilably so — on public policy, this relegation of Congress to the periphery of vision is understandable. But it is a mistake if for no other reason than that executive branch conflicts themselves frequently can be made intelligible by watching the way they are expressed in the Congressional arena.[6]

Thus the first special feature of the American political system to which outside observers need to attend — the constitutional separation of powers — has as its most acutely problematic manifestation the powers and activities of the United States Congress.

Let us now consider federalism, also an explicit feature of the American constitutional order. Just as there are in the world at large nations other than the United States with constitutionally given separations of power, so also there are devolved federal systems other than the American one.[7] Federalism interacts with the separation of powers, as well as making its independent contribution to the confusion of observers. As an independent factor, federalism means at a minimum that separate account must be taken of autonomous centres of power in each of the fifty states and the District of Columbia. Schooling, transportation, and the maintenance of public order are examples of policy domains that cannot possibly be understood without a disaggregated look at the activities, policies, decisions and inclinations of the several states.

At more than one point in American history, as is well known, the federal structure of the union served as a theoretical foundation for the shaping of the nation as a whole. In this connection I mention only three such episodes: the adoption of the Connecticut compromise in the constitutional convention which gave the United States a bicameral Congress, one branch of which, the Senate, provides equal representation for each state; attempts at nullification of federal laws by autonomous state action during the troubled course of the Constitution's first six decades; and the Civil War itself.

More recently, it seems to me that the federal structure of the American political system contributes most importantly to confusion about the United States because of the way in which federalism interacts with the American party system.[8] Evidently a significant reason that Americans make do with only two major political parties, unlike other much smaller Western European countries, among others, who are accustomed to what they perceive to be a far greater range of partisan choices, is because each of the two American major parties is in most respects a loose coalition of state parties. Americans find it possible to express many aspects of their diversity through politics by virtue of the fact that party structures are based primarily on local authority, and nominations to public office are locally made and sustained. Thus the American political system embraces not a two-party system but rather close to a one-hundred-party system.[9] It is necessary to hedge on the exact number because of the anomalies of local political cultures: Nebraska, for example, maintains a state legislature that is not only unicameral but nonpartisan.[10] In some parts of the country, public officials run unopposed because of the weakness of opposition political parties. On the whole, however, it is possible to speak of Vermont Republicans and Vermont Democrats, and to compare and contrast them with Democrats and Republicans from South Carolina, Montana, New Jersey and so on.

States and regions have their own distinctive political cultures arising from the peculiarities of their original and subsequent settlement, their historic and contemporary economic interests, and the local political institutions that have emerged in their varied climates and soils. These cultures, these institutions, send to Congress widely varying representatives who in turn participate in the system of separation of powers, thus linking two of the exceptional elements of the American political order.

On top of these we have the peculiar institution of judicial review, a process by which judges appointed to serve during good behaviour – that is, until they retire or die or are impeached – interpret the laws and the constitution and make final determinations about the legality of governmental acts. Opinions differ about the grounds upon which judicial review might be justified.[11] It seems to be reasonably clear, in any event, that the existence of such an institution is un-avoidable once a Bill of Rights comes into being. These first ten amendments to the Constitution, ratified in 1791, contained plain texts mostly prohibiting Congress from acting so as to impair various enumerated rights reserved to inhabitants of the United States or the states. Who but the courts, empowered to hear and settle cases and controversies under the Constitution, were in a position to listen to complaints and adjudicate between differences of opinion on the subject of whether Congress had in any given instance violated these rights?

Thus from my perspective, a Bill of Rights carries with it an entailed structural consequence; it brings into being a strong form of judicial review. This structural feature in turn carries a great deal of baggage in its train. It inflates the importance of judges in the system. It makes of the law suit a preferred method for resolving issues of status – rights and obligations – as between government and citizen and citizen and citizen. It empowers lawyers as intermediaries of choice for settling claims.

By 1836 our visitor de Tocqueville could exclaim over the richness and the obtrusiveness of the American legal culture, the prevalence of lawyers, and litigation.[12] And so it has remained. Matters that are settled either by customs or by informal operations of the status system in some political systems are settled by litigation and the explicit rendering of written opinions in the United States.

This seems, somehow, entirely apt for a system in which newcomers to the population have played such a large part and in which relations among socially heterogeneous elements must be peacefully maintained and more than occasionally renegotiated. The rigid social separations of a caste system might have worked in some circumstances to order the relations of a heterogeneous people, but not in the presence of a Bill of Rights that extends to cover all inhabitants. Under such a regime, the emergence of legalism as a means of introducing flexibility into human relations seems, if not inevitable, at least plausible.

Thus no fewer than three unusual features of the American political system are woven into the very centre of our constitution. All three can be found in some form or other in other political systems, but not, I think, all three together. And each gives rise to further anomalies that have been institutionalised in important ways: the separation of powers to a uniquely powerful Congress, federalism to a devolved and variegated hundred-party system, and the Bill of Rights to an advanced form of legalism as a method of ordering relations in the society.

III

It seems almost unnecessary to argue that very great complexity is an emergent property of a political system thus designed and evolved. The complexity of the American political system may as well be directly acknowledged, however: it is, after all, frequently the complexity of the system that stymies proposed reforms based on false analogies with simpler systems.

Perhaps the classic such case is the perennial barrage of complaints about American national elections that they go on too long and are too expensive. What is needed, it is frequently said, is a national election on the British model where expenses are tightly controlled and the whole thing takes only six weeks.[13] Advocates of this particular set of reforms may overlook the fact that American elections require long ballots – indeed sometimes very long ballots – to accommodate all the electoral contests that take place concurrently with Presidential elections and that British Parliamentary elections with one contest per constituency require very short ballots. To simplify elections entails simplification of the underlying government which elections serve to populate. Complexity in democratic government – among other factors – requires complex electoral arrangements, and American government is both democratic and complex.

A second point along the same lines is perhaps less obvious, but equally consequential. This has to do with the sheer size of the decision-making community in American politics. One way to grasp the elemental force of this point is to pose the issue as an ambassador's problem. An ambassador newly arrived in most of the world's capital cities can, over a reasonable length of time, get to know virtually everybody who is instrumental to governmental decision-making. Even in the most greatly advanced and civilized democratic nations, there is a not impossibly large group of parliamentarians and civil servants who, to all intents and purposes, run the country. In authoritarian regimes, of course, the number of key actors is much smaller.

In the United States, that number is dauntingly large. It is large in part because policy-making is not contained within the government, or even within the interplay between the two political branches of government, but spills out into think tanks, law firms, and interest groups. Different policies, from public housing to military procurement to the management of trade deficits, activate different congeries of political leaders, Congressional staff members, bureaucrats and interested bystanders. Over relatively short periods of time occupants of these varied roles change jobs, and new people are rotating in all the time.[14] The idea that a new ambassador could get to know all the American players that matter to his country in any reasonable time seems very doubtful; and to attempt to have them all in for dinner, as ambassadors sometimes do, would bankrupt the home economies of all but the most robust nation states.

It is, of course, not merely the responsibility of newly arrived ambassadors to keep track of the players in American policy-making. In some respects, players are obliged to keep track of one another, and of the ongoing state of policy-making in the arenas that interest them. For subject matter specialists this is not an impossible job. For generalists, it may be. In any event, the very size of American policy-making communities frequently requires recourse to means of internal communication unheard of in other nations, namely, publication in the national general circulation press (as well as in trade papers) as a device for sending messages among political leaders.[15] This means that a rich menu of information about proposed, tentative and internally contested governmental action is regularly available in Washington to observers who can afford the price of the daily newspapers. It means also that many policies that become publicly known do not necessarily become the law of the land.

These are some of the consequences of the complexity and size of the American policy-making community: complicated elections and policy-making in the open, both processes importantly mediated by news media that are far more integral to elite political behaviour than is commonplace abroad.

IV

In very short compass it has been possible to generate a discussion of a sizeable number of features that not only underwrites the notion that there is indeed something exceptional about the American government, but also shows in a preliminary way that many of these features do not stand alone, but are linked functionally with others in a true system that has properties of organic wholeness. I do believe, however, that it is not wholly the responsibility of observers abroad to learn as best they can what manner of beast the American government is. It is possible to conceive of an American-sponsored programme of international communication that addresses the sizeable problem of improving foreign knowledge about American government and its working.

There are, as I see it, two main strategies that a nation might use in conducting a programme of international communication. One is targeted to general publics, and sticks fairly closely to the ebb and flow of current events. This is the strategy that supports and sustains such projects as the Voice of America, or overseas tourist bureaus, or that puts on publicity campaigns such as the 'Let Poland be Poland' effort of the early Reagan administration.[16]

An alternative strategy targets elites, and attempts a longer-range form of education. International visitor programmes fall into this category, as do such efforts as the Rhodes Scholarships, the Harkness and Fulbright programmes.

Clearly, a nation having large resources and global interests like the United States is obliged to pursue both strategies. There is an issue, however, having to do with the proper proportions in the mixture. I should argue that there has been an overinvestment in the first strategy and an underinvestment in the second in recent years.

Most government-sponsored activities targeted to general publics abroad attempt to reach populations that, as regards foreign affairs, are politically powerless, may be only marginally attentive, and are often short of memory. Moreover governmental efforts targeted in this fashion are bound to be utterly swamped by private sector cultural imperialism — the cumulative effects of movies exported for foreign showing and US television shows. In light of the great popularity of American popular entertainment abroad, there is little or nothing to be done by governments to add or detract from the images of American life that leak through the pores of ordinary American movies or television programmes.

Undervalued, meanwhile, is the strategy that targets elites abroad, and is oriented to political education of a more fundamental sort. The evidence suggests that a rudimentary understanding of the operations of our complex democratic republic is beyond the powers of more than a handful of those overseas political elites, friends and adversaries alike, who must deal with us on a serious basis. This even includes elites in client states overwhelmingly dependent on American good-will, like Israel, and allies with 'special relationships' like the UK and Canada.

On the whole, political elites abroad live within systems that are authoritarian or parliamentary in character. Reasoning from analogy out of experience of their own systems in attempts to fathom what goes on in ours leads them nowhere, or worse, leads them to erroneous conclusions about what to expect of US performance. Yet it is, or should be, obvious, that the asymmetries between the United States and most nations are very great. Because of America's size and resourcefulness, when the US fails to understand others, the others frequently suffer. When others fail to understand the United States, the others still suffer.

Wisely, many foreign governments attempt to compensate for their lack of understanding of the intricacies of American government by hiring American advisors and lobbyists. This merely locates the difficulty back another step and the problem then becomes how to be a sophisticated and discerning client of one's American lobbyist. How to reconcile conflicting advice, or evaluate advice that is given without benefit of a second opinion? There seems to me to be an irreducible need for some greater level of understanding than currently prevails.

One approach, focused on the long range, asks whether a better job might be done in enhancing the teaching of American government and politics in universities abroad where foreign elites are educated. The need is not met by the vast preponderance of faculty and student exchange programmes, which enable thousands of students from abroad to study engineering, for example, in America, or which sends hundreds of American faculty in every imaginable subject to universities in other countries to teach and do research. In such programmes the study of American government and politics is a very small drop in the bucket.

Large scale philanthropy is probably needed to address the problem directly, philanthropy such as that which created the first chair in American government ever endowed outside the United States at Oxford two years ago. Creation of a number of such chairs is not beyond the resources of the American government. On a smaller scale, far more can and should be done to reach out to those students of American government who already teach outside the United States. At a bare minimum it should be possible to create a network of communication among such scholars, in mitigation of what John Lees called 'the loneliness of the long-distance observer of American politics'.[17]

Notes

I thank Timothy S. Prinz, Maura Barrios and Nancy Palmer for their excellent help on this chapter. Geoffrey Smith, Bernt Haas and Joseph LaPalombara supplied useful information and encouragement.

1   Alexis de Tocqueville, *Democracy in America*, New York, 1945. (First published 1836).

2   For a general overview of psychological principles that can be put to constructive use in describing the understanding of leaders and analysts who deal (mostly antagonistically) with foreign nations see Robert Jervis, *Perception and Misperception in International Politics*, Princeton, NJ, 1976, esp. pp. 283–7.

3   Richard E. Neustadt, *Alliance Politics*, New York, 1970, p. 69.

4   See, for example, Lloyd Cutler, 'To form a government', *Foreign Affairs*, 59, Fall 1980, pp. 126–43, and James L. Sundquist, *Constitutional Reform and Effective Government*, Washington, D.C., 1986.

5   This point is elaborated with comparative detail in Nelson W. Polsby, 'Legislatures', in Fred I. Greenstein and Nelson W. Polsby, eds, *Handbook of Political Science*, vol. 5, Reading, Mass., 1975, pp. 257–319.

6   This observation is also made by David Broder, *Behind the Front Page*, New York, 1987, pp. 209–10.

7   Jean Blondel identifies seventeen federal systems in existence at the end of the 1960s: United States, Switzerland, Australia, Canada, West Germany, Austria, USSR, Czechoslovakia, Yugoslavia, India, Malaysia, Burma, Nigeria, Argentina, Brazil, Venezuela, and Mexico. He also finds sixteen separation of powers systems, and though he does not explictly identify them, these no doubt include the United States, the Philippines, Liberia, and twelve Latin American nations. The United States is the only member of both sets. See Jean Blondel, *An Introduction to Comparative Government*, New York, 1969, pp. 294 (n. 9) and 319.

8   Still the best single discussion of this relationship is David B. Truman, 'Federalism and the party system' in Arthur W. MacMahon, ed., *Federalism: Mature and Emergent*, New York, 1955, pp. 115–36.

9   A useful empirical demonstration of the ideological diversity of state parties carrying the same labels (incidentally by a thoughtful Australian political scientist) is K. G. Armstrong, "Party, state and ideology in the US House of Representatives, 1967–1976'. Paper prepared for delivery at the annual meeting of the American Political Science Association, September 1981. Much anecdotal material on local differences among the various congressional districts is contained in Michael Barone and Grant Ujifusa, eds, *The Almanac of American Politics 1987*, New York, 1987; and Alan Ehrenhalt, *Politics in America*, Washington, D.C., 1982.

10   Even its state capitol building in Lincoln is atypically built in the shape of a skyscraper rather than around the conventional dome.

11   For recent examples see: Jesse Choper, *Judicial Review and the National Process: A Functional Reconsideration of the Role of the Supreme Court*, Chicago, 1980; John Hart Ely, *Democracy and Distrust: A Theory of Judicial Review*, Cambridge, Mass., 1980; and Alexander M. Bickel, *The Least Dangerous Branch: The Supreme Court at the Bar of Politics*, 2nd edn, New Haven, 1986. In *Federalist 78*, Alexander Hamilton says,

The complete independence of the courts of justice is peculiarly essential in a limited Constitution. By a limited Constitution, I understand one which contains certain specified exceptions to the legislative authority; such, for instance, as that it shall pass no bills of attainder, no ex post facto laws, and the like. The limitations of this kind can be preserved in practice no other way than through the medium of courts of justice, whose duty it must be to declare all acts contrary to the manifest tenor of the Constitution void. Without this, all the reservations of particular rights and privileges would amount to nothing. (Max Beloff, ed., *The Federalist*, Oxford, 1987, pp. 347−51.)

12   De Tocqueville wrote: 'Democratic government favors the political power of lawyers. When the rich, the noble and the prince are excluded from the government, the lawyers then step into their full rights, for they are then the only men both enlightened and skillful, but not of the people, whom the people can choose.' And a little later in the same discussion his famous statement occurs: 'There is hardly a political question in the United States which does not sooner or later turn into a judicial one.' Alexis de Tocqueville, *Democracy in America*, pp. 285−6, 290.

13   See, for example, 'Interviews with three former chief executives: what's wrong with the way we pick our presidents?', *US News and World Report*, 23 July 1984, pp. 28−30; and George Grassmuck, ed., *Before Nomination: Our Primary Problems*, Washington, D.C., American Enterprise Institute, 1985. On effects of the long nominating process, see William Crotty and John S. Jackson III, *Presidential Primaries and Nominations*, Washington, D.C., Congressional Quarterly, 1985, pp. 62−8.

14   Assistant Secretaries of Cabinet departments, for example, stay an average of two years. Dean E. Mann with Jameson W. Doig, *The Assistant Secretaries: Problems of Process and Appointment* Washington, D.C., Brookings Institution, 1965; G. Calvin MacKenzie, *The Politics of Presidential Appointments*, New York, 1981. There are 109 assistant secretaries currently listed in the 1987 *Federal Staff Directory*, Mt. Vernon, VA, Congressional Staff Directory, Ltd., 1987. On the effects of turnover in the executive branch, see Hugh Heclo, 'Issue networks and the executive establishment' in Anthony King, ed., *The New Political System*, Washington, D.C., American Enterprise Institute, 1981. In addition to a vast executive policy network, more than half of the majority members in the House and virtually all of the majority members in the Senate chair at least one committee or subcommittee. Stephen S. Smith and Christopher J. Deering, 'The rise of subcommittee government', in Lawrence C. Dodd and Bruce I. Oppenheimer, *Congress Reconsidered*, 3rd edn, Washington D.C., Congressional Quarterly, 1985.

15   Illuminating on this point is the classic by Bernard C. Cohen, *The Press and Foreign Policy*, Princeton, NJ, 1963. Cohen describes a number of instances where elites used the press to communicate their ideas to one another. For example:

A freshman Congressman wanted to reach the State Department, the White House, and his fellow members of Congress with his foreign policy ideas, but he felt that his junior status in itself gave him no platform from which to reach his audience. So he chose to communicate to the foreign policy-making community by writing letters to the editor of the *New York Times*, for publication, hoping to make a substantive contribution to policy that way. (p. 135)

Cohen quotes one State Department official as saying, 'the embassies do not attempt to cover the news; they assume that people in the State Department read newspapers'. (p. 209)

16   A shrewd observer, John Spencer Nichols, writes, 'in 1984, Washington will spend more than three quarters of a billion dollars on propaganda, much of it on overtly persuasive programming that, for the most part, will fall on deaf ears. At the same time, President Ronald Reagan's policy has been slighting the more information-oriented programmes that can better promote US interests abroad.' John Spencer Nichols, 'Wasting the propaganda dollar', *Foreign Policy*, 56, Fall 1984, pp. 129–30. See also Kenneth L. Adelman, 'Speaking of America: public diplomacy in our time', *Foreign Affairs*, 59, Spring 1981, pp. 913–36.

17   John D. Lees, *The Political System of the United States*, 3rd end, London, 1983, p. 11.

Index